Given by family and friends
in honor of
Dorothy P. Donalson.

# GENDER AND ELECTIONS

# Gender and Elections

## SHAPING THE FUTURE OF AMERICAN POLITICS

Edited by

**Susan J. Carroll**
Rutgers University

**Richard L. Fox**
Union College

CAMBRIDGE
UNIVERSITY PRESS

CAMBRIDGE UNIVERSITY PRESS
Cambridge, New York, Melbourne, Madrid, Cape Town, Singapore, São Paulo

Cambridge University Press
40 West 20th Street, New York, NY 10011-4211, USA

www.cambridge.org
Information on this title: www.cambridge.org/9780521844925

First published 2006

Printed in the United States of America

A catalog record for this publication is available from the British Library.

Library of Congress Cataloging in Publication Data

Gender and elections : shaping the future of American politics / edited by
Susan J. Carroll, Richard Logan Fox.
   p.  cm.
Includes bibliographical references and index.
ISBN-13: 978-0-521-84492-5 (hardback)
ISBN-10: 0-521-84492-4 (hardback)
ISBN-13: 978-0-521-60670-7 (pbk.)
ISBN-10: 0-521-60670-5 (pbk.)
1. Women in politics – United States.   2. Elections – United States.   3. Voting – United
States.   4. Women political candidates – United States.   5. Sex role – Political aspects –
United States.   I. Carroll, Susan J., 1950–   II. Fox, Richard Logan.   III. Title.
HQ1236.5.U6G444   2006
324.973'0931 – dc22        2005026255

ISBN-13   978-0-521-84492-5 hardback
ISBN-10   0-521-84492-4 hardback

ISBN-13   978-0-521-60670-7 paperback
ISBN-10   0-521-60670-5 paperback

# Contents

# List of Figures, Text Boxes, and Photo

**Figures**

**Text Boxes**

**Photo**

# List of Tables

# Acknowledgments

This volume had its origins in a series of three roundtable panels at professional meetings in 2002 and 2003 focusing on how women fared in the 2002 elections. Most of the contributors to this book were participants on those roundtables. As we gathered together at these professional meetings, we began to talk among ourselves about a major frustration we faced in teaching courses on women and politics, campaigns and elections, and American politics. We all had difficulty finding suitable, up-to-date materials on women candidates, the gender gap, and other facets of women's involvement in elections, and certainly, none of us had been able to find a text focused specifically on gender and elections that we could use. We felt the literature was in great need of a recurring and reliable source that would first be published immediately following a presidential election and then updated every four years so that it remained current.

At some point in our discussions, we all looked at each other and collectively asked, "As the academic experts in this field, aren't we the ones to take on this project? Why don't we produce a volume suitable for classroom use that would also be a resource for scholars, journalists, and practitioners?" In that moment *Gender and Elections* was born. We are enormously grateful to Barbara Burrell for organizing the first of our roundtable panels and thus identifying and pulling together the initial core of contributors to this volume.

This book would not have been possible without the assistance of the Center for American Women and Politics (CAWP) at Rutgers University. Debbie Walsh, Director of CAWP, has embraced and encouraged this project and been supportive in numerous ways, including inviting Richard Fox to spend a semester at CAWP as a visiting scholar. Gilda Morales, who is in charge of information services at CAWP, proved to be an invaluable source of knowledge about women and politics, and several contributors relied upon her expertise as well as the data she has compiled over the years for CAWP. We also would like to thank Linda Phillips and Danielle Heggs, who offered technical and logistical support at various points.

While everyone at CAWP was helpful, we want to single out Kathy Kleeman, a senior program associate at CAWP, for assistance above and beyond what we ever could have expected. Kathy spent numerous hours making this volume much better than it otherwise would have been. She brought a third set of critical eyes to the reading of every chapter, and as an extremely skilled writer, she helped to make all of our chapters more readable, accessible, and polished. We are especially indebted to her.

Finally, we also would like to thank Cambridge University Press and our editor, Ed Parsons, in particular, for unwavering enthusiasm and patience. We have both thoroughly enjoyed working with Ed.

# Contributors

**Barbara Burrell** is an associate professor in the political science department at Northern Illinois University and the associate director of the university's Public Opinion Laboratory. She is the author of *A Woman's Place Is in the House: Campaigning for Congress in the Feminist Era* (University of Michigan Press, 1994) and *Public Opinion, the First Ladyship and Hillary Rodham Clinton* (Routledge, 2001). Burrell also has published numerous articles on how gender interacts with the electoral process.

**Dianne Bystrom** is the director of the Carrie Chapman Catt Center for Women and Politics at Iowa State University. A frequent commentator about political and women's issues for state and national media, she is a co-author, co-editor and contributor to ten books – including *Gender and Candidate Communication* (Taylor & Francis, 2004), *The Millennium Election* (Bowman & Littlefield, 2003), *Anticipating Madam President* (Lynne Rienner, 2003), *Women Transforming Congress* (University of Oklahoma Press, 2002), and *The Electronic Election* (Lawrence Erlbaum, 1998) – and has written several journal articles. Her current research focuses on the styles and strategies used by female and male political candidates in their television advertising and their news coverage by the media.

**Susan J. Carroll** is a professor of political science and women's and gender studies at Rutgers University and senior scholar at the Center for American Women and Politics (CAWP) of the Eagleton Institute of Politics. She is the author of *Women as Candidates in American Politics* (Indiana University Press, Second Edition, 1994) and editor of *The Impact of Women in Public Office* (Indiana University Press, 2001) and *Women and American Politics: New Questions, New Directions* (Oxford University Press, 2003). Carroll has published

numerous journal articles and book chapters focusing on women candidates, voters, elected officials, and political appointees.

**Georgia Duerst-Lahti** is a professor of political science and department
chair at Beloit College, where she has served in a number of administrative
posts. Her research has focused on gender in U.S. political institutions and
the ideologies that shape its dynamics, were first developed in her book
with Rita Mae Kelly, *Gender Power, Leadership, and Governance* (University
of Michigan Press, 1995). These ideas have been extended in chapters,
such as her essay in *Women Transforming Congress* (University of Oklahoma
Press, 2002), and articles, particularly one in the journal *Sex Roles*. Her
current research project explores gender in the 2004 presidential election,
focusing upon the way masculinity manifests itself and its consequences
for women and the presidency.

**Richard L. Fox** is an associate professor of political science at Union College in Schenectady, NY. He is the author of *Gender Dynamics in Congressional
Elections* (Sage, 1997) and co-author of *Tabloid Justice: The Criminal Justice
System in the Age of Media Frenzy* (Lynne Rienner, 2001). More recently he
has co-authored, with Jennifer Lawless, *It Takes a Candidate: Why Women
Don't Run for Office* (Cambridge University Press, 2005). His articles have
appeared in the *Journal of Politics, American Journal of Political Science, Political Psychology, PS, Women & Politics, Political Research Quarterly,* and *Public
Administration Review.* His research focuses on the manner in which gender
affects voting behavior, state executive elections, congressional elections,
and political ambition.

**Susan A. MacManus** is the distinguished university professor of public
administration and political science in the department of government and
international affairs at the University of South Florida. She is the author of
*Young v. Old: Generational Combat in the 21ˢᵗ Century* (Westview Press, 1996)
and *Targeting Senior Voters: Campaign Outreach to Elders and Others with Special Needs* (Rowman & Littlefield, 2000); editor of *Reapportionment and Representation in Florida: A Historical Collection* (Intrabay Innovation Institute,
University of South Florida, 1991) and *Mapping Florida's Political Landscape:
The Changing Art & Politics of Reapportionment & Redistricting* (Florida Institute of Government, 2002); co-editor, with Kevin Hill and Dario Moreno,
of *Florida's Politics: Ten Media Markets, One Powerful State* (Florida Institute of
Government, 2004); and co-author, with Thomas R. Dye, of *Politics in States
and Communities* (Prentice-Hall, Eleventh Edition, 2003). Her research

on women candidates, officeholders, activists, and voters has been published in *Social Science Quarterly, Public Administration Review, Journal of Politics, Women & Politics, Urban Affairs Quarterly, National Civic Review,* and *The Municipal Year Book,* among others.

**Kira Sanbonmatsu** is an associate professor of political science at The Ohio State University. She is the author of *Where Women Run: Gender and Party in the American States* (University of Michigan Press, forthcoming) and *Democrats, Republicans, and the Politics of Women's Place* (University of Michigan Press, 2002). Sanbonmatsu has also published articles concerning political parties and candidate recruitment as well as research on voters' gender stereotypes in journals such as the *American Journal of Political Science* and the *Journal of Politics.*

**Wendy G. Smooth** is an assistant professor of public policy in the department of women's studies at The Ohio State University and a faculty affiliate with the Kirwan Institute for the Study of Race and Ethnicity. Before joining the faculty at Ohio State, she served as an assistant professor of political science at the University of Nebraska-Lincoln. Her research focuses on the impact of gender and race in state legislatures. Smooth is the recipient of the 2001 Best Dissertation in Women and Politics Award presented by the Women and Politics Section of the American Political Science Association. Currently, she is working on a manuscript entitled *Perceptions of Power and Influence: The Impact of Race and Gender on Legislative Influence.*

SUSAN J. CARROLL AND RICHARD L. FOX

# Introduction: Gender and Electoral Politics into the Twenty-first Century

The 2004 elections in the United States will surely be remembered most for the hotly contested and deeply divisive presidential election between incumbent Republican President George W. Bush and Democratic challenger John F. Kerry. Because of the international and domestic controversy over the U.S.-led invasion of Iraq, the entire world was watching this election. The Democrats and John Kerry both tried to reassure voters that they could keep the country safe and to turn attention to domestic issues, such as jobs and the economy, where polls showed they had an advantage. In contrast, the Republicans and George W. Bush preferred to keep the public focused on homeland security and the fight against terrorism, where they had the upper hand. After Kerry wrapped up his party's nomination in March, more than seven months before the election, most polls forecasted a close race. Indeed, the race remained tight through election day. In fact, for the first time in history, the Gallup organization's final pre-election poll in 2004 projected the race as dead even,[1] and the intensity of the campaign propelled a higher percentage of voters to the ballot box than at any time in the last forty years. Ultimately, President George W. Bush was re-elected by a margin of 51 to 48 percent, and Republicans strengthened their majorities in both the U.S. House and Senate.

To the casual observer, the storyline of the 2004 election would appear to have little to do with gender. However, we contend that underlying gender dynamics are critical to shaping the contours and the outcomes of elections in the United States. The purpose of this volume is to demonstrate the importance of gender in understanding and interpreting American elections and to provide an overview of the multiple ways in which gender enters into and affects contemporary electoral politics.

1

## THE GENDERED NATURE OF ELECTIONS

Elections in the United States are deeply gendered in several different ways. Most obviously, the electoral playing field is dominated by men. Ten of the eleven major party candidates for President in 2004 were men. Similarly, men comprised the vast majority of candidates for governor and Congress in 2004. Most behind-the-scenes campaign strategists and consultants – the pollsters, media experts, fundraising advisors, and those who develop campaign messages – are also men. Further, the best-known network news reporters and anchors (such as Dan Rather, Peter Jennings, Tom Brokaw, Brian Williams, and Brit Hume), who were charged with telling the story of the 2004 and previous elections, are men. On cable television news, the highest rated programs on Fox News, MSNBC, and CNN, all of which cover politics extensively, are hosted by men. Also, more than 75 percent of political newspaper columnists and editorial writers across the country are male.[2] The leading voices in political talk radio, such as Rush Limbaugh and Sean Hannity, to whom millions of Americans listen every week, are men. And the majority of those contributing the largest sums of money, perhaps the most essential ingredient in American politics, to the campaigns and parties are, of course, men.

Beyond the continued dominance of men in politics, gendered language permeates our political landscape. Politics and elections are most often described in terms of analogies and metaphors drawn from the traditionally masculine domains of war and sports. Contests for office are often referred to by reporters and political pundits as "battles" requiring the necessary strategy to "harm," "damage," or even "destroy" the opponent. The headquarters of presidential campaigns are called "war rooms." Candidates "attack" their opponents. They raise money for their "war chests." The greatest amount of attention in the 2004 presidential race was focused on critical "battleground" states. Candidates across the country in 2004 touted their toughness in "hunting down" and "killing" the terrorists who attacked the United States on September 11, 2001.

Along with the language of war, sports language is also prevalent in campaigns and in the coverage of campaigns by the media. Considerable attention is devoted to discussion of which candidate is ahead and behind in the "horse race." Similarly, commentators talk about how campaigns are "rounding the bend," "entering the stretch drive," or "in the final lap." But while language drawn from the race tracks is common, so too is language drawn from boxing, baseball, football, and other sports. Coverage of political debates often focuses on whether one of the candidates has scored a "knockout punch." When a candidate becomes aggressive, he or she is described as "taking the gloves off." A popular political cable television talk show is named "Hardball." Candidates running for elective office frequently talk about making a "comeback," "scoring a victory," or being "in the early innings" of a campaign. When a campaign is in trouble, the candidate may need "to throw a hail Mary pass." If something unexpected occurs, commentators report that a "candidate has been thrown a curve ball."

The language of war and sports, two of the most traditionally masculine domains in American society, is so prevalent in our political discourse that it is even used by those who wish to increase women's political involvement. For example, to provide more opportunities for women to enter politics, advocates frequently argue that we need to "level the playing field."

As the language used to analyze politics suggests, our expectations about the qualities, appearance, and behavior of candidates also are highly gendered. We want our leaders to be tough, dominant, and assertive – qualities much more associated with masculinity than femininity in American culture. In the post- 9-11 environment, a military background, especially with combat experience, is a very desirable quality for a candidate to have, but military credentials remain almost exclusively the domain of male candidates. A military background is particularly desirable for a presidential candidate, who, if elected, will assume the responsibilities of "commander-in-chief." However, since the American public has seen very few women among generals or top military officials, the idea of a female commander-in-chief still seems an oxymoron to many Americans.

Even the expectations Americans have about how candidates and political leaders should dress are gendered. While women politicians are no longer expected to wear only neutral-colored, tailored business suits, jogging attire or blue jeans still are not acceptable. Americans have grown accustomed to seeing their male political leaders in casual attire. During the 1990s we frequently saw pictures of Bill Clinton jogging with members of the Secret Service. More recently, we have all seen images of President George W. Bush on his ranch in jeans and cowboy boots. Yet, never have we seen a picture of Condoleezza Rice or Hillary Clinton outfitted in jogging shorts or dressed in blue jeans and cowboy boots.

Finally, elections in the United States are gendered in the strategies candidates employ in reaching out to women and men in the general public. Candidates, both men and women, strategize about how to present themselves to voters of the same and opposite sexes. Pollsters and campaign consultants routinely try to figure out what issues or themes will appeal specifically to women or to men. Increasingly, candidates and their strategists are designing different messages to be delivered to voters based on their gender and other demographics. Specially devised appeals are directed at young women, working class men, senior women, hunters (mostly men), single women, married women, suburban women, white men, and women of color, to name only some of the targeted groups.

In short, when we look at the people, the language, the expectations, and the strategies of contemporary politics, we see that gender plays an important role in elections in the United States. Even when gender is not explicitly acknowledged, it often operates in the background, affecting our assumptions about who are legitimate political actors and how they should behave.

This is not to say, however, that the role of gender has been constant over time. Rather, we regard gender as malleable, manifesting itself differently at various times and in different contexts in the electoral process. In women's candidacies for elective office, for example, there has been obvious change. As recently as twenty years ago, a woman seeking high-level office almost anywhere in the United States was an anomaly and in many instances might have faced overt hostility.

Clearly, the electoral environment is more hospitable now. Over the years, slowly but steadily, more and more women have entered the electoral arena at all levels. In 2004 for the first time, a woman, former First Lady and New York Senator Hilary Clinton, was forecast as the prospective frontrunner of her party if she were to seek the nomination to become president of the United States. Senator Clinton was the subject of intense media speculation about whether she would indeed run for president in 2004. In fact, toward the end of 2003, Tim Russert, the host of the political talk show *Meet the Press,* asked Senator Clinton eight separate times in one interview whether she might throw her hat into the ring and run for president in 2004. And as we head toward the 2008 presidential election, Senator Clinton is viewed as the early frontrunner for the Democratic nomination.

## POLITICAL REPRESENTATION AND SIMPLE JUSTICE: WHY GENDER MATTERS IN ELECTORAL POLITICS

In addition to the reality that gender is an underlying factor shaping the contours of contemporary elections, examining and monitoring the role of gender in the electoral process is important because of concerns over justice and the quality of political representation. The United States lags far behind many other nations in the number of women serving in its national legislature. Prior to the 2004 elections, the United States ranked 57th among countries throughout the world in the proportion of women serving in their parliaments or legislatures; in early 2005, only 15 percent of all members of Congress were women. No woman has ever served as president or vice-president of the United States. Only eight of the fifty states had women governors in 2005, and women constituted only 22.5 percent of all state legislators across the country according to the Center for American Women and Politics.

Despite the relatively low proportion of women in positions of political leadership, women constitute a majority of the voters who elect these leaders. In the 2004 elections, for example, 67.3 million women reported voting, compared with 58.5 million men, according to U.S. Census figures. Thus, 8.8 million more women than men voted in those elections! As a matter of simple justice, something seems fundamentally wrong with a democratic system that has a majority of women among its voters, but leaves women so dramatically under-represented among its elected political leaders. As Sue Thomas has explained, "A government that is democratically organized cannot be truly legitimate if all its citizens from . . . both sexes do not have a potential interest in and opportunity for serving their community and nation."[3] The fact that women constitute a majority of the electorate but only a small minority of public officials would seem a sufficient reason, in and of itself, to pay attention to the underlying gender dynamics of U.S. politics.

Beyond the issue of simple justice, however, are significant concerns over the quality of political representation in the United States. Beginning with a series of studies supported by the Center for American Women and Politics in the 1980s, a great deal of empirical research indicates that women and men support and devote attention to somewhat different issues as public officials.[4] At both the national and state levels, male and female legislators have been found to have different policy priorities and preferences. Studies of members of the U.S. House of Representatives, for example, have found that women are more likely than men to support policies favoring gender equity, day care programs, flex time in the work place, legal and accessible abortion, minimum wage increases, and the extension of the food stamp program.[5] Further, both Democratic and moderate Republican women in Congress are more likely than men to use their bill sponsorship and co-sponsorship activity to focus on issues of particular concern to women.[6] Similarly, a number of studies have found that women serving in legislatures at the state level are also more likely than men to give priority to, introduce, and work on legislation related to women's rights, health care, education, and the welfare of families and children.[7] When women are not present in sufficient numbers among public officials, their distinctive perspectives are under-represented.

In addition to having priorities and voting records that differ from those of men, women public officials exhibit leadership styles and ways of conducting business that differ from those of their male colleagues. A study of mayors found that women tend to adopt an approach to governing that emphasizes congeniality and cooperation, whereas men tend to emphasize hierarchy.[8] Research on state legislators has also uncovered significant differences in the manner in which female and male committee chairs conduct themselves at hearings; women are more likely to act as facilitators, whereas men tend to use their power to control the direction of the hearings.[9] Other research has found that majorities of female legislators and somewhat smaller majorities or sizable minorities of male legislators believe that the increased presence of women has made a difference in the access that the economically disadvantaged have to the legislature, the extent to which the legislature is sympathetic to the concerns of racial and ethnic minorities, and the degree to which legislative business is conducted in public view rather than behind closed doors.[10] Women officials' propensity to conduct business in a manner that is more cooperative, communicative, inclusive, public, and based on coalition-building may well lead to policy outcomes that represent the input of a wider range of people and a greater diversity of perspectives.[11]

The presence of women among elected officials also helps to empower other women. Barbara Burrell captures this idea well:

> Women in public office stand as symbols for other women, both enhancing their identification with the system and their ability to have influence within it. This subjective sense of being involved and heard for women, in general, alone makes the election of women to public office important.[12]

Women officials are committed to insuring that other women follow in their foot steps, and large majorities mentor other women and encourage them to run for office.[13]

Thus, attention to the role of gender in the electoral process, and more specifically to the presence of women among elected officials, is critically important because it has implications for improving the quality of political representation. The election of more women to office would likely lead to more legislation and policies that reflect the greater priority women give to women's rights, the welfare of children and families, health care, and education. Further, the election of more women might well lead to policies based on the input of a wider range of people and a greater diversity of perspectives. Finally, electing more women would most likely lead to enhanced political empowerment for other women.

## ORGANIZATION OF THE BOOK

This volume applies a gendered lens to aid in the interpretation and understanding of contemporary elections in the United States. Contributors examine the ways that gender enters into, helps to shape, and affects elections for offices from president to state legislature across the United States. As several chapters in this volume demonstrate, gender dynamics are important to the conduct and outcomes of presidential elections even though, to date, a woman has not won a major party's nomination for president. Many women have run for Congress and for offices in state government, and this volume analyzes the support they have received, the problems they have confronted, and why there are not more of them. Women of color face additional and distinctive challenges in electoral politics because of the interaction of their race or ethnicity and gender, and this volume also attempts to contribute to an understanding of the status of and electoral circumstances confronted by women of color, particularly African American women.

In Chapter 1, Georgia Duerst-Lahti discusses the gender dynamics of the presidential election process. She begins by examining the meaning of the phrase "presidential timber" to demonstrate how masculinity has shaped ideas of suitable presidential candidates. Duerst-Lahti argues that embedded in presidential elections and the traditions that accompany them are implicit assumptions that make presidential elections masculine space, including the test of executive toughness, a preference for military heroes, and the sports-related metaphors employed in describing presidential debates. Americans have carefully sought the right *man* for the job as the single great leader and commander-in-chief of "the greatest nation on earth." She demonstrates how this construction of the presidency leads to struggles over different forms of masculinity and has implications for women as candidates and citizens.

In Chapter 2, Susan A. MacManus focuses on the changing dynamics of gender and political participation, and particularly on the new, imaginative techniques that political parties and women's groups used to bolster female

registration, turnout, and candidate selection in the 2004 election. She
chronicles the historic fight for women's suffrage and gender differences
in political participation before focusing on recent reforms of the electoral
system. The reforms, adopted in many states after the 2000 election and
the passage of the national Help America Vote Act in 2002, include: streamlined registration processes; stepped up voter education efforts; expanded
voting timetables (early voting); improved absentee voting processes; and
new high tech voting machinery (touch screens). MacManus details the
razor-sharp targeting of women through the use of various advertising
and mobilization tools, and she provides examples of direct mail ads and
Internet web sites (with their catchy logos) that were used in the 2004
election to boost female political participation rates, particularly those of
infrequent and non-voting women.

In Chapter 3, Susan J. Carroll examines voting differences between
women and men in recent elections. A gender gap in voting, with women
usually more likely than men to support the Democratic candidate, has
been evident in every presidential election since 1980 and in majorities of
races at other levels of office. Carroll traces the history of the gender gap
and documents its breadth and persistence. She examines the complicated
question of what happens to the gender gap when one of the candidates
in a race is a woman. Carroll reviews different explanations for the gender gap, and identifys what we do and do not know about why women
and men in the aggregate differ in their voting choices. She also analyzes
the different strategies that candidates and campaigns have employed for
dealing with the gender gap and appealing to women voters.

In Chapter 4, Richard L. Fox analyzes the historic evolution of
women running for seats in the U.S. Congress. The fundamental question addressed in this chapter is why women continue to be so under-
represented in the congressional ranks. Fox examines the experiences of
women and men candidates for Congress by comparing fundraising totals
and vote totals. His analysis also presses into the more subtle ways that gender dynamics are manifested in the electoral arena by examining regional
variation in the performance of women and men running for Congress,
the difficulty of change in light of the incumbency advantage, and gender
differences in political ambition to serve in the House and Senate. The
chapter concludes with an assessment of the degree to which gender still
plays an important role in congressional elections and the prospects for
gender parity in the future.

In Chapter 5, Wendy G. Smooth traces African American women's participation in electoral politics from Shirley Chisholm's historic campaign

for president of the United States in 1972 to former Senator Carol Moseley Braun's 2004 campaign for the White House. This chapter provides an historical overview of African American women's political participation as candidates in American politics. Following the passage of the Voting Rights Act of 1965, African Americans made unprecedented strides in electoral politics. Since the passage of this legislation, the number of African American elected officials serving at every level of government has soared from less than 500 in 1965 to more than 9,000 today. Smooth chronicles the successes of African American women in politics, the continued barriers they face as they seek greater inclusion in the American political system, and their activism in overcoming these barriers.

In Chapter 6, Barbara Burrell examines the roles played by political parties and women's organizations in promoting and facilitating the election of women to public office. The traditional view of the relationship between political parties and women's candidacies for public office has been that parties primarily have recruited women in "hopeless" races and as sacrificial candidates in contests where the party had little prospect of winning. Over time, political parties have become somewhat more supportive of women's candidacies even as their role in campaigns has been challenged by other groups such as women's political action committees. Burrell describes the increasing involvement of women in the party organizations and the evolving focus on electing women to public office as a means to achieve equality. The role of national party organizations and women's groups in increasing the numbers of women running for and elected to Congress is examined, with particular attention to the financial support these organizations have provided for women candidates.

In Chapter 7, Dianne Bystrom examines the impact of the media on candidates' campaigns for political office. Studies have shown that newspapers often cover women less than their male opponents, focus on image attributes over issue stances, and raise questions about the women's viability. Consequently, candidate-mediated messages – television advertising and web sites – are particularly important to women candidates as they attempt to present their issues and images directly to voters during a political campaign. This chapter reviews the state of knowledge about women candidates, their media coverage, television commercials, and web sites, and provides examples of how women candidates may be able to capitalize on their controlled communication channels to influence their media coverage and create a positive, integrated message that connects with voters.

Finally in Chapter 8, Kira Sanbonmatsu turns to the often overlooked subject of gender in state elections. She addresses two central questions in this chapter: How many women ran for state legislative and statewide offices in 2004? How did the performance of women candidates in 2004 compare with previous elections? Sanbonmatsu analyzes the cross-state variation in the presence of women candidates, including the role of political parties in shaping women's candidacies. She also considers the reasons for the variation across the American states in women's presence in statewide executive office. Understanding why women are more likely to run for and hold office in some states and not others is critical to understanding women's status in electoral politics today – as well as their prospects for achieving higher office in the future.

Collectively these chapters provide an overview of the major ways that gender affects the contours and outcomes of contemporary elections. Our hope is that this volume will leave its readers with a better understanding of how underlying gender dynamics shape the electoral process in the United States.

## NOTES

1. Poll: Bush, Kerry Split Six Key States. November 1, 2004. CNN. <http://www.cnn.com/2004/ALLPOLITICS/10/31/poll.sunday/> 2005, January 8.
2. Clarence Page. March 20, 2005. Hot Air and the X Chromosome. Chicago Tribune.
3. Sue Thomas and Clyde Wilcox. 1998. Introduction: Women and Elective Office: Past, Present, and Future. In *Women and Elective Office: Past, Present, and Future*, eds. Sue Thomas and Clyde Wilcox. New York: Oxford University Press, 1.
4. Debra Dodson, ed. 1991. *Gender and Policymaking: Studies of Women in Office.* New Brunswick, NJ: Center for American Women and Politics.
5. Most recently, see Michele Swers. 2002. *The Difference Women Make: The Policy Impact of Women in Congress.* Chicago: University of Chicago Press.
6. Swers, 2002.
7. For examples, see Sue Thomas. 1994. *How Women Legislate.* New York: Oxford University Press; Michael B. Berkman and Robert E. O'Connor. 1993. Women State Legislators Matter: Female Legislators and State Abortion Policy. *American Politics Quarterly* 21(1): 102–24; Susan J. Carroll. 2001. Representing Women: Women State Legislators as Agents of Policy-Related Change. In *The Impact of Women in Public Office*, ed. Susan J. Carroll. Bloomington: Indiana University Press. Lyn Kathlene. 1989. Uncovering the Political Impacts of Gender: An Exploratory Study. *Western Political Quarterly* 42: 397–421.
8. Sue Tolleson Rinehart. 2001. Do Women Leaders Make a Difference? Substance, Style, and Perceptions. In *The Impact of Women in Public Office*, ed. Susan J. Carroll. Bloomington: Indiana University Press.
9. Lyn Kathlene. 1995. Alternative Views of Crime: Legislative Policy-Making in Gendered Terms. *Journal of Politics* 57: 696–723.

10. Impact on the Legislative Process. 2001. In *Women in State Legislatures: Past, Present, Future*. Fact sheet kit, New Brunswick. NJ: Center for American Women and Politics.
11. Most recently see Cindy Simon Rosenthal. 1998. *How Women Lead*. New York: Oxford University Press.
12. Barbara Burrell. 1996. *A Woman's Place is in the House*. Ann Arbor, MI: University of Michigan Press, 151.
13. Debra L. Dodson and Susan J. Carroll. 1991. *Reshaping the Agenda: Women in State Legislatures*. New Brunswick, NJ: Center for the American Woman and Politics.

# 1 Presidential Elections

## Gendered Space and the Case of 2004

Shortly after the 2004 election, a tongue-in-cheek Associated Press (AP) article led with the following: "Wanted: a former altar boy from the South-west who speaks Spanish, married into a rich Republican family from Ohio and revolutionized the Internet after working as a volunteer firefighter in Florida. Position: president of the United States."[1] Using findings from exit polls to construct the profile of the perfect presidential candidate for 2008, the article went on to propose that he:

- "[is] a Medal of Honor winner" with combat experience, who helped normalize relations with Vietnam;
- loves outdoor sports and drops his "'g's' when talkin' about huntin' and fishin' and car racin'";
- is a former quarterback for the University of Michigan Rose Bowl team;
- is a "trained economist who taught in Minnesota, where he met his wife, a nurse," whose father is a former governor;
- "was a volunteer fireman" who "drove his pickup truck to help out the World Trade Center site";
- and is "a billionaire in his own right who developed software..."

Although not fitting this profile, five prominent men and Hillary Rodham Clinton were mentioned in this article as potential candidates. It closed with, "Mr. Perfect might be a Mrs. – the first woman to head a majority party ticket. But it would be a lonely job, what with her husband fighting in Iraq."

For presidential candidacies, the press serves as the great mentioner, without whose attention no candidate can be seen as viable. The power of mentioning, or not, has implications beyond individual candidates. What the press assumes, and the way it frames its coverage of presidential elections and candidacies, has consequences for what readers think about, and to a lesser extent, how they think about it.

The AP article described here focuses on the next election and the candidate characteristics needed to win. Distributed on November 6, 2004, it is among the first articles to frame elements of the 2008 presidential election. Importantly, its framing is highly gendered (see Text Box 1.1), and one suspects that neither the author nor the readers thought much about it. As a result, its assumptions about masculinity as an implicit criterion for the presidency – combat experience, huntin', quarterback, fireman – go unexamined.

Yet, the article's headline, " . . . finding Mr. or Mrs. Right for a run in 2008," and closing paragraph both assume that a woman can be president. In other words, they cue the reader to think about a woman as the right or perfect presidential candidate in 2008. This cuing is no small matter. Because only men have ever been president, and because certain functions of the presidency, such as commander-in-chief, are particularly associated with masculinity, the assumption that a woman could be "Mrs. Right candidate" represents a major shift in cultural understandings of both women and the institution of the presidency. So potent is the association between masculinity and the presidency that an organization called The White House Project has been established with a core purpose of making this cultural shift.[2] One of its primary strategies, in fact, is to have the media treat a woman in the presidency as normal, much as the AP article seems to do.

However, most of the characteristics ascribed to the ideal candidate in this AP article suggest a profile consistent with men rather than women in U.S. society. Taking note of this fact helps to reveal how presidential elections are gendered space.

- Although a woman could easily be from the Southwest, speak Spanish and have married into a rich Republican family, the Catholic church only allowed altar boys, not altar girls, at the time current presidential candidates were growing up.
- Firefighters remain overwhelmingly men, especially in volunteer corps.
- Until very recently, women have been barred from combat duty, so few have been positioned to win the Medal of Honor. However, a woman might well have negotiated with the Vietnamese: women have long been associated with peace, more are in the diplomatic corps, and two have become secretary of state.

**TEXT BOX 1.1: A Gender primer: Basic concepts for gender analysis**

To do gender analysis of presidential elections, some basic concepts and definitions are needed.

Gender can be defined as the culturally constructed meaning of biological sex differences. Males and females share far more physiologically than they differ, yet in culture we largely divide gender roles and expectation into masculine and feminine even though biologically and culturally more than two genders exist. Importantly, in contrast to sex, gender is not necessarily tied to a human body.

Gender is assigned as:

- An attribute or property of an individual, entity, institution, etc.
  She's a wise woman.
  Men dominate physics.
- Ways of doing things – practices or performance.
  He throws like a girl.
  She fights like a man.
- Normative stances toward appropriate and proper ways of behaving, allocating resources, exercising power, and so on.
  Men shouldn't cry.
  Fathers must provide and mothers give care.
  A woman's place is in the home.

The process of assigning gender is "to gender" or "gendering."

- To gender or gendering is to establish a gender association.
  Metrosexuality describes Yuppie urban men with a softer side.
  The highly feminized field of nursing.
- To regender or regendering is to change from one gender to another gender.
  Before typewriters, secretaries were men.
  Girls now outperform boys in school.
- To transgender or transgendering is to cross gender boundaries, weakening gender norms and associations, and is open to both men and women.
  Half of medical students now are women so medicine is changing.

Gender ethos is defined as the characteristic spirit or essential and ideal attributes that correspond to gender expectations.
  Football is among the most manly of all U.S. sports.
  A Madonna with child quintessentially expresses femininity.
  The military is imbued with masculinity.

*Source:* Compiled by author.

- No woman has yet played quarterback for a Big Ten team. In 1999–2000, a female place kicker on the Colorado State University football team encountered extreme sexual harassment. (Interestingly, Condoleezza Rice may benefit from an association with football simply because she claims that her dream job is some day to be National Football League commissioner.)

- While economics has the smallest proportion of female Ph.D.s in the social sciences, women have entered the field in growing numbers, so a woman might have strong economic credentials. However, only about 10 percent of nurses are male, so she probably would not have one as her husband.

- Finally, if a woman became president, she might well be lonely, as is the first woman to serve in any position. However, no commander-in-chief has ever faced the challenge of leading a nation in war with a spouse on the battlefront, because the wives of presidents have always functioned as helpmates, regardless of their other career interests and professional credentials.

In other words, while a widely distributed AP article mentioning that a woman could be a viable candidate may help to normalize the idea of a woman as president, much more needs to happen. We cannot simply "add and stir" in a woman without changing the elements associated with masculinity. Such "equal treatment" ignores important differences and (dis)advantages. Because so much that is perceived as contributing to presidential capacity is strongly associated with men and masculinity, presidential capacity is gendered to the masculine; as such, women who dream of a presidency must negotiate masculinity, a feat much more difficult for them than for any man.

Text Box 1.2 rewrites the AP article to approximate a perfect candidate based upon culturally feminine roles and associations in order to illustrate the central claim of this chapter: that presidential elections are gendered space, that much of what happens in a presidential election becomes a contest about masculinity that is integrally intertwined with understandings of what makes a candidate suited for this masculinized office and institution. This chapter's primary purpose is to show ways masculinity emerges in campaigns. I attempt to raise awareness of this implicit dynamic and to counteract some of the potency masculinity gains from simply being "ordinary." This chapter also touches upon the process of opening, or regendering, presidential election space for women.

**TEXT BOX 1.2: Finding Mrs. Right for a Run in 2008: Not the same as Mr. Right**

A November 6, 2004, AP article used exit polls to "build a perfect candidate for 2008."[*] Despite suggesting that Mrs. Right could fit the bill equally well as Mr. Right, the article concentrated on aspects consistent with masculinity. Given the considerable difference in life experiences between women and men, what factors known from exit polls and other sources in 2004 could be used to create an ideal female candidate for 2008?

- A fifth generation Latina American from Arizona, she comes from a long line of Democrats, including political office holders from New Mexico.
- As a child she considered becoming a nun, which endeared her to a favorite uncle, a Catholic bishop in Florida who has close ties to the Cuban community. They share a love of the outdoors, gardening, camping, and fly-fishing.
- She took first place in the individual medley on the U.S. national swim team, missing the Olympics only due to an injury.
- As an Army nurse, she served in the waning days of the Vietnam War. She received a medal of commendation for helping evacuate mixed race children.
- She married an Anglo Army officer who specialized in military intelligence. He retired as a general in 1992. He speaks Arabic fluently, and President George H. W. Bush recognized him for outstanding service during the Persian Gulf War.
- She founded a company that placed temporary nurses, becoming a multimillionaire when she franchised the business. She has helped many women start their own businesses as a result.
- Throughout this time, she raised four children and transformed the public education system in her city as a volunteer activist. She interrupted her career to care for her son for three months when he suffered life-threatening injuries caused by a drunk driver. She sits on the national board of Mothers Against Drunk Driving.
- Her company created software, now used nationwide, that digitized and standardized patient medical records and enabled patients to access them 24-7. She made even more money from the software than the nursing business.
- She became governor of Michigan, and is in her second term. Her husband intends to campaign hard on her behalf, as he has done in the past.

---

[*] Ron Fournier. November 6, 2004. Exit Polls Can Lead the Way in Finding Mr. & Mrs. Right for a Run in 2008. *Wisconsin State Journal.*

Of course, women find a contest about masculinity a distinct hurdle compared to male candidates, but men who run for the presidency must also negotiate masculinity. Masculinity takes many forms, each competing to be considered hegemonic – that is, the controlling, best, and most valued version.[3] Drawing upon work by R. W. Connell, this chapter looks into masculinity more carefully and explores the gendering of presidential timber – an ill-defined but commonly employed concept about suitability for the presidency. I examine overt references to masculinity as well as the ongoing struggle for hegemony between two forms of masculinity in the United States, "dominance" masculinity and "technical expert" masculinity. I do so in order to make explicit the implicit masculine qualities of the presidency deemed essential in a successful presidential candidate. Not incidentally, this chapter will shed light on the possible openings for women who seek to wear the presidential mantle.

This chapter explores presidential elections through the concept of gendered space, rather than just discussing elections. While elections – with their aspects of candidate recruitment and winnowing, formal primary and general elections, caucuses, conventions, debates, and the like – certainly are part of election space, so is much more. For example, the presidency as an institution occupies a place in history, inside the U.S. government system, in relationship to Congress, other national institutions, and political parties. Each of these places is part of presidential election space. So is the entire environment of those elections, with their places in the public mind, the news and opinion media, American culture, and all the people – present and past – who help to create and sustain presidential elections. These people include the candidates, the elite political gatekeepers, pollsters, campaign consultants, campaign workers, voters, even apathetic citizens. Each of them occupies a place in presidential election space. This large and somewhat amorphous space that includes everything related to presidential elections is the locus of analysis.

I will demonstrate that presidential selection processes are themselves implicitly imbued with masculinity and therefore (non)conscious beliefs that masculine persons should be president. To do so, the chapter tackles "a recurring paradox. The categories of men and masculinity are frequently central to analyses, yet they remain taken for granted, hidden and unexamined . . . [They are] both talked about and ignored, rendered simultaneously explicit and implicit . . . at the centre of the discourse but they are rarely the focus of the interrogation."[4] As will become clear, some media coverage – especially from op/ed pages – explicitly deals with men and masculinity in the presidential election. More often however, as in the AP article examined at the beginning of this chapter, coverage treats masculinity paradoxically by ignoring its central place in presidential elections even while highlighting it. In the process, it ignores ways in which presidential elections are gendered, thereby perpetuating men's greater potential to be seen as presidential to the detriment of female candidates.

## STAGES OF PRESIDENTIAL ELECTIONS: PARTS OF GENDERED SPACE

The early stages of any presidential election are an insider's game, with party elites and elected officials talking to the press about potential candidates and the press reporting upon them. Year one begins the day after the previous campaign – for example, on November 8, 2000, for the 2004 election. For the press to mention a candidate regularly is exceptionally important: no press mention, no candidacy. The press covers candidates who undertake "testing the water" activities and also can create potential candidates simply by mentioning that some individuals could be candidates.

Years one and two of any election cycle focus upon factors that provide candidates strategic advantages to win the next election. Chief among these factors is whether the race includes an incumbent president or is an open seat. In 2004, George W. Bush ran as an incumbent president, and he was assumed to be running for re-election as of the day he was declared the winner in 2000.

Another relevant factor is the influence of the previous election, reflected in such elements as the margin of victory, big mistakes made by a candidate or a campaign, and strategies that worked particularly well. Of course, the 2000 election between Al Gore and George W. Bush proved exceptionally close, with Gore securing a plurality of the popular vote, but Bush winning the electoral college vote after intervention by the Florida and U.S. Supreme Courts. Because the election was so close, Bush seemed a particularly vulnerable incumbent. Hence an unusually large field of Democratic challengers emerged, especially after Gore announced on December 16, 2002, that he would not run again.

Press coverage for each election cycle begins in the days and months immediately after the end of the previous one. News coverage during the first year of any election cycle focuses upon "aspirants," or individuals doing things that would clearly help them with a presidential bid. Aspirants might be traveling the country giving speeches, meeting with an unusual assortment of interest group leaders, forming exploratory committees, visiting states important to early selection processes, such as New

Hampshire and Iowa, and otherwise getting more positive press coverage than usual.

A second set of individuals might better be thought of as "potential aspirants"; they do a few things that bring them press coverage, but prove not to be serious candidates for that election cycle. Such coverage in one cycle becomes a resource for future cycles, however.

A third set of potential candidates is spotlighted because they have characteristics consistent with presidential candidates, although they may not have given serious consideration to a presidential bid. These individuals can be thought of as "recruits"; the mere fact that the press mentions them as potential candidates begins to build the perception of their viability. The press plays an influential role in this process. When the media mention an individual as a presidential candidate, they create the perception that s/he could be one. With no mention in the press, regardless of aspirations and credentials, an individual will not be seen as a potential or actual candidate.

Despite the unusual ending of the 2000 election, press coverage for the 2004 race began right away. Table 1.1 shows the names of individuals mentioned as possible candidates during the first three years of the cycle leading up to the 2004 election, the date each was first mentioned, and whether each proved to be an aspirant, a potential aspirant, or a recruit.

For the gendering of presidential elections a few matters are clear. Only three women made the list of those mentioned by the press as potential Democratic candidates for the 2004 presidential election. Hillary Rodham Clinton was, in fact, the first to be mentioned, the day after the November 8th election and more than a month before the 2000 election was decided by the Supreme Court. New Hampshire's former governor Jeanne Shaheen appeared only one time in a list of possible candidates, as did several other governors and senators. Because Shaheen made no gestures toward a run, this mention reflects a recruiting attempt. It also indicates that the press has begun to seriously consider women with presidential credentials, such as governor or senator, as possible candidates. Finally, Carol Moseley Braun is mentioned for the first time on January 6, 2003, very late in the cycle, during the third year, second to last of all candidates.

During the third year of a presidential election cycle, the pace quickens. Candidates become active in early states, strive for viability by raising considerable campaign funds, and use the opportunity of an official announcement of their candidacy to garner press coverage. The aspirants become separated from others during this time. Former first lady and newly minted Senator Hillary Rodham Clinton was particularly subject to speculation, despite repeated claims that she was not running. These

**TABLE 1.1:** Presidential candidates in 2004 were named in newspaper articles soon after the 2000 election

| Date of first mention | people | Most significant current and prior positions | Type of candidate |
|---|---|---|---|
| 11/9/2000 | Hillary Rodham Clinton | Senator, NY, First Lady | recruit |
| 12/8/2000 | Joe Lieberman | Senator, CT, Vice-presidential candidate | aspirant |
| 12/13/2000 | Al Gore | Vice-president, Senator, TN | potential |
| 12/14/2000 | Evan Bayh | Senator and Governor, IN | recruit |
| 12/14/2000 | Bill Bradley | Senator, NJ | recruit |
| 12/14/2000 | Gray Davis | Governor, CA | recruit |
| 12/14/2000 | Bob Kerrey | Senator, NE | recruit |
| 12/14/2000 | John Edwards | Senator, NC | aspirant |
| 12/14/2000 | Dick Gephardt | Congressman, MO, House Minority Leader | aspirant |
| 12/14/2000 | John Kerry | Senator, MA | aspirant |
| 12/14/2000 | Jeanne Shaheen | Governor, NH | recruit |
| 12/15/2000 | Russ Feingold | Senator, WI | recruit |
| 12/15/2000 | Tom Vilsack | Governor, IA | recruit |
| 12/15/2000 | Paul Wellstone | Senator, MN | recruit |
| 12/17/2000 | Joseph Biden Jr. | Senator, DE | potential |
| 12/17/2000 | Tom Daschle | Senator, SD, Senate Majority and Minority Leader | potential |
| 12/17/2000 | Rev. Al Sharpton | Activist, NY | aspirant |
| 4/22/2001 | Roy Barnes | Governor, GA | recruit |
| 9/6/2001 | Howard Dean | Governor, VT | aspirant |
| 11/10/2002 | Wesley Clark | General | aspirant |
| 12/26/2002 | Bob Graham | Senator and Governor, FL | aspirant |
| 1/6/2003 | Carol Moseley Braun | Ambassador, Senator, IL | aspirant |
| 2/10/2003 | Dennis Kucinich | Congressman and Mayor, OH | aspirant |

*Source:* Compiled by author.

speculations subsided in 2003. By speculating often that a woman might become a candidate, the press helps to change the gendering of presidential election space, simply because the idea is in front of the attentive public. Speculation about Hillary Clinton likely came more easily because Elizabeth Dole had sustained high levels of support in public opinion polls when she made a short-lived bid for the presidency in the 2000 cycle.

The election took shape, especially for Democrats, during 2003. Interestingly, President Bush received very little coverage explicitly related to his role as a candidate then. But everything he did as president reflected upon his candidacy, and his campaign staff was well aware of this fact. Press coverage of a president is always extensive, giving him considerable advantage. With a large cast of contenders, and an impassioned desire to retake the White House, the Democrats opted to hold an unprecedented series of debates among their aspiring candidates. These began with a widely televised debate in South Carolina May 3, 2003, and ran until January 2004. After Labor Day, the pace of polls conducted by news outlets and polling organizations, as well as campaigns, quickened and the polls themselves provided candidates frequent press coverage. However, such coverage tends to be limited and can become detrimental if a candidate is not polling well. Candidate viability and prospects in the primaries and caucuses – measured in part by fundraising success – begin to solidify. Although no candidate withdrew in 2003, it is not uncommon for aspirants to do so during year three if they are polling too low, are unable to raise campaign funds, or fail to attain adequate press coverage.

Year four of an election cycle begins in early November, with press coverage intensifying after January 1. During the final two months of 2003, candidates undertook a whirlwind of visits to the early primary and caucus states of New Hampshire and Iowa, and to a lesser extent, South Carolina and Oklahoma. Polls and press coverage of these visits become critical. Do poorly in either and a candidate loses the "press election" in which the press vets candidates for their presidential viability and presidential timber. This pattern spills over into January. While all the 2004 male Democratic candidates stayed in the race, the sole female candidate, Carol Moseley Braun, withdrew on January 16, 2004, three days before the Iowa caucus, throwing her support to Howard Dean.

In the last ten months of any campaign season, press coverage escalates greatly and presidential election space becomes highly visible and national, beginning to draw interest from a much broader audience. Candidates generally withdraw from contention as their performance in polls, primaries, and caucuses falls short of expectations set by news coverage. The Iowa caucuses and New Hampshire primary, which always come first, hold substantially more sway than any others. These are followed by a series of state primaries and caucuses whose rules are determined by states and political parties. For the past several presidential elections, "Super Tuesday," a collection of many states' primaries taking place the second week of March, has determined the presumptive nominees, even though primaries continue until June. In 2004, John Kerry emerged for the Democrats and George Bush never had challengers, so in practice, the general election began after Super Tuesday. In the past, campaigns have lulled during late primaries and early summer, but in 2004 the Bush camp launched its attack vigorously during this time period. As will be discussed below, much of this attack directly challenged Kerry's masculinity.

During late summer of presidential election years, press coverage shifts to each respective party as it approaches its convention. In 2004, the Democratic convention took place the last week of July, and the Republican convention ran August 30 to September 2. Conventions officially nominate a party's candidate, but they also showcase the candidate and other party notables, including potential future nominees. The duration between conventions was unusually long during 2004.

The final throes of the general campaign begin in earnest after the conventions, becoming ever more frenzied as Election Day nears. For the 2004 elections, presidential debates, which always attract considerable press coverage, were held on September 30, October 8, and October 13, and a vice-presidential debate took place on October 5. The polls showed a race that was too close to call, producing frenetic activity and press coverage up until the general election on November 2.

Because television networks faced severe criticism for the way they "called" the election in 2000, they gave greater care in 2004. Nonetheless, by midnight on election day, all agreed that George W. Bush had won. With fraud reported in Ohio and provisional ballots – a product of reforms from the 2000 debacle – not yet counted, Kerry delayed his concession call to Bush until 11:00 Wednesday morning.

Three days later, on November 6, in the earliest days of the first year of the 2008 presidential election cycle, the AP article that began this chapter mentioned potential candidates for 2008.

## THE GENDERED PRESIDENCY AND PRESIDENTIAL TIMBER

The term presidential timber implies the building products used to construct a president. So far, the human material that makes presidents has been male. Masculinity has been embedded through the traditions that dominate the presidency, but inside those traditions lie more implicit assumptions that make presidential elections masculine space: the test of executive toughness, a preference for military heroes, the sports and war metaphors of debates, and more. Implicit in the gendering of presidential election space is the common belief that the election picks a single leader and commander-in-chief of "the greatest nation on earth." This belief stands in a post-World War II context that includes the Cold War,

the fall of communism, the emergence of the United States as the world's
sole hyperpower, and the rise of terrorism.

In these conditions, Americans have carefully, albeit not necessarily
systematically or rationally, sought the right man for the job. As judged
from the number of candidates and the reaction to candidacies thus far,
women have not yet been seriously considered as suitable to serve as president. Although many reasons can be proffered to explain this dearth of
female attempts for the post, observations about the heavily masculinized character of the office, and hence masculinized selection process,
remain among the strongest, yet most difficult, explanations to establish. In essence, because the institution is itself perceived as masculine,
contests for the presidency are, among other things, struggles over dominant or hegemonic masculinity. Presidential elections also present real
challenges for women who must exhibit masculine characteristics (probably better than males) while retaining their femininity if they want to
succeed.

The idea that institutions have been gendered toward masculinity
became obvious when women entered them; their novel presence made
visible the ways masculinity is "normal." Thinking of men as having gender
instead of "naturally" coinciding with a universal standard has occurred
only quite recently. An institution becomes gendered because it takes on
characteristics or preferences of the founders, incumbents, and important
external actors who influence it over time. In doing so, these founders and
influential incumbents create the institution's formal and informal structures, rules, and practices, reflecting their preferred mode of organizing.
If men have played an overwhelming role in an institution's creation and
evolution, it is only "natural" that masculine preferences become embedded in its ideal nature. It takes on a masculine gender ethos. This is what
has happened to the U.S. presidency.

But gender is not static and neither is the gendering of an institution
that operates inside a social context. One can expect continual gender
transformations as a result of women's activism, equal employment opportunity policies in education and the workplace, and cultural experiences
of Americans' daily lives. Similarly, campaigns and elections evolve from
a particular history influenced by key people and processes that have gendered aspects. This evolutionary process favors those whose preferences
become reflected in presidential election processes, but those preferences
can change over time. So, although men have clearly had the advantage
in shaping the presidency and presidential elections over time, gender has
been in considerable flux over the past forty years. Even if only men have

been seen as having presidential timber thus far, these assumptions may change in the future.

So how might presidential timber be gendered? Informal use would suggest that it combines a blend of overlapping elements of charisma, stature, experience, and viability in a particular election. It also has included ideas of proper manliness. Presidential historian Forrest McDonald provides insights into presidential timber through his description of presidential image:

> [T]he presidential office ... inherently had the ceremonial, ritualistic, and symbolic duties of a king-surrogate. Whether as warrior-leader, father of his people, or protector, the president is during his tenure the living embodiment of the nation. Hence, it is not enough to govern well; the president must also seem presidential. He must inspire confidence in his integrity, compassion, competence, and capacity to take charge in any conceivable situation. ... The image thus determines the reality.[5]

The "king-surrogate, ... warrior-leader, father ..., protector" roles and images indisputably evoke men and masculinity.

Yet one could imagine a queen, mother, and protector with Joan of Arc warrior qualities. Former British Prime Minister Margaret Thatcher is often cited as having evoked these images, but British comedy often showed her baring a muscular, manly chest. Many argue that Britain's experience with highly successful queens opened the way for Thatcher.

In contrast, the United States has no such historical experience, so voters have a harder time seeing women as capable of fulfilling traditionally masculine leadership roles of the institution. This cultural (in)capacity to understand women as able public leaders likely is exaggerated because, according to Michael Kimmel, an expert on masculinity, the gendered public and private divide was much stronger in the United States than in Europe.[6]

Even more challenging, and perhaps most important for electing presidents, presidential timber derives from the perception of others. That is, others must see a potential candidate as possessing it. Forrest McDonald declares that a president must "seem presidential" and inspire confidence in his "capacity to take charge in *any* (emphasis added) conceivable situation ... with image determining reality."

If only men have been president, then having a presidential image presents a significant challenge for women who need political elites, party activists, and ultimately voters to perceive them as presidential. Further, men have more often been culturally been imbued with a "take charge" capacity, although women certainly do and can take charge, so this aspect of timber might be open for transgendering, for being understood as suitable for either women or men. However, the requirement that one be perceived as able to take charge in any conceivable situation undermines women, particularly during war or security threats such as 9-11. Jennifer Lawless found in post-9-11 America that considerable gender stereotyping re-emerged, with a willingness to support a qualified female candidate falling to its lowest point in decades.[7] For these reasons, the ordinary usage of the term presidential timber and potential gendering of it deserve scrutiny, because its use is both the center of analysis and invisible.

By examining how the term "presidential timber" is used in press accounts, we can better establish its meaning and its explicit and implicit gendering. A search of over 10,000 articles published in seven newspapers (nationally influential newspapers including the *Washington Post*, *The New York Times*, and the *Los Angeles Times* as well as the regionally important papers *The Atlanta Journal Constitution*, the *St. Louis Post-Dispatch*, the *Houston Chronicle*, and *The Boston Globe*[8]) and occasionally a few other news sources from January 1, 2003, through November 16, 2004, yielded a surprising total of a mere eight articles that contain the phrase "presidential timber," most of which came early in this period and none of which related to the sitting president.[9] George W. Bush's campaign repeatedly pointed to his post 9-11 performance and approval ratings whenever questions were raised about his credentials for the job. In essence, they positioned him as possessing timber by virtue of serving as president, although this has not always worked for other recent presidents. Jimmy Carter purportedly lost because he anguished too much in public, and many commentators – and arguably voters – perceived George H. W. Bush as lacking sufficient timber. Often, this perceived lack of timber has been linked to a "whimp factor" or otherwise not fulfilling the requisite image of presidential masculinity.[10] In apparent response to this danger, George W. Bush has positioned himself as exceptionally masculine, a steadfast cowboy willing to stand firm as he takes on the world.

During 2003, the concept of presidential timber figured prominently in one newspaper article and was merely a passing point in two others where a neutral author's voice reports that a particular candidate failed the timber test in the perception of others. For example, John Edwards left some wondering if he had sufficient presidential timber after his debut on the Sunday talk show circuit. For Howard Dean, the problem arose because he, rather than others, saw timber in himself. "The governor who had never seriously been challenged, who viewed himself as presidential timber, very nearly got tossed from office."[11] The press often uses the concept of presidential timber to cast doubt on a candidate's capacity.

The third mention proves more revealing about the concept and its meaning. Presidential timber figures as the central topic of an extended article about the nine Democratic candidates who participated in the South Carolina Forum, an initial opportunity to compare them. According to the article, one of three likely goals for each candidate would be "striving to present themselves as presidential timber."[12] The importance of the idea of timber resides in "impressions," which are still largely unformed. "So the debate is considered an important chance to form opinions that could help shape later aspects of the campaign."[13] Key to the impression and the opinions are "passion" and "appeal" that would help party activists "gauge which candidate could mount the strongest challenge to Bush." In other words, presidential timber involves a candidate's passion, appeal, and competitiveness as conveyed through first impressions. None of these aspects appears to be particularly gendered, although a woman might be eliminated if she is not perceived – for reasons of sexism or feminine personal characteristics – as competitive against the other party's candidate.

The litany of each candidate's distinguishing characteristics is familiar, but bears closer scrutiny in light of an analysis of presidential timber.

- Kerry sought to "capitalize on his medal-winning service in the Vietnam War...to establish in voters' minds his competence on national security issues." His appeal: he can beat a wartime president.
- Dean distinguished himself as a strong critic of Bush on Iraq, appealing to peace activists.
- Edwards "raised more money than any of the candidates during the first three months of this year." He appealed by matching Republican funding.
- Lieberman touted his vice-presidential candidate experience and appealed to centrists.
- Gephardt, a policy wonk from the House, strove to provide health coverage for nearly all Americans, which appealed to many Democrats.
- Graham, a Southern governor and Senator, touted his experience. Southern roots appealed to strategists, who know the South has been key for Democratic victories.
- Moseley Braun, Sharpton, and Kucinich were lumped together as liberal underdogs, "seeking to present themselves as realistic alternatives to the more prominent candidates."

The fact these three candidates were combined, instead of being considered separately, further undermines perceptions of timber; they were not even worthy of individual press attention. Moreover, since the 1988 election when Republicans succeeded in denigrating liberals as weak and out of touch, most successful center-to-left officeholders use the term "progressive" rather than liberal; hence, being called liberal may undermine perceptions of presidential timber. Finally, being seen as an underdog so late in the presidential election cycle also likely undermined positive perceptions. The last underdog to break from the pack was Jimmy Carter, and he failed to win his second term.

In what ways is this newspaper account of presidential timber gendered? It would seem at first glance very few. The only female candidate, Carol Moseley Braun, is combined with two other male candidates. Gender analysis can highlight this fact, but also suggests a need to focus on the race and class based dynamics of these three underdogs. While the fact is left unstated, both Sharpton and Moseley Braun are African Americans. Given the deep pattern of racism in the United States, one cannot help but acknowledge the obstacle being black presents in wooing white voters, even though Colin Powell received positive press and was mentioned as possessing the necessary stature to be president. None of the three Democrats lumped together had individual wealth, nor had they attracted ample campaign contributions. Further, none was polling well.

More directly to the point of gender, women may more often find themselves categorized as liberal underdogs, which is both gendered and disadvantageous in current political settings. They are seen as liberal because, more than their male counterparts, they tend to be interested in social programs and equal rights, which are deemed liberal. Such policies tend to benefit women so to work on women's behalf is, in a masculinist Catch-22, to be liberal. Women are underdogs in large part because they have been excluded from high-level political office for most of U.S. history. They are not likely to be seen as frontrunners due to a realistic assessment of women's record thus far. Again a Catch-22: women won't win because they haven't yet won.

Gender analysis makes visible a less obvious disqualifier for women: experience. Presidents have traditionally come from four positions: governor, senator, vice president, or military hero. Again due to long-term exclusion, all of the top male candidates except Edwards had logged considerably more time in these roles than had Moseley Braun. Further, Graham had held both senate and gubernatorial seats, something no woman has done. Because recent presidents have emerged from governorships more than other positions, Dean and Graham held an edge. Fewer than thirty women in the history of the country have ever been governors, and even fewer have come from the South where recent gubernatorial candidates-turned-presidents have served. At the time of this writing, the only southern governor is Kathleen Blanco from Louisiana, and she is new to the post. As a senator, Edwards had limited experience; however, he had the advantage of proving his prowess raising money while Moseley Braun encountered serious problems in this area. And, of course, Kerry most of all touted his combat heroism to challenge the Bush wartime presidency. Having been barred from combat until very recently, and only allowed into the general military for several decades, women's opportunity for military heroism has been negligible, and holding the home front does not have the same cachet for timber. Apparently, neither does diplomacy, because Moseley Braun had been an ambassador, albeit to a post in peaceful United States ally New Zealand. Perhaps a female diplomat with requisite elective experience who successfully negotiates a major world trouble-spot would be viewed as possessing more presidential timber.

Considerable danger exists in taking the case of one woman and generalizing to all women, but the larger point remains. While the characteristics each candidate reportedly uses to create a perception of presidential timber do not seem innately determined by sex, the opportunity structures for requisite timber experiences still have strongly gendered constraints.

## CONTESTING MASCULINITY

Masculinity is neither fixed nor uniform. Just as there are several versions of a "proper" woman – often varying by class, cultural subgroup, and gender ideology – men and masculinity are not singular. For presidential candidates, the political gatekeepers, and voters, certain expectations of masculinity exist for a president. Nonetheless, within broader ranges of gender expectations, analysis suggests that much of the heat around gender performances, or the way individuals "do gender," derives from contests to make one version of gender the hegemonic form, the form that is recognized as right, just, proper, and good and the form that is afforded the most value. It is the form most able to control all other forms, and therefore it becomes most "normal."

R. W. Connell has analyzed contemporary masculinity, finding ongoing contests between two major forms: dominance and technical expertise.[14] Dominance masculinity is preoccupied with dominating, controlling, commanding, and otherwise bending others to one's will. Often rooted in physical prowess and athleticism, this competitive and hierarchical masculinity also can be rooted in financial prowess in the corporate world or elsewhere. Michael Jordan and Arnold Schwarzenegger serve as archetypal examples.

Expertise masculinity emerges from capacity with technology or other intellectualized pursuits. Such masculinity also values wealth, a key marker of masculine status, but the hegemony arises from mastery of and capacity to deal with complex technology or ideas. Bill Gates and Carl Sagan serve as exemplars of technical expertise masculinity.

Connell says that these modes of masculinity "sometimes stand in opposition and sometimes coexist," because neither has succeeded in displacing the other.[15] Connell further argues that these modes of hegemonic masculinity always stand in relationship to other subordinated masculinities and to femininity.

If this struggle for hegemonic masculinity plays out in presidential elections, then it also has consequences for female candidates, since expertise has been a prime base of power for women in leadership roles. Whereas women gain credibility in leadership situations when they are perceived as possessing expertise, they face a considerably greater challenge in being perceived as leaders if they try to dominate. In fact, women often are punished for seeming too dominating. Therefore, the nature of the contest for hegemonic masculinity has implications for women, too. A strong showing of expertise masculinity would allow women easier access; a strong showing of dominance masculinity would cause women to face greater difficulty in the contest, or even in being seen as suited to participate in the contest.

How might have this contest played out in the past? In 1992, George H. W. Bush had won the Persian Gulf War, but had also been labeled as a "whimp" who could not project a vision for the nation. Bush had the possibility of employing dominance masculinity as commander-in-chief, but failed. Bill Clinton portrayed himself as intelligent, as a Rhodes Scholar, and as a policy wonk. He projected expertise masculinity and won through a focus on "the economy, stupid"; that is, he was smart about the economy. Once in office, however, he quickly encountered problems when he backed down from a disagreement with the Joint Chiefs of Staff over gays in the military and was pegged as weak. Letting his wife lead his major health care initiative also cast doubt upon his manly autonomy. This perception plagued him until a showdown over the budget with House Speaker Newt Gingrich and the Republican majority in the 104th Congress. Then, Clinton dominated and won. Strangely, when he was again attacked, this time over sexual misconduct, his popularity rose. While far too complicated to suggest a single cause, the manly vitality at stake – perhaps proof that he was not controlled by his strong wife, Hillary – figures as an aspect of dominance masculinity. Clinton did best as president when he projected dominance masculinity, not expertise masculinity.

The 2000 election might seem the perfect contest between expertise and dominance masculinity with Al Gore, the smart and technically savvy vice president, against George W. Bush, former professional baseball team owner whose intelligence was regularly questioned. In the 2004 election, the contest for masculinity was seemingly modified somewhat from 2000. As in 2000, Bush entered the contest from an explicit position of dominance masculinity. He could not, and likely would not choose to, project expertise masculinity. Although ironic, when Bush called upon his "expertise" with the office of the presidency, he did so from a dominance masculinity stance, claiming that expertise mostly in terms of a war presidency. Kerry tried to project both expertise and dominance masculinity. He was both smart and heroic. Kerry certainly had plenty of resources for expertise masculinity, displaying his knowledge of foreign policy and general mastery of a wide range of subjects, from Chinese assault weapons to nineteenth-century British poetry. However, his basis for victory in primary elections was his war hero status, firmly rooted in dominance masculinity. He also projected his athleticism at every available opportunity. Apparently, his campaign recognized the potential liability of expertise masculinity, even though the liberal base values intelligence and expertise greatly. Kerry, it seemed, tried to have both.

In order to test the prevalence of each broad category of masculinity, I identified words that could be associated with each. Because these words might be used frequently, I limited the searches to short but critical election stages (April and October 2000 and January 2004) and searched for words in newspaper articles that suggested either dominance or technical expertise in candidates.[16] Quite simply, for both time periods, as Tables 1.2 and 1.3 show, words common to dominance masculinity outnumbered expertise masculinity words roughly two to one and four to one, respectively. This pattern strongly suggests that dominance, rather than expertise, drives the ethos of presidential campaigns. Women therefore face particular gendered challenges in their bid for the masculinized presidency.

Somewhat surprisingly, a closer look at the 2000 election shows that Gore was connected with more of all of these words than Bush, and his news coverage used language of both dominance and expertise. When expertise words were applied to Bush, they were used in the negative; he

**TABLE 1.2:** Dominance words were used twice as often as expertise words in articles about presidential candidates in 2000

| Technical expertise masculinity | | Dominance masculinity | |
|---|---|---|---|
| Words | # of times used | Words | # of times used |
| Technical | 41 | Dominate | 57 |
| Intelligent | 63 | Strong | 229 |
| Smart | 43 | Aggressive | 84 |
| Advocate | 92 | Attack | 210 |
| Wonk | 10 | Blast | 8 |
| Total | 249 | Total | 588 |

*Notes:* Articles analyzed from April and October 2000 in the *Washington Post, New York Times, Los Angeles Times, Atlanta Journal Constitution, St. Louis Post-Dispatch, Houston Chronicle,* and *Boston Globe.*
*Source:* Compiled by Author.

was pegged as not intelligent or not smart. However, while Bush received less coverage that included these terms, Bush was equal to Gore in coverage about dominance. Nonetheless, Gore did not "do" dominance masculinity well, with many references to his aggressiveness and attacks being cast negatively. For example, the AP quotes Bruce Buchanan, a University of Texas political scientist, as saying, "There's a kind of sanctimonious

**TABLE 1.3:** Dominance words were four times more common than expertise words in articles about presidential candidates in 2004

| Technical expertise masculinity | | Dominance masculinity | |
|---|---|---|---|
| Words | # of times used | Words | # of times used |
| Technical | 48 | Dominate | 169 |
| Expert | 122 | Strong | 788 |
| Intelligent | 114 | Control | 170 |
| Smart | 50 | Aggressive | 95 |
| Advocate | 12 | Attack | 63 |
| Lecture | 2 | Blast | 12 |
| Wonk | 5 | Athlete | 10 |
| Total | 353 | Total | 1,307 |

*Notes:* Articles analyzed from January 2004 in the *Washington Post, New York Times, Los Angeles Times, Atlanta Journal Constitution, St. Louis Post-Dispatch, Houston Chronicle,* and *Boston Globe.*
*Source:* Compiled by Author.

**TABLE 1.4:** "Tough" appeared more often in presidential election coverage than any other masculinity word

| Manly | Masculine | Wimp | Testosterone | Tough |
|-------|-----------|------|--------------|-------|
| 101   | 26        | 69   | 22           | 3,280 |

*Notes:* Numbers indicate the actual number of times the word appeared. Articles analyzed from January 1, 2003 to November 16, 2004, in the *Washington Post, New York Times, Los Angeles Times, Atlanta Journal Constitution, St. Louis Post-Dispatch, Houston Chronicle,* and *Boston Globe.*

*Source:* Compiled by Author.

aggressiveness to Al Gore that I would call his principal weakness when he gets mobilized in an attack mode in a debate. If he seems to be bullying, his talents don't do him any good."[17]

Performing dominance masculinity, especially if seen as too aggressive, may not be advantageous in presidential elections. Howard Dean frequently suffered the same consequence in the 2004 election.

## EXPLICIT REFERENCES TO MASCULINITY

The use of particular words related to masculinity became the subject of explicit analysis and explicit campaign strategy during the 2004 election. Table 1.4 shows such words as they appeared in newspaper coverage of the election; the counts include all forms of the word, such as manly and manliness, or masculine and masculinity. "Tough" was included because it became so integral to the discourse of the election, even though it can be applied to a "tough situation faced by our soldiers in Iraq" as readily as to President Bush's tough posture on Palestinian leadership or a tough primary in South Carolina. In fact, the most pronounced finding is the extent to which presidential election space is infused with the concept of toughness; hence, one can predict that its regendering will hinge upon the extent to which women can be seen as tough enough.

Masculinity, manliness, testosterone, and whimp make far less of a showing than tough, but articles including these words place masculinity as the subject of analysis. One critical fact is that both campaigns strategized about projecting hegemonic masculinity. Even in 2003, conservatives were "draping George W. Bush in a masculine mystique.... [T]he president is hailed as a symbol of virility – a manly man in contrast to the allegedly effeminate Bill Clinton."[18]

But not only Republicans were concerned. One extended headline read, "Who's the Man? They Are; George Bush and John Kerry stand shoulder to shoulder in one respect: Macho is good. Very good. It's been that way since Jefferson's day."[19] Many experts claimed, "a good portion of the presidential image-making in 2004 will center on masculinity.... Both candidates appear to come by their macho naturally." Both candidates also take every chance to overtly cultivate machismo images, whether through images of Bush powering his father's cigarette boat in Maine or Kerry taking shots and checks on the hockey rink. Despite use of explicit terms, most manly themes will be "cast in more subtle and euphemistic terms, as pundits talk about the candidates' 'authenticity,' 'decisiveness,' and 'toughness.'"[20]

Toughness has had masculine associations, and discourse throughout the space of presidential elections drips with evocations of it. Despite women making tough decisions all the time, decisiveness has generally been associated with men. Therefore, the extensive Republican effort to paint John Kerry as indecisive, a "flip-flopper," was also a way to cast him as like a stereotypical woman who keeps changing her mind. Charges of flip-flopping attacked Kerry's authentic masculinity by evoking expertise rather than dominance themes.

> [T]elevision commentators repeatedly describe Kerry as too verbose and intellectual to connect with average voters, in contrast to the plainspoken Bush.... "It's a particularly American definition of mas-culinity that, somehow, if you are intellectual and have a lot of book learning and talk in ways that make that clear, then you are femi-nized," said Messner, who researches gender stereotypes. "You are seen as someone who could waffle when it comes time to make a big decision. All of that is code for not being masculine enough."[21]

Authenticity presents a puzzle as to a masculine association. The answer, however, emerged in perceptions of authentic masculinity itself. Authenticity was linked to masculinity because the Republicans particu-larly displayed a strategy of:

> ... portraying opponents as less than fully masculine. Republicans retooled a Nixon plan from the 1972 campaign, and designed a plan to enable Bush to "capture the hearts and votes of the nation's white working men.... Nixon's plan was to build an image as 'a tough, courageous, masculine leader.'"[22]

Bush's advisors intended to do the same. A key component of such mas-culinity is dominance. To be the manly leader who can raise other men requires the enemy to "be feminized."[23] But this is not new. "American politicians have not been above feminizing their opponents dating back to the era of powdered wigs, playing on the stereotypical notion that only the "manly" can lead."[24] Bush supporters called John Edwards the "Breck girl" and John Kerry "French-looking."[25] They mocked John Kerry for windsurfing, and in a series of campaign advertisements, "made him look a little bit ridiculous by editing" in particular ways.[26] They accomplished this emasculation even though windsurfing is a very difficult sport that requires enormous athleticism. Republicans undermined Kerry's genuine war hero status through the Swift Boat group's ads. They succeeded in raising questions even though Kerry's status as a hero was grounded much more strongly in dominance masculinity than Bush's military record.

Such attacks pushed Kerry into ever more explicit displays of his own dominance masculinity. His advisors began to declare it. "Different voters... were really struck by John's presidentialness. He's big, he's masculine, he's a serious man for a serious time."[27] As nuanced foreign policy became the object of Republican ridicule, and sensitivity to other nations a reason for scorn, Kerry donned ever more manly costumes: snow boarding, pheasant hunting, the football toss at each stop. Mocking Kerry's use of camouflage gear for a hunting trip where he had proven a good enough shot to bag a goose, senior Bush aides dressed in their own camouflage for Halloween. Kerry moved away from his expertise because it highlighted his "patrician airs" and did not play well with audiences, and the Bush camp systematically undermined Kerry's key weapon for the presidency, his manliness.

## PROSPECTS FOR WOMEN AS PRESIDENT

Like 2000, the election of 2004 proved a fierce battle between the major party candidates, with a core front of the battle being waged over the type of leadership demanded by the nation, especially in a time of war. Integral to that battle has been a contest for hegemonic masculinity. For over 125 years, the women who have run for president have confronted this competition for masculinity. Still, the pace of women aspiring to the presidency has picked up in recent decades, although it remains glacial (see Text Box 1.3).

Following Pat Schroeder in 1987 who only tested the water, Elizabeth Dole made a bid in 1999. Despite early polls that consistently placed her second behind George W. Bush among Republican contenders, she received far less press attention than others, especially John McCain, and dropped out October 20, 1999. She ran in part because she had successfully captured the spotlight at the 1996 Republican convention. However, her credentials as wife were derived from Bob Dole, and hence her experience

## TEXT BOX 1.3: Women have been candidates for President and Vice President since 1872

**1872**

Victoria Woodhull, a stockbroker, publisher, and protégé of Cornelius Vanderbilt, ran for president of the United States on the Equal Rights Party ticket.

**1884**

Belva Lockwood, the first woman admitted to practice law before the U.S Supreme Court, ran for president on the Equal Rights Party Ticket; she did so again in 1888.

**1925**

Nellie Tayloe Ross, a Wyoming Democrat, became the nation's first woman governor, elected to replace her deceased husband. She served for two years. Later, she became vice chair of the Democratic National Committee and director of the U.S. Mint. At the 1928 Democratic National Convention, she received thirty-one votes on the first ballot for Vice President.

**1952**

Two women – India Edwards and Judge Sarah B. Hughes – were proposed as Democratic vice presidential candidates. Both withdrew their names before the balloting so the choice of presidential nominee Adlai Stevenson, Senator Estes Kefauver, could be nominated by acclamation.

**1964**

Senator Margaret Chase Smith, a Maine Republican, was nominated for the presidency by Vermont Senator George Aiken at the Republican national convention. Smith had campaigned briefly for the post, limiting herself to periods when the Senate was not in session. Elected to the House of Representatives in 1940 (to replace her dying husband) and the Senate in 1948, Smith had already made history by becoming the first woman to serve in both houses of Congress.

**1972**

Congresswoman Shirley Chisholm ran for president in the Democratic primaries. At the party's national convention, she garnered 151.25 delegate votes before Senator George McGovern clinched the nomination. At the same convention, Frances (Sissy) Farenthold, a former Texas state legislator who twice ran for governor of that state, finished second in the balloting for the vice presidential nomination, receiving more than 400 votes.

*(continued)*

**TEXT BOX 1.3** *(continued)*

**1984**

Third-term Congresswoman Geraldine A. Ferraro (D-NY), secretary of the House Democratic Caucus, became the first woman ever to run on a major party's national ticket when she was selected by Walter F. Mondale as his vice presidential running mate. The ticket was decisively defeated, capturing only thirteen electoral votes, and few analysts felt that Ferraro's presence had a strong impact – positive or negative – on the outcome.

**1987**

Congresswoman Patricia Schroeder (D-CO), the dean of women in Congress, disappointed supporters in her exploratory campaign when she decided not to pursue a candidacy for president. The fact that she shed a few tears upon hearing the crowd's reaction to her announcement produced extended debate about women's fitness for the job.

**1999**

Elizabeth Dole, former secretary of the Departments of Transportation and Labor, president of the American Red Cross, and wife of 1996 presidential candidate Bob Dole, entered the Republican presidential campaign, but withdrew on October 20, 1999, in advance of the primaries.

**2003**

Carol Moseley Braun, the first black woman elected to the U.S. Senate (D-IL) and former ambassador to New Zealand, made a bid for the presidency. She withdrew just before the Iowa caucuses on January 16, 2004.

*Source:* Center for American Women and Politics, Rutgers University, as extended by the author.

as a seasoned campaigner was easy to dismiss. Further, she had never held the posts heretofore deemed proper experience for a president: senator, governor, vice president, or military hero. Instead, she had twice been cabinet secretary and headed the American Red Cross. She nonetheless garnered broader support than Shirley Chisholm had when she sought the Democratic nomination in 1972 and stayed in the race longer than Pat Schroeder. As a result, Dole continued the incremental process of women progressing closer toward a successful presidential candidacy.

In 2004, a female candidate progressed even further along the steps of a successful presidential election bid. Carol Moseley Braun mounted a campaign similar to Dole's in that she became an official candidate but dropped out before the primaries commenced. Moseley Braun stayed in the race longer than Dole had, but received little press coverage overall. Much of it was positive about her personally, yet highlighted the weakness of her campaign. She was described as poised in the debates, wise and gracious, with a resplendent smile. At the same time, she was characterized as "a contentious figure" during her 1992 Senate campaign and while in office. About her campaign, coverage stated, "Ms. Braun has struggled to raise money and build support"...and, "she has struggled to have her campaign taken seriously."[28] While only brief and suggestive, some comparison between coverage of Carol Moseley Braun and the male candidates helps elucidate ways presidential elections are gendered space.

First, as the "woman candidate" and especially as a "black woman," she received attention as a novelty candidate. Women's groups were among the few active and visible supporters of her candidacy. Further, because she was the lone woman and Al Sharpton, another African American candidate was running, coverage arguably magnified her sex rather than her race. She often spoke of the difference women bring as well, calling attention to her gender.

Coverage of high-level female candidates has tended to focus upon their physical appearance, clothes, and personal life, otherwise known as the "hair, husband, and hemline" problem. The focus upon their family or personal life tends to diminish the credentials and accomplishments of female candidates, treating them always as connected to other people, rather than autonomously. It is hard to be perceived as the "single great leader alone at the top" if one is always mentioned in connection with a husband.

The importance of women's spouses became exceptionally clear during Geraldine Ferraro's vice-presidential candidacy in 1984 when her husband's financial dealings became an issue for her. Elizabeth Dole certainly struggled with this dimension of presidential timber. Male candidates also receive scrutiny on the merits of their mates, however. Howard Dean was considered damaged because his wife, Judith Steinberg, chose not to campaign with him. Many suggested that Teresa Heinz Kerry proved a liability to her husband and Laura Bush an asset to hers.

In terms of autonomy, Moseley Braun had the potential advantage of being single, although her fiancé found frequent mention as the cause of several problems in her Senate campaign. So, despite not having a husband, her character was still cast in terms of her mate, and her mate was highly problematic.

More mention is made of all candidates' dress than in the past, so this aspect is not limited to women, although Moseley Braun did receive consistently more comment on her clothes. More importantly, the way dress is used in campaigns is gendered, sometimes in ways that exclude women. For example, male candidates commonly roll their sleeves up, which "is the candidates' awkward attempt to step outside the safety of their dark-suited uniforms and show themselves as manly men who could lay bricks to support their family and throw a punch to defend its honor."[29] This ceremonial gesture traditionally occurs when a male candidate seeks to connect with a young, working class, or rural audience, and simply does not apply the same for women.

> The hoisting of the sleeves announces that the candidate has come to speak the truth, both plainly and earnestly. He has stripped himself of the formality associated with blazers, suits and navy gabardine. By the nakedness of his forearms he has rendered the setting informal and he is announcing to the audience that it will be treated to unscripted responses, sincerity and ultimately the real man. The pushed-up sleeves are the fashion equivalent of the knowing wink, the two-handed handshake and all of those other gestures intended to make a stranger feel like an old pal. In its purest form, sleeve-rolling is an artifice that declares the candidate is average, never mind that the point of all of his back-patting, chili-eating and speech-making is to convince folks that he is better than average.[30]

All the Democratic candidates did this "symbolic gesture of informality, camaraderie and machismo" regularly "except of course Carol Moseley Braun, who always looks as though she is headed to an afternoon worship service. Such is the burden of being the only female candidate struggling to appear wise, moral, feminine, tough, and yet not intimidating."[31] In other words, Moseley Braun did not participate in the "manly" gesture of sleeve-rolling, arguably deemed critical to an appealing image by male candidates. She instead needed to negotiate contradictory demands, such as being tough but not intimidating and also feminine, aspects outside ordinary notions of masculine presidential timbre. Her dress also seemed intended to evoke culturally positive characteristics credited more to women than men, wisdom and morality. Ironically, the single most important article about her assets as a presidential candidate began by focusing on her clothes and how she played it "so safe" in her dress.[32]

The Moseley Braun candidacy was not destined to survive for a variety of reasons, regardless of whether she was a man or woman. She lacked extensive pre-presidential experience and had lost her senate seat. Her lapses in judgment were highlighted, especially those related to a trip to Nigeria at a time when the State Department recommended against it because of the human rights violations of the country's leader. Most of all, perhaps, voters were not yet willing to take seriously, to confer the perception of presidential timber to, a liberal, black woman regardless of her background.

Her candidacy remains important regardless. She dared to suggest ambassadorial foreign policy experience might be as important to a presidency as the military experience historically touted by male candidates. By not appealing mostly to black constituencies, she opened the door for mainstreaming black candidates. By her very presence as a candidate, she made Americans, political insiders, and the press more accustomed to the idea of a woman president. Arguably, Moseley Braun has helped bring the idea of a black women president into the realm of the "thinkable." This dynamic may aid Condoleezza Rice and account for at least some of the talk of recruiting her as a candidate for 2008.

Early signs point to the 2008 election as a time when female candidates may be considered seriously. For example, as early as February, 2005, one website offers campaign materials such as buttons and bumper stickers that urge a long list of candidates to run, about one-quarter of whom are women: Condoleezza Rice, Dianne Feinstein, Elizabeth Dole, Hillary Clinton, Carol Moseley Braun, and Barbara Boxer. Clearly, Rice is being recruited to run, whether or not she is interested.[33]

Hillary Rodham Clinton continues to be mentioned widely as a presidential candidate. She was mentioned throughout the 2004 cycle, despite her denials of interest. Having served successfully as a senator, she gains credibility in her own right. No longer must she rely upon derivative power as first lady; she is positioned very differently now. Political insiders and the public alike see her as a frontrunner candidate and powerful Democrat. Bill O'Reilly, host of a popular television talk show, considers Hillary Clinton to be "the most powerful Democrat in the country."[34] The Associated Press quoted Bill Clinton as saying, "Hillary would be an excellent choice as the first female leader of the world's most powerful nation." In the same article, Senator Joseph Biden (D-DE), a potential presidential aspirant himself, declared, "She is likely to be the nominee. She'd be the toughest person and I think Hillary Clinton is able to be elected president of the United States."[35] Notice that, consistent with the masculine words above, she is described as "the toughest person." A recent poll showed Americans warming to the idea of a female president, and named Clinton as the clear frontrunner, followed by Condoleezza Rice.[36] In other words, whether or not she runs, presidential election space has shifted its gendering enough for political elites across the spectrum to name a woman as *the* early frontrunner. Perhaps the presidency is regendering, making it possible for a female candidate to cross the next benchmark of successful candidacies by making it into the primaries as an aspirant. Clinton might even cross the next hurdle of becoming the party's nominee for general election. With each step, female candidates regender presidential elections, making them more open to women.

Though the thoroughly masculinized character of the presidency – its election, and perceptions crucial to presidential viability and leadership – still pose major challenges for women's success as candidates, the fact that masculinity has become more exposed makes it more likely to change. When the ordinary and non-conscious assumption that only manly men are presidents comes into awareness, the citizenry can think more clearly about the implications of dominance masculinity as a primary qualifier for office. Ideas of leadership, which have been adjusting to women leaders' successes in other realms, can inform judgments in presidential elections, too. "With women like Sen. Hillary Rodham Clinton (D-N.Y.) and Condoleezza Rice, Bush's national security advisor, looming as potential presidential candidates, the nation may have to find new ways to think and talk about qualities traditionally attributed to men . . . 'When you think about it, Hillary is viewed in all those leadership ways,' [political scientist Susan] McManus said. 'So the discussion may not just include men anymore.'"[37] To think explicitly about masculinity in presidential elections is to open the door wider for women.

## NOTES

1. Ron Fournier. November 6, 2004. Exit Polls Can Lead the Way in Finding Mr. or Mrs. Right for a Run in 2008. Wisconsin State Journal.
2. For information about The White House Project go to http://www.thewhitehouseproject.org/.
3. R. W. Connell. 1995. *Masculinities*. Berkeley: University of California Press, and Whitehead and Barrett.
4. David Collinson and Jeff Hearn. 2001. Naming Men as Men: Implications for Work, Organization, and Management. In *The Masculinities Reader*, eds. Stephen M. Whitehead and Frank J. Barrett. Cambridge, MA: Polity Press, pp. 144–169.
5. Forrest McDonald. 1994. *The American Presidency: An Intellectual History*. Lawrence, KS: University of Kansas Press.
6. Michael Kimmel. 1996. *Manhood in American*. New York: The Free Press.
7. Jennifer L. Lawless. 2004. Women, War, and Winning Elections: Gender Stereotyping in the Post-September 11th Era. *Political Research Quarterly* 57: 479–90.
8. Articles from 2001–2002 must have more than 50 percent of their content focused upon a candidate to be included. For 2003 through Super Tuesday

2004, articles from seven papers have been collected using the Nexis word search command for presidential candidate ("candida!" and "president!") For the remaining stages, I searched for all articles mentioning Kerry and/or Bush, eliminating those on Bush not directly related to the election campaign. Throughout, I eliminate news briefs, AP articles, and other non-relevant articles, such as movie reviews.

9. Articles from the New York Times, July 13 to September 16, 2004, are not included in this count.
10. McDonald, *The American Presidency: An Intellectual History*; Stephen J. Ducat. 2004. *The Wimp Factor*. Boston: Beacon Press.
11. December 12, 2003. At Home in Vermont/Dean and His State Like to Go Their Own Way, Many Say. St. Louis Post-Dispatch.
12. James Gerstenzang and Mark Z. Barabak. May 3, 2003. Democrats Gather for a Debate in Deep South; Nine contenders for the presidential nomination assemble tonight in South Carolina in a bid to form opinions and capture voter interest. Los Angeles Times.
13. Gerstenzang and Barabak 2003. All of the quotations in the remaining analysis of timber are from this article, unless otherwise indicated.
14. Connell 1995.
15. Connell 1995, 194.
16. For the 2000 election, I looked at news accounts in the *Washington Post* and the *St. Louis Post-Dispatch* for the months of April and October; I thank Peter Bartanen for his research assistance. For 2004, I looked in all seven papers for the month of January, a key time for winnowing Democratic candidates; Sarah Bryner and Sara Hyler provided excellent research assistance.
17. The Associated Press. October 2, 2000. In Gore-Bush Debates, Voters Will See Personal As Well As Political Differences, TV Setting May Magnify Strengths and Weaknesses. St. Louis Post-Dispatch.
18. Cathy Young. September 8, 2003. We're Still Playing the Gender Card. Boston Globe.
19. James Rainey. March 18, 2004. Who's the Man? They are; George Bush and John Kerry stand shoulder to shoulder in one respect: Macho is good. Very good. It's been that way since Jefferson's day. Los Angeles Times.
20. Rainey 2004.
21. Rainey 2004.
22. Arlie Hochschild. October 5, 2003. NASCAR Dads Fuel Strategies for Bush in '04. Los Angeles Times.
23. Ducat 2004.
24. Rainey 2004.
25. Maureen Dowd. March 11, 2004. Whence the Wince? New York Times.
26. Howard Kurtz. September 23, 2004. Presidential Attack Ad Move From Land To Water – and Back. Washington Post.
27. Todd S. Purdum and David M. Halbfinger. February 1, 2004. With Cry of "Bring It On," Kerry Shifted Tack to Regain Footing. The New York Times.
28. Jennifer Lee. September 23, 2003. Ex-Senator Announces For Presidency. New York Times.

29. Robin Givhan. December 5, 2003. Something Up Their Sleeves; Gesture Is the Epitome of "Candidate Casual." Washington Post.
30. Givhan 2003.
31. Givhan 2003.
32. Robin Givhan. January 16, 2004. The Lady in Red Played It So Safe. Washington Post.
33. Helen Kennedy. February 14, 2005. Rice Mentioned as GOP 2008 Presidential Candidate. Wisconsin State Journal.
34. Bill O'Reilly. February 14, 2005. The New Dean on Campus. Janesville Gazette.
35. The Associated Press. February 27, 2005. Clinton: Hillary Would Be Great President. <abcnews.go.com/US/wireStory?id=536651> 2005, May 13.
36. Erin Duggan. February 23, 2005. Americans Warming to the Idea of a Female President, Poll Says. Wisconsin State Journal.
37. Rainey 2004.

SUSAN A. MacMANUS[1]

# 2   Voter Participation and Turnout

## It's A New Game

Women make up a majority of the U.S. voting age population, registered voters, and actual voters. These facts explain why both major political parties – Democrats and Republicans – and women's advocacy groups from across the ideological spectrum worked harder to mobilize women voters in 2004 than in the past. Women's votes were viewed as critical to victory, and getting women to the polls became a key strategy.

Women's dominance at the ballot box is a relatively recent phenomenon. Women did not possess the right to vote in all the states until 1920, with the ratification of the Nineteenth Amendment to the U.S. Constitution. Since then, "We've come a long way, baby" ["sister," "mama," "grandma"].

But it's not far enough yet, say political activists who pushed for greater female involvement in the 2004 campaign. Thanks to these crusaders, both the Democratic and Republican National Committees beefed up their efforts to educate, mobilize, and support women voters.

Outside the political parties, women's advocacy groups sprang into action – first to get more women registered, and then to get them to the polls. Groups ranged from the more traditional, and nonpartisan, League of Women Voters (founded in 1919) to new ones with catchy, sassy names like MTV's Chicks Rock, Chicks Vote; Running in Heels; and 10 for Change.

Throughout the 2004 campaign, political parties and advocacy groups alike used a variety of voter mobilization tools – everything from web sites and recorded phone calls from celebrities to precisely targeted mail, radio spots, and television ads (broadcast and cable). Films, concerts, books, buttons, clothing, bumper stickers – you name it – aimed at slices of women voters. Long gone are any assumptions (or wishes) that women think or vote alike.

Today's political mobilization strategies borrow heavily from marketing, where strategies differ depending upon age, income, education, marital status, sexual orientation, issue priorities, and even geographical location. As in the private sector, political parties, candidates, and advocacy organizations use focus groups and public opinion surveys to carefully test message content, format, and placement.

Heading into the 2004 campaign, Donna Brazile, chair of the Democratic National Committee's Voting Rights Institute, manager of the Gore-Lieberman campaign in 2000, and author of *Cooking With Grease: Stirring the Pots in American Politics*, gave this advice to the political parties:

> To pull more women into the voting process – and to win votes – the two major parties should drop any idea of a "one size fits all" approach to women. Instead, they should target their messages to diverse groups of women. . . . Political campaigns will have to address single women, married women, suburban soccer moms, security moms, on-the-go female professionals, urban-base[d] voting women, Jewish women, Latinas, senior moms, want-to-be-moms and soon-to-be moms.[2]

Getting more women to vote got a big push from election reforms. After the heavily disputed 2000 election, many states moved to correct flaws in their election systems. Some, including Florida, bought new voting equipment to replace punch-card systems with their infamous hanging, dangling, and pregnant chads. Others improved ballot formats (no more butterfly ballots), intensified poll worker training, and/or mandated more voter education and registration efforts. A number of states made it easier to vote early or absentee. (Thirty-two states now offer some form of advance voting.)

In 2002, Congress passed the Help America Vote Act (HAVA). The Act allows a voter to cast a provisional ballot if that voter's name does not appear on the registered voter roll at the assigned polling place but the voter believes he or she is registered. Afterward election officials review the master registration list and count the ballot if the person is indeed registered.

The goal of all these reforms was to increase voter participation – raise registration and turnout rates – and reduce errors, particularly among new and inexperienced voters and those with below-average reading and comprehension skills.

In this chapter, we begin with a short history of how women won the right to vote and then look at changes in registration and turnout rates over the years through the election of 2004. The remainder of the chapter focuses on new strategies and high tech-based ways of targeting and mobilizing women voters in 2004. Among these were: the emergence of new women's groups; the creation of catchy interactive web site addresses and logos; direct mail encouraging women to vote early or by mail (absentee); creative uses of fashion, music, and meeting places; and very sophisticated ads aimed at energizing specific slices of the women's vote. As the chapter shows, the Get-Out-The-Vote (GOTV) game has gotten more important over the years and women have become more highly sought after players. This is nothing short of amazing considering that women were denied the right to vote under the original U.S. Constitution.

## A BRIEF HISTORY OF WOMEN'S SUFFRAGE

The struggle for women's voting rights began at the nation's birth. In 1776, women like Abigail Adams urged the men writing the Declaration of Independence to include women. "Remember the Ladies," wrote Adams to her husband, John, a delegate to the Continental Congress. "If particular care and attention is not paid to the ladies, we are determined to foment a rebellion, and will not hold ourselves bound by any laws in which we have no voice or representation." Was she ever right!

In the 1800s, white women began working outside the home, mostly at mills, as America changed from an agrarian to a more industrialized society. The long working hours and dangerous conditions led many women to organize. Meanwhile, stay-at-home, middle-class women began banding together for charity work, temperance (abstinence from alcohol), and the abolition of slavery. Black women like Sojourner Truth and Harriet Jacobs rose to oppose sexism, slavery, and the white activists who "saw themselves as the sole liberators of passive, childlike slaves."[3]

The official birthday of the women's suffrage movement occurred on July 20, 1848, at the country's first women's rights convention in Seneca Falls, New York. The 300 attendees issued a document proclaiming that men and women were created equal and, therefore, that women should be allowed to vote.[4]

After the Civil War, groups led by Susan B. Anthony and others organized to push for universal suffrage. They made substantial progress in 1870 when the Fifteenth Amendment extended the franchise to African American men.

In 1890, rival suffrage groups merged to form the National American Woman Suffrage Association (NAWSA). Conservative and liberal women's groups alike, including the Woman's Christian Temperance Union, the Young Women's Christian Association, and the National Association of Colored Women, began to see that voting was the only way for women to affect public policy.

### Western States Ahead of the Nation

Ultimately, it was in the wild, wild West where women first tasted success. Historically, most public policy innovations in America occur not at the national level but in the states. So it was with women's suffrage. In 1890, Wyoming became the first women's suffrage state upon its admission to the Union. In 1893, Colorado extended the right to vote to women through an amendment to its state constitution. Neighboring western states soon jumped on the bandwagon. By 1900, women could vote in thirteen western and midwestern states as well as in Michigan and New York.

### The Ladies Get Testy

The successes of the women's suffrage movement spurred strong opposition from anti-suffragists, many of whom were also women. Then, as now, differing views on women's societal and political roles resulted in a traditionalist (anti-suffragist) versus revisionist (suffragist) schism.

Even within their own ranks, suffragists disagreed about the pace of the movement. One faction of NAWSA broke off to form another group that became the National Woman's Party in 1916. They used protests and hunger strikes to rally support for an amendment to the U.S. Constitution. (It was known as "the Anthony Amendment" in honor of Susan B. Anthony and ultimately became the Nineteenth Amendment to the U.S. Constitution in 1920.)

During World War I, women suffragists split into pro- and anti-war blocs. (The same schism characterized women voters in 2004 over the war in Iraq.) But the leaders of suffragist groups, like Alice Paul of the National Women's Party and Carrie Chapman Catt of the Woman's Peace Party, put aside their personal feelings about the war, fearing a backlash against women's suffrage. The tactic paid off. Their refusal to campaign against the war made it more politically palatable for President Wilson and other politicians to support the Nineteenth Amendment.

### At Last, Ratification!

It was not until June 4, 1919, that the U.S. Congress formally proposed the Nineteenth Amendment to the states for ratification.[5] Over a year later, on August 18, 1920, Tennessee became the thirty-sixth state to approve

**TEXT BOX 2.1: The history of the women's vote**

Today every U.S. citizen who is eighteen years of age by election day and a resident of the local precinct at least thirty days is eligible to cast a ballot. However, women, African Americans, Native American Indians, and members of certain religious groups were not allowed to vote during the colonial period and the early years of the country's history. In [1787] the U.S. Constitution granted each state government the power to determine who could vote. Individual states wrote their own suffrage laws. Early voting qualifications required that an eligible voter be a white man, twenty-one years of age, Protestant, and a landowner. Many citizens who recognized the importance of the right to vote led the suffrage movement.

**One Hundred Years Toward the Women's Vote**

Compiled by E. Susan Barber

**1776**

Abigail Adams writes to her husband, John, at the Continental Congress in Philadelphia, asking that he and the other men – who are at work on the Declaration of Independence – "Remember the Ladies." The Declaration's wording specifies that "all men are created equal."

**1848**

The first women's rights convention in the United States is held in Seneca Falls, New York. Many participants sign a "Declaration of Sentiments and Resolutions" that outlines the main issues and goals for the emerging women's movement. Thereafter, women's rights meetings are held on a regular basis.

**1861 to 1865**

The American Civil War disrupts suffrage activity as women, North and South, divert their energies to "war work." The war, however, serves as a "training ground," as women gain important organizational and occupational skills they will later use in post-war organizational activity.

**1866**

Elizabeth Cady Stanton and Susan B. Anthony form the American Equal Rights Association, an organization for white and black women and men dedicated to the goal of universal suffrage.

*(continued)*

**TEXT BOX 2.1** *(continued)*

**1868**

The Fourteenth Amendment is ratified. It extends to all citizens the protections of the Constitution against unjust state laws. This Amendment is the first to define "citizens" and "voters" as "male."

**1870**

The Fifteenth Amendment enfranchises black men.

**1870 to 1875**

Several women – including Virginia Louisa Minor, Victoria Woodhull, and Myra Bradwell – attempt to use the Fourteenth Amendment in the courts to secure the vote (Minor and Woodhull) and right to practice law (Bradwell). They all are unsuccessful.

**1872**

Susan B. Anthony is arrested and brought to trial in Rochester, New York, for attempting to vote for Ulysses S. Grant in the presidential election. At the same time, Sojourner Truth appears at a polling booth in Grand Rapids, Michigan, demanding a ballot; she is turned away.

**1874**

The Woman's Christian Temperance Union (WCTU) is founded by Annie Wittenmyer. With Frances Willard at its head (1876), the WCTU becomes an important force in the struggle for women's suffrage. Not surprisingly, one of the most vehement opponents to women's enfranchisement was the liquor lobby, which feared women might use the franchise to prohibit the sale of liquor.

**1878**

A Woman Suffrage Amendment is introduced in the U.S. Congress. (The wording is unchanged in 1919, when the amendment finally passes both houses.)

**1890**

Wyoming becomes the first women's suffrage state upon its admission to the Union.

**1893**

Colorado becomes the first state to adopt a state amendment enfranchising women.

**1896**

Mary Church Terrell, Ida B. Wells-Barnett, Margaret Murray Washington, Fanny Jackson Coppin, Frances Ellen Watkins Harper, Charlotte Forten Grimké, and former slave Harriet Tubman meet in Washington, D.C., to form the National Association of Colored Women (NACW).

**1903**

Mary Dreier, Rheta Childe Dorr, Leonora O'Reilly, and others form the Women's Trade Union League of New York, an organization of middle- and working-class women dedicated to unionization for working women and to women's suffrage. This group later becomes a nucleus of the International Ladies' Garment Workers' Union (ILGWU).

**1911**

The National Association Opposed to Woman Suffrage (NAOWS) is organized. Led by Mrs. Arthur Dodge, its members include wealthy, influential women and some Catholic clergymen – including Cardinal Gibbons who, in 1916, sends an address to NAOWS's convention in Washington, D.C. In addition to the distillers and brewers, who work largely behind the scenes, the "antis" also draw support from urban political machines, Southern congressmen, and corporate capitalists – like railroad magnates and meatpackers – who support the "antis" by contributing to their war chests.

**1912**

Theodore Roosevelt's Progressive (Bull Moose/Republican) Party becomes the first national political party to adopt a women's suffrage plank.

**1913**

Alice Paul and Lucy Burns organize the Congressional Union, later known as the National Women's Party (1916). Borrowing the tactics of the radical, militant Women's Social and Political Union (WSPU) in England, members of the Woman's Party participate in hunger strikes, picket the White House, and engage in other forms of civil disobedience to publicize the suffrage cause.

**1914**

The National Federation of Women's Clubs – which by this time includes more than two million white women and women of color throughout the United States – formally endorses the suffrage campaign.

*(continued)*

**TEXT BOX 2.1** *(continued)*

**1916**

Jeannette Rankin of Montana becomes the first American woman elected to represent her state in the U.S. House of Representatives.

**August 26, 1920**

The Nineteenth Amendment is ratified. Its victory accomplished, NAWSA ceases to exist, but its organization becomes the nucleus of the League of Women Voters.

*Source:* Adapted from *Election Focus 2004*, Issue 1, No. 8, April 14, 2004. Available at: http://usinfo.state.gov/dhr/img/assets/5796/elections04_14_043.pdf.

of the amendment by a single vote in its legislature. The young legislator who cast the deciding vote confessed that he had been led to do so by a telegram he had received from his mother urging him to vote in favor of the amendment. On August 26, 1920, the U.S. Secretary of State officially proclaimed that the required thirty-six states had ratified the Nineteenth Amendment giving women the right to vote. (However, it would be years later before African American women had full voting rights. Discriminatory practices such as literacy tests and poll taxes, along with threats and violence, kept many from voting until these barriers were outlawed by court rulings, voting rights acts passed by Congress, and a constitutional amendment eliminating poll taxes.)

The Nineteenth Amendment as proposed and ratified read:

> The right of citizens of the United States to vote shall not be denied or abridged by the United States or by any State on account of sex.

> Congress shall have power, by appropriate legislation, to enforce the provisions of this article.

The suffragists finally prevailed. It had been a long haul – 140 years after the Declaration of Independence was signed in 1776 and seventy-two years after women had issued their first formal demand for the right to vote at Seneca Falls, New York (in 1848). In its Sunday, August 29, 1920, editorial, the *New York Times* applauded those who had worked so long and hard for this right: "Women in fighting for the vote have shown a passion of earnestness, a persistence, and above all a command of both tactics and strategy, which have amazed our master politicians." But the editorial went on to warn against presuming that women would all vote alike: "It is doubtless true that women will divide much as men have done among several parties. There will be no solid 'woman vote.'" It certainly

Figure 2.1: **Women Have Registered to Vote at Higher Rates Than Men in Recent Elections.**

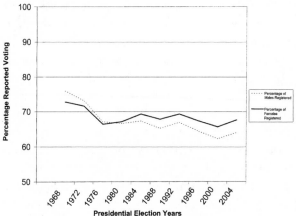

*Source:* U.S. Census, Current Population Survey, November 2004 and earlier reports.

was that way in Election 2004: Democrat John Kerry got 51 percent of the women's vote and Republican George W. Bush, 48 percent – a difference of only 3 percentage points.

## REGISTRATION RATES

Convincing people to register is often more difficult than getting them to vote once they have registered. Some states, like Maine, Minnesota, Wisconsin, Wyoming, New Hampshire, and Idaho, allow citizens to register on Election Day. But most states require them to register in advance, usually fifteen to thirty days before the election.[6]

U.S. Census figures show that in every election cycle since 1980, a higher percentage of women than men has registered to vote. (See Figure 2.1.) Younger women (under age forty-four) have out-registered younger men since the 1970s. It is only among the oldest cohort, sixty-five and older, that women's registration rates consistently lag behind men's.

After the close presidential election in 2000, both the Democratic and Republican parties realized they had to spend considerably more time and money registering voters for 2004. The parties knew they would have to identify non-registrants more precisely and begin registration drives earlier to win. Naturally, women were a prime target, especially those who had never registered to vote.

Registration drives were conducted on college campuses, at concert and movie locations, outside churches and bookstores, at political rallies and civic group meetings – anywhere eligible but unregistered persons were likely to be. (Voter eligibility requirements typically include age – eighteen years of age or older – U.S. citizenship, and permanent residency at the location where one is registering. In most states, one is not eligible to register if convicted of a felony and not yet finished with the sentence. The same is true of persons declared mentally incapacitated by the state.)

Citizens' mailboxes (postal and Internet) were flooded with voter registration forms, along with the telephone numbers and mail and Internet addresses of election officials. Parties and advocacy group representatives went door-to-door offering to help people register or leaving forms for them to complete. Naturally, the registration outreach efforts were targeted at high-growth areas and places with heavier concentrations of unregistered people. Public service announcements (PSAs) reminding voters of how and when to register ran on just about every television (cable and broadcast) and radio station. These PSAs were tailored to fit the demographics of a station's viewers or listeners.

## Parties Use Different Strategies

The approaches used by the two major political parties to register new voters differed markedly. Democrats relied more heavily on outside groups such as America Coming Together, MoveOn.org, and various labor union PACs (political action committees) to register new voters who would be sympathetic to Democratic Party candidates, although some local Democratic organizations were involved in registration drives. Republicans relied more heavily on the party organization itself – at all levels – to register GOP-leaning new voters. Some post-election analyses attributed the Republicans' greater registration successes to their almost exclusive use of party volunteers rather than volunteers from sympathetic outside groups. But others say Republicans succeeded because they started earlier – right after the U.S. Supreme Court ruled on the 2000 election outcome – and set their goals higher.

Each "side" derived – and met – specific numeric goals of unregistered women. Democratic-leaning groups heavily targeted young, single, and blue-collar working women. Republicans targeted married women with children and social conservatives in suburban and rural areas. Both parties targeted women without college educations because they were less likely to be registered than college-educated women.

## TURNOUT RATES

In 2004, after intense Get-Out-The-Vote (GOTV) efforts, ranging from calls and transportation assistance to heavily-targeted television, radio,

**Figure 2.2: Women Have Voted at Higher Rates Than Men in Recent Elections.**

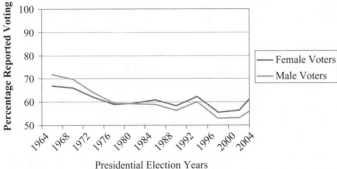

Presidential Election Years

*Note:* The turnout rate for each gender is the percent of the eligible population that voted (the number voting as a percent of the total number of voting age persons of that gender).

*Source:* U.S. Census, Current Population Survey, November 2004 and earlier reports.

Internet, and direct mail ads, the turnout rate went up, especially among women. As a result, women increased their share of the electorate from 52 percent in 1996 and 2000 to 54 percent in 2004.

## Women Catch Up With – and Pass – Men

For years after passage of the Nineteenth Amendment, the participation rates of men were greater than those of women (even though there were more women than men of voting age). This was true whether male-female comparisons were made using the sheer *number* of men and women voting or the relative *percentage* of each gender who voted (the turnout rate). It was not until 1964 that the number of women voters surpassed the number of men voting in presidential elections. But women continued to vote at a lower rate until 1980, when the percentage of women voting slightly exceeded that of men. (See Figure 2.2.) Since 1980, the turnout rate of women has exceeded that of men, and with each successive election, women have outvoted men at increasingly higher rates. The civil and women's rights movements of the 1960s and 1970s played a large role in improving the turnout rate among women.

Among women, as among men, turnout rates are lowest among the young, the poor, the unemployed, and the least educated. Voting studies have found that turnout rates are also lower than average among renters, newcomers to a community, infrequent and non church-goers, Asians, Latinos, single parents living in poor neighborhoods, persons with physical disabilities, blue-collar and service-sector workers, and Independents.

The relative turnout rates of men and women differ across age groups. For decades, older men (sixty-five and older) have turned out to vote at higher rates than older women. The same pattern held true among the forty-five to sixty-four age group until 1992, when female turnout rates surpassed male voting rates. In contrast, since the early 1970s, women eighteen to forty-four have voted at higher rates than males their age. The lone exception was in 1996, when the turnout rate of women eighteen to twenty-four dipped below that of their male counterparts. Higher turnout rates among younger women are attributed to a rise in the educational level of women. Today, more women than men attend college.

## Women Benefit from Election Reforms

One reason women made up a larger proportion of the electorate in 2004 is the increased number of female registrants. But another reason is the improvements in election systems, especially those that allow more flexibility in *when* one votes.

Since 2000, a number of states have adopted or expanded laws permitting early, or convenience, voting. Many have also made it easier to vote absentee (by mail). Both of these are examples of pre-Election Day balloting – a growing trend throughout the United States. In Florida in 2004, for example, 30 percent of the electorate voted before November 2 via either early (18 percent) or absentee voting (12 percent).

Where early voting is permitted, voters may go to designated voting sites before Election Day to cast their ballots. A 2004 statewide survey of 800 Florida voters found that almost one-fifth voted early, and slightly more (51 percent) of these were female than male. Early voting is increasingly popular, especially among the youngest and oldest voters. Among voters eighteen to twenty-four years of age, women made up 67 percent of the early voters; among voters sixty-five years of age and older, 59 percent were females.[7] African American and Native American women were more likely to vote early than women of other races or ethnicities.

Among all voters by party, independents were the most likely to vote early (20 percent), and Republicans, to vote absentee (14 percent). Among women, early voting was the choice of 22 percent of independents, 19 percent of Republicans, and 15 percent of Democrats. Absentee voting was preferred by 17 percent of Republican women, 14 percent of Democratic women, and only 4 percent of independent women.

## Targeted Ads Promote Early and Absentee Voting

Educating women about early and absentee voting was a major component of GOTV efforts in many states. The direct mail pieces in

Direct Mail Ad 1

Ad sponsor: AFL-CIO (pro-Kerry)
Target: Working women in low-to-mid-paying jobs

Direct Mail Ad 2

Ad sponsor: Republican National Committee (pro-Bush)
Target: College-age women and their parents

**Photo Section 2.1:** Direct Mail Ads Showing Appeals to Women Voters.

Photo Section 2.1 are visual proof of how precisely the pieces were targeted to women of different ages, races or ethnicities, and family situations in the key battleground state of Florida by both parties.

## WOMEN-TO-WOMEN MOBILIZATION EFFORTS RULE THE DAY

Six months prior to the 2004 election, a poll of 1,426 voters conducted for the Pew Research Center for the People and the Press showed women

Direct Mail Ad 3

Ad sponsor: Florida Democratic Party (pro-Kerry)
Target: Working Hispanic women who may not be able
to vote on election day

Direct Mail Ad 4

Ad sponsor: Human Rights Campaign in cooperation with
Equality Florida and TurnOut Florida (pro-Kerry)
Target: Women workers who fear discrimination on the basis
of sexual preference or gender

**Photo Section 2.1** (*continued*)

made up 58 percent of the nation's "swing voters" – registered voters who
were undecided or who said they might change their minds before Election
Day. Another poll by Lake, Snell, Perry, & Associates found the proportion
to be even higher – 65 percent.

Historically, women are the late deciders – about whether to vote at
all and, if so, for whom. Many nonvoters feel frustrated and unprepared.
Because of their life situations, they do not have the time to study up on
the election as much as they would like. In fact, this is a more common
reason for not voting than being alienated or cynical, as research after the
2000 election revealed.

Direct Mail Ad 5

Ad sponsor: United Seniors Association (pro-Bush)
Target: Older citizens on Medicare—more women than men

Direct Mail Ad 6

Ad sponsor: Republican Party of Florida (pro-Bush)
Target: Working and professional women who may be
willing to vote early

**Photo Section 2.1** (*continued*)

This new knowledge led to "women-helping-women" GOTV efforts
in 2004. The formula called for frequent personal contacts to bolster
the confidence of women feeling inadequately prepared to vote, which
yielded innovative ways of mobilizing different subsets of women voters.
Certainly, the nation's largest women's advocacy groups – the League
of Women Voters, NOW, and the National Women's Political Caucus –
plunged into the fray. But the emergence of new women-oriented groups,

a few of which are described below, created a whole new ball game. The logos and descriptions are taken from their respective web sites. Even though the books have closed on Election 2004, many of these groups have vowed to remain active.

## INVOLVING WOMEN IN THE POLITICAL PROCESS: NONPARTISAN EFFORTS

A number of new and established women's organizations, mostly nonpartisan in nature, created interactive and informative web sites during the 2004 campaign. Their goals were to register new women voters, provide in-depth information about critical issues, arrange meet-ups, recruit volunteers (and candidates for office), and get women to the polls on Election Day.

### WomenMatter (www.womenmatter.com)

This nonpartisan organization is "dedicated to empowering women to participate in the political process" by better informing them about key issues. "It is a nonpartisan, web-centric, non-profit organization whose goal is to empower women by helping them become part of the political process."

The group's key concerns were not only registration and turnout, but also informing women about how to use new voting equipment such as the touch screen voting machines that were added in many states. "It is only through our actually showing up at the polls that the government will take us seriously. . . . So we need to guarantee that women of all ages, incomes, and ethnic groups are taught how to register and how to use the new machines."

### 10 for Change (www.10forchange.org)

The National Organization for Women started 10 for Change with people who had marched in its April 25 March for Women's Lives in Washington, D.C. The group used an interactive online program to help users learn how to register voters "to help make women voters a powerful voice in this and every election."

The group described its registration drive: "Changing people's lives, changing voter participation, changing how people look at our political process – 10 steps, 10 minutes and 10 people at a time. That's what 10 for Change is all about." "The number 10 represents a manageable goal for the busy individual. Take 10 minutes and make sure you're registered to vote. Tell 10 friends about this great campaign. Bring 10 voter registration forms to your next campus function, PTA meeting or any get-together." "Ten also multiplies quite nicely. If we can turn 1 voter into 10...and 10 voters into 100...and 100 voters into 1,000...and so on...we can really make a difference in this country! We achieve this mathematical magic by creating new voters and re-invigorating lapsed ones. And by getting all these voters to the polls on Nov. 2."

**Vote, Run, Lead.** (www.voterunlead.org)
Vote, Run, Lead is a program of The White House Project, a national non-partisan organization dedicated to putting women in positions of leader-ship, including the presidency. The group captured its goals in its GOTV slogan: "Go vote. Go run. Go lead. Go girl." The web site urged viewers to recruit women to vote, get politically active, and run for office. "Calling All Women! You CAN and MUST Make A Difference! Learn More About Why Women Matter."

## AIMING AT UNMARRIED WOMEN: A TRADITIONALLY LOW-TURNOUT GROUP

Women's Voices. Women Vote, the first nonpartisan organization created for the specific purpose of increasing the registration and voting rates of unmarried women, was quite visible in many of the hotly contested states in the election of 2004. The group ran a very effective information cam-paign. According to a post-election study by Greenberg, Quinlan, Rosner Research, Inc., unmarried women participated in larger numbers than in any previous presidential election: "As a percentage of the electorate, they moved from 19 percent in 2000 to 22.4 percent in 2004, an increase of roughly 7 million votes."

**Women's Voices. Women Vote.** (http://wvwv.org/)

The nonprofit Tides Center, which provides man-agement and infrastructure services to charities, formed WVWV to target unmarried women (never married, divorced or separated, and widowed). This group's compilation of U.S. Census statistics was invaluable to other groups and ended up being cited on many web sites, campaign brochures, and television and radio ads.

The most widely cited statistics were:

- Unmarried women are 46 percent of all voting-age women and 56 percent of all unregistered women.
- Sixteen million unmarried, unregistered women and another 22 million unmarried, registered women did not vote in the 2000 presidential election.
- If unmarried women had simply voted at the same rate as married women, more than 6 million additional votes would have been cast in 2000. Only 52 percent of unmarried women voted in 2000 compared to 68 percent of married women – the marriage gap.

WVWV surveys found that unmarried women who do not vote think that politics is too complicated, politicians do not listen to them, and politics is controlled by powerful interests (e.g., corporations), so it doesn't matter whether they vote or not.

The group encouraged the use of women celebrities, politicos, and the wives and daughters of the presidential candidates. "Unmarried women want to hear from strong, independent women who have made it, such as women members of Congress, Senator Hillary Clinton, and Oprah Winfrey. They want to hear about politics from authentic credible sources including friends and family." (Both the Kerry-Edwards and Bush-Cheney campaigns heavily involved the candidates' spouses and daughters as surrogates on the campaign trail.)

The group enlisted Jennifer Aniston, star of the television show "Friends," to appear in a thirty-second GOTV television ad. The script went like this:

"Let me ask you a question. Woman to woman.
Would you let someone else choose your clothes? Your friends?
OK. What about your husband?
No?
Then why would you let someone else choose your President? Your leaders?
Four years ago, 22 million single women didn't vote. And left the choice to someone else.
November 2nd, every single one of us can make a difference.
So unless you want someone else to decide for you. Make yourself heard. And vote.
A message from Women's Voices. Women Vote. A project of the Tides Center."

More issue-specific ads focused on educating women about how important their votes are to economic and security matters, health care, and education.

## AIMING AT MARRIED WOMEN OF FAITH: MORAL VALUES MATTER

Some women's groups, like the Concerned Women for America, focused their efforts on mobilizing married women of faith by stressing the importance of moral values. The Greenberg, Quinlan, Rosner Research, Inc. post-election analysis reported than married women made up 32 percent of the electorate in 2004 – a larger portion that unmarried women (22 percent). Moral values turned out to be the most often cited reason for voters' choice of presidential candidates, according to the national exit poll.

**Concerned Women for America** (www.cwfa.org)

 During Election 2004, this "pro-family," "pro-life" group encouraged the formation of Prayer/Action chapters where women could meet to discuss the decline of moral values in the United States. "The vision of CWA is for women and like-minded men from all walks of life to come together and restore the family to its traditional purpose and thereby allow each member of the family to realize their God-given potential and be more responsible citizens." Defending traditional definitions of marriage was a key concern.

The Elections 2004 portion of the CWA web site compared and contrasted President Bush's and Senator Kerry's campaign platforms on abortion, cloning, education, marriage, taxes, terror, energy, environment, gun control, health care, and jobs.

## AIMING AT MOTHERS: VOTE FOR BUSH; NO, VOTE FOR KERRY

For every action, there is an equal and opposite reaction. So says the law of physics – and politics, especially when it comes to targeting mothers. So it was with the Moms4Bush and Women in Support of the President versus the Mothers Opposing Bush (MOB) and the Mainstreet Moms Oppose Bush groups. The emergence of these diametrically opposed groups is further proof that there is no monolithic women's vote.

**Moms4Bush** (www.moms4bush.com)

 "Are you a mother, grandmother, aunt, sister? Did 9-11 impact you as a woman? Are you concerned about the future of our country's security? Are you upset about the media's negative spin with our War on Terror? Are you someone that knows we need to win this War on Terror now? If you answered 'Yes' to any of the above, then you are a 'Security Mom.'"

Moms4Bush urged its supporters to "Talk to your neighbors, the moms you meet at the playground, the pool, or at a summer picnic." They urged the re-election of George W. Bush for their children: "The future for our children – a future that is safe from terrorists!"

Music permeated this web site. Log on, and you heard a "Re-elect George W" medley.

**Women in Support of the President (WISP)** (www.gowisp04.org)
WISP was formed in an Annapolis restaurant by women who were angered by the "anti-Bush movement and propaganda." The initial idea was to create a bumper sticker, but it soon became a much bigger grassroots organization.

As with so many activist groups, WISP targeted the infrequent female voter: "We believe women who feel passionately about this election are not necessarily women who have ever been politically active before." "We are career women, and moms from all walks of life who feel strongly about having a President that is a dependable leader."

GOTV actions by WISP included placing automated phone-call messages to undecided women, initiating letter-writing campaigns to local newspapers, and call-ins to talk-radio programs.

**Mothers Opposing Bush** (www.MOB.org)
This group of women activists sprang up to oppose the re-election of George W. Bush because they feared his administration was "leading our country away from our core values of honesty, compassion, community, and patriotism."

The group's web site encouraged women to form local MOB chapters. To assist supporters in this effort, it provided downloadable handout cards (featuring women of different races and ethnicities) and sign art for events.

*Source:* Mothers Opposing Bush

**Mainstreet Moms Oppose Bush** (www.themmob.com)
MMOB is a Democratic-leaning organization of mothers that worked hard to register and turn out women supporting Democratic candidates. The group's belief was that children were the common ground that could be used to bridge the red state/blue state divide.

## AIMING AT WOMEN OF DIFFERENT AGES: FROM GRANNIES TO BARBIES

The symbols used to represent age-specific groups ranged from rocking chairs to "real-life" Barbie dolls. Organizations focusing on senior women stressed turnout, while those aiming at eighteen to twenty-four-year-olds stressed registration. The cleverly-designed Barbie for President campaign, sponsored by the White House Project, was created to entice young girls into following politics well ahead of their eighteenth birthdays when they would become eligible to vote.

**Granny Voter** (www.grannyvoter.org)

Formed by eleven grandmothers – all older than sixty – with thirty-two grandchildren among them, this nonpartisan group aimed to mobilize grandparents to "use your political power to make a difference in your grandchildren's future." Said the grannies, "We want to use our political capital as seniors – the largest voting bloc in the American electorate – to shape solutions to pressing problems with our grandchildren's future in mind."

**Get Out Her Vote** (http://www.getouthervote.org/)

The Feminist Majority Foundation created this effort to educate and register young women, particularly eighteen to twenty-four-year-olds, who vote less than any other age group. The group's web site, with the charge to "Vote as if your life depends on it," featured photographs of celebrities Laura Dern, Alfre Woodard, Sheryl Crow, and Nia Vardalos – each of whom recorded a radio PSA answering the question "Why Get Out Her Vote?"

The group homed in on organizing young women on college campuses to help them register and rally other women on campus (young women helping young women). Why? Because college students can be mobilized more easily than their non-college-educated peers.

**"Barbie for President"** (www.Barbie.com)
Hoping to grab the attention of girls too young to vote and get them interested in politics, The White House Project "recruited" Barbie to run for president. In a widely publicized announcement, Barbie entered the race in 2004 as a candidate from the "Party of Girls." Her slogan? "Empower Girls." In August, the "Party of Girls" convention was held at Toys "Я" Us Times Square in New York City. The party's platform (to create world peace, help the homeless and poor, and take care of animals) was devised with input from girls voting online on Barbie.com.

## AIMING AT MINORITY WOMEN: HEALTH, EDUCATION, AND EQUALITY ISSUES PREDOMINATE

Groups aiming at mobilizing black and Hispanic women heavily emphasized inequities in health care, education, and employment opportunities as reasons to "get political." Post-election analyses show that in 2004, Hispanic and African American women made up a larger portion of first-time voters than did white females.

### Black Women's Health Imperative
(www.BlackWomensHealth.ORG/Vote)

More than 14 million African American women are of voting age, and many are in poor health. The Black Women's Health Imperative's "Vote, damn it!" campaign was a partnership with other Black women's groups including the National Council of Negro Women, National Coalition of 100 Black Women, Black Women's Agenda, National Association of Negro Business and Professional Women's Clubs, National Association for Equal Opportunity in Higher Education, Zeta Phi Beta Sorority, Chapters of Alpha Kappa Alpha Sorority, Chi Eta Phi Sorority, Black Women of Essence, National Black Nurses Association, and the Women of Color Partnership, Religious Coalition for Reproductive Choice.

The Imperative's web site provided online voter registration, voter guides to women's issues, an e-postcard activity, and a free download-able poster. It promoted presidential and vice presidential debate watch parties, and Election Day as "Take Somebody to the Polls Day."

**Mujeres Latinas En Accion** (www.mujereslatinasenaccion.org)
**MANA National Latina Organization** (www.hermana.org)
**HOPE Hispanas Organized for Political Equality** (www.latinas.org)

The primary focus of Latino women's groups is public policy, with an emphasis on sharing infor-mation about public policy and how to influence it, and teaching leadership skills to Latinas in all sectors of society. Naturally, during a presidential election year, encouraging and assisting Latinas in registering and turning out to vote was a high priority for groups like Mujeres Latinas, HOPE, Mi Familia Vota, and MANA.

A survey of Latino voters conducted in February 2004 by Democracy Corps reported that working women make up one-third of the Latino electorate, and unmarried women make up 22 percent. (Married women are a larger portion than unmarried women.)

## AIMING AT PRO-CHOICE AND PRO-LIFE WOMEN: GROUPS ON BOTH SIDES OF THE ABORTION ISSUE

Prior to the 2004 election, there were already well-established politically-oriented groups representing both sides of the abortion, or reproduc-tive rights, issue. Among the two most powerful and well-known were EMILY'S List (pro-choice) and the Susan B. Anthony List (pro-life). Both were quite active in 2004. Each raised money to mobilize its sympathizers and fund candidates for public office who shared the group's position on this highly divisive subject.

### EMILY's List WOMEN VOTE! (www.emilyslist.org)
"EMILY's List WOMEN VOTE! touts itself as "the nation's largest voter mobilization strategy designed specifically for women voters." (EMILY stands for "Early Money Is Like Yeast" because, as the group points out, "it

makes the dough rise.") Since its formation in 1995, EMILY's List WOMEN VOTE! has raised funds and used them to motivate women voters to go to the polls to support pro-choice candidates, especially women. The group uses television, radio, direct mail, Internet, and personal contacts.

### Susan B. Anthony List (www.sba-list.org)

 This group, named for suffragist leader Susan B. Anthony, who was pro-life, works for goals opposite those of EMILY's List. The SBA List and its Candidate Fund raised more than $5 million in the 2004 campaign cycle. Membership has grown from 10,000 to more than 111,000 over the past three election cycles.

In the 2004 election, the SBA List sent out 800,000 pieces of election literature and funded two million GOTV phone calls. Some of the women who made these calls included U.S. Senator Elizabeth Dole (R-NC), and Jane Abraham – wife of U.S. Energy Secretary Spencer Abraham – who served as the SBA List Candidate Fund president. An October 11 article on the web site told users: "Your Vote-Your Voice- is important and has the potential to save babies' lives! Make a difference and vote on November 2nd!"

### AIMING AT WOMEN AGAINST VIOLENCE AND WAR

Historically, women have been more concerned about domestic violence and more opposed to war than men. Thus, it was not surprising that a number of anti-violence, pro-peace women's groups emerged to rally like-minded females into action at the voting booth on November 2, 2004.

### V is for Vote (www.vday.org)

 V is for Vote was founded in 2004 by Eve Ensler, *The Vagina Monologues* playwright. This grassroots organization was formed to mobilize, register, and get out the women's vote. In Election 2004, the group urged the presidential candidates "to make Violence Against Women a central issue of their campaign platforms, not a sideline or 'women's' issue."

Collective action by sympathetic women was at the heart of the group's "V-actions" – forming V-Posses to register, educate, and get each other to the polls; plastering "V is for Vote" messages throughout campuses and

**1000 Flowers** (www.1000flowers.org)

This group targeted hair and nail salons in low-registration areas in eight states (Nevada, New Mexico, Oregon, Ohio, Florida, Pennsylvania, New York, and California). "Nail the Vote!" urged women to commit to vote and paint their nails red, white, and blue with V-O-T-E decals: "Your beautiful nails can persuade others to become voters too!" The group offered voter registration Beauty Kits to salons and manicure party supplies, including a special lipstick, to donors.

The web site gave tips on hosting manicure parties to discuss the candidates and issues, use the media to spread the word, and get organized for voting day (find polling places, arrange for carpools and babysitting, and get time off from work).

## PRECISION TARGETING OF WOMEN VOTERS

Women were a key target of both the Bush and Kerry campaigns. Throughout the campaign, each camp constantly sought better ways to communicate and connect with the critically important female voter. The candidates and their campaign strategists worked hard to find the winning combination of personal appearances, events featuring their wives or other powerful females, television and radio ads, and direct mail pieces.

Analysts agree that the 2004 election was characterized by the most precise demographic targeting in American campaign history. As evidenced by the direct mail pieces highlighted, ads were specially-crafted to appeal to different groups of women on the basis of their age, race/ethnicity, marital and parental status, employment and income, ideology, and religion, among others.

### Drawing Female Crowds: The First Lady Versus Women on the Move

Campaign professionals on both sides of the political aisle agreed that Laura Bush was more effective at drawing big crowds of women voters wherever she went than was Teresa Heinz Kerry. As a result, Democrats formed the "Women on the Move" bus tour rather than rely on visits by

Mrs. Kerry alone, whereas Republicans were quite happy to depend on the popular first lady to attract large female audiences of all ages.

The Democrats' Women on the Move bus tour featuring female celebrities from Hollywood and the nation's capital hit key battleground states like Florida, Iowa, and New Hampshire in the closing days of the campaign. Among the riders were actresses Ashley Judd of *De-Lovely*, Kirsten Dunst of *Spiderman II*, and Julia Louis-Dreyfus of the TV series "Seinfeld." Political and government officials included Ann Lewis, chair of the Democratic National Committee's Women's Vote Center; Laura Tyson, national economic advisor for the Clinton Administration; John Kerry's sister, Diana; Elizabeth Bagley, former ambassador to Portugal; Brigadier General (Ret.) Pat Foot; and Congresswomen Eddie Bernice Johnson (D-TX) and Louise Slaughter (D-NY). These "stars" generated lots of media coverage.

### Using the Media and Direct Mail

In recent years, radio spots and television ads have been critical in winning voters. Radio and television are especially powerful in reaching young and new voters, including women. By contrast, newspaper circulation is declining, and readers tend to be older voters. Neither Republicans nor Democrats spent much on newspaper and magazine ads in 2004, but both spent millions on television, radio, and direct mail ads.

In buying radio and TV time, campaigns carefully targeted media markets in key battleground states. Democrats ran more ads on broadcast television stations than Republicans, and Republicans placed more ads on cable television and radio. The campaigns selected the stations whose viewers or listeners the candidates wanted to reach and the times those viewers would mostly likely be tuned in. In each ad, the words and images were finely tuned to give a specific message to the targeted viewers. In 2004, Republicans tapped into the First Lady's popularity[8] and prominently featured her in Bush's campaign ads. Television ads with Mrs. Bush, according to focus groups, tended to draw a more positive rating for her husband.

Although radio and TV ads can beam specific campaign messages to specific audiences, direct mail is considered the most precise. It can reach far narrower audiences (by ZIP code, for example) and also reaches only registered voters who are eligible to vote in a particular electoral contest. Campaign managers can subdivide or cross-reference registered voter lists according to some personal characteristic (race, gender) or issue (membership in religious or environmental group, for example) and mail pieces to only those names. In 2004, campaigns divided women voters into several different niches, as shown by the direct mail ads included in this chapter.

One might argue that direct mail is, after all, junk mail and that recipients are likely to toss it in the trash. That may be true up to a point. Only about 10 to 15 percent of those who receive a mailer ever even look at it, and older persons are the most likely to read direct mail.

The trick is to capture the recipient's attention. The time to do that is short. According to direct mail specialists, it has to happen between the time a person picks up a mailer and the time she reaches the first trash can. It's more likely to happen if the recipient can immediately see something of herself and her sentiments in the piece. That means compelling pictures and a simple, straightforward message. The outside panels are often designed to look less like a political ad and more like a human interest informational piece because, as direct mail specialists know, politics is a lower priority with many voters than children, work, health, and other aspects of their lives. Mailers in 2004 were considerably more visual and creative than those sent in 2000.

The timing of when to send mail ads is getting trickier, especially in the growing number of states that have early voting. If an advertisement is mailed too early, nobody remembers it. If it is mailed too late, it gets lost in the shuffle and has no impact on a voter's decision. In addition, the more mail pieces a candidate sends, the more likely a voter is to remember the candidate's name. All direct mail consultants preach that repetition is critical.

In 2004, direct mail sent by the presidential candidates, the political parties, and various advocacy groups clearly targeted female voters – and aimed at them often.

## EFFECTIVENESS OF MOBILIZING WOMEN IN 2004

All of the emphasis on registering women and turning them out to vote paid off. Women voters made up 54 percent of all voters – up from 52 percent in 2000. White women made up the bulk of female voters – 41 percent of all voters, compared to 12 percent who were nonwhite women. However, there was a higher proportion of minority women among first-time voters.

Efforts to turn out unmarried women also succeeded. As noted earlier, they increased from 19 percent of all voters in 2000 to an estimated 22 percent in 2004. A majority of unmarried women chose Kerry (62 percent) while a majority of married women supported Bush (55 percent).

Getting working women to the polls turned out to be a more difficult task. They declined from 31 percent of all voters in 2000 to an estimated 29 percent in 2004. Among working women, Kerry did slightly better than Bush (51 percent v. 48 percent). But among non-working women, Bush pulled 53 percent of their votes compared to 46 percent for Kerry.

The number of young voters went up from 2000, but their share of the electorate did not (remaining at 28 percent). The increase in eighteen to twenty-year-olds who voted was 9.3 percentage points, going from 42.3 percent in 2000 to 51.6 percent in 2004. A majority (56 percent) of female voters younger than thirty supported Kerry, as did a majority of men younger than thirty (51 percent). Young voters were the only age group to give a majority of their votes to the Democratic candidate for president, although a post-election study by The Center for Information & Research on Civic Learning & Engagement reported that in terms of party identification, "18–29 year old voters closely resembled the overall voting population – 37% Democrat, 35% Republican, and 29% independent – just one point more Democratic and two points less Republican than the electorate as a whole."

## THE FINAL WORD

In this chapter, we began with a short history of how women won the right to vote in 1920 and then tracked changes in female registration and turnout rates over the years through the election of 2004. By 1964, more women than men were voting and by 1980, the percentage of women voting was higher than the percentage of men voting. The female-male participation gap has continued to widen. The growing clout of female voters is attributable to the simple facts that women outnumber men among the population at-large and have higher voter turnout rates.

The election of 2004 resulted in record registration and turnout levels among female voters. Candidates, political parties, and women's advocacy groups all worked hard to get more women registered and to the polls. They used virtually every advertising and mobilization tool available in this high-tech era: interactive web sites; catchy and creative logos splashed across web sites and printed on fashionable t-shirts; meet-ups and rallies; phone calls from celebrities; and precisely targeted mail, radio spots, and television ads (broadcast and cable).

Infrequent- and non-voting women were an especially highly sought-after demographic. For Republicans, it was the conservative, stay-at-home moms, while for Democrats, it was working moms, often single parents,

in minimum wage jobs. Both groups had histories of low voter participation rates prior to 2004. Democrats increased turnout among single
women, mostly young, but lost ground among white, working, and married women.[9] Republicans increased turnout of non-working married
women living in rural and suburban areas and gained some ground among
working women.

Of course, neither camp ignored the more consistent woman voter
either. Borrowing a page from the playbooks of the marketing and advertising worlds, strategists on both sides of the political aisle relied on public
opinion surveys and focus groups to craft successful mobilization efforts.
Women were targeted on the basis of their age, income, education, marital
and parental status, race/ethnicity, religion, sexual orientation, issue priorities, and/or geographical location with razor-sharp precision. Reaching
women voters in the 2004 campaign was clearly a new game.

## NOTES

1. This work could not have been completed without the invaluable assistance
   of Thomas A. Watson, Brittany L. Penberthy, and Amber M. Davis.
2. Donna Brazile. July 3, 2004. Energize the Women's Vote in 2004. Women's
   eNews.
3. Carol Andreas and Katherine Culkin. 2003. Women's Rights Movement: The
   Nineteenth Century. In *Dictionary of American History*, 3rd edition, ed. Stanley
   I. Kutler. New York: Charles Scribner's Sons.
4. For an excellent history of the suffrage movement, see Dorothy McBride
   Stetson. 1991. *Women's Rights in the U.S.A.: Policy Debates and Gender Roles.* Pacific
   Grove, CA: Brooks/Cole.
5. On June 4, 1919, the U.S. Senate voted to add the Nineteenth Amendment
   to the U.S. Constitution by a vote of fifty-six to twenty-five. The House had
   passed it two weeks earlier by a vote of 304 to 89.
6. North Dakota has no registration requirement. Excellent sources of information about state voter registration laws are the Council of State Governments
   and the National Conference of State Legislatures (NCSL).
7. Statewide telephone survey of a random sample of 800 Floridians who voted
   in the 2004 presidential election. The survey was conducted for The Collins
   Center for Public Policy, Inc. by a bipartisan team of pollsters – Barcelo &
   Company (R) and Hamilton, Beattie (D) – on November 2–3, 2004.
8. A poll by the Los Angeles Times in early fall showed that 71 percent of registered
   voters viewed First Lady Laura Bush favorably, while just 35 percent said the
   same about Teresa Heinz Kerry. National Journal Poll Track, Aug. 31, 2004.
9. Post-election survey of 2000 voters, 500 of whom were unmarried women,
   by Democracy Corps conducted Nov. 2–3, 2004; margin of error of
   +/− 2.2 percent.

# 3   Voting Choices

## Meet You at the Gender Gap

The date is October 22, 2004, less than two weeks before the November 3 election that will determine whether the Republican incumbent, George W. Bush, or the Democratic challenger, John Kerry, will serve as President of the United States for the next four years. Polls show the race is very close.

John Kerry has recently been interviewed on "Live with Regis and Kelly" and has appeared with his wife, Teresa Heinz Kerry, on the "Dr. Phil" show to talk about his marriage, divorce, and children. On October 22, he campaigns in Milwaukee, Wisconsin, with Caroline Kennedy Schlossberg, daughter of the late President John F. Kennedy, at his side. In his speech to a Milwaukee audience, Kerry tells women voters:

> You worry when you hear a child, a son or daughter, cough in the middle of the night.... You worry when they go out in the morning just to play, because you can't afford an illness. You can't afford an accident. You and your husband worry at the kitchen table after the kids have gone to bed, and when the month's paychecks don't cover all the bills.... No matter how tough it gets, no one in the White House seems to be listening.[1]

He claims that both health care premiums and the pay gap between men and women have increased under President Bush, and he vows that as President he will raise the minimum wage, helping millions of women who work in low-paying jobs. Kerry also briefly reminds voters that he will be tough on terrorism and will hunt down and kill or capture terrorists who threaten our country.

On the same day, October 22, 2004, President George W. Bush, who along with First Lady Laura Bush also recently appeared on the "Dr. Phil" show to discuss parenting and other family issues, makes a campaign stop in Wilkes-Barre, Pennsylvania. He tells voters that keeping American families safe from terrorism is the most important issue in the presidential contest, and he reminds them that the country is at serious risk of future terrorist attacks. Just a few days earlier, a group supporting President Bush had begun airing a campaign ad featuring a teenager from Ohio whose mother had been killed on September 11, 2001, in the attack on the World Trade Center. The poignant ad, widely acclaimed as one of the most effective of the 2004 campaign, shows the teenager, Ashley Faulkner, being embraced by President Bush, whom she met at a campaign rally. The teenager proclaims, "He's the most powerful man in the world, and all he wants to do is make sure I'm safe, that I'm okay."[2]

These snapshots of the presidential campaigns from October 2004 illustrate that both John Kerry and George W. Bush attempted to reach out to women voters in the 2004 election. However, the appeals they used and the specific subgroups of women they targeted were different. George W. Bush emphasized over and over during his campaign that he was the candidate who could better protect American families from terrorist threats. In doing so, he was appealing primarily to white, married women with children who were concerned about the safety of their families – women who in the 2004 campaign were commonly referred to as "security moms" – while attempting to raise concerns among other women voters about Kerry's capabilities as a leader in the war against terrorism.

John Kerry tried to counter the Bush campaign by reassuring so-called "security moms" and other women voters that he, too, would be tough on terrorism. However, polls showed that women who had not yet made a choice between the two candidates tended to be less affluent than many other voters and were concerned about issues like health care and equal pay for equal work. In order to win over these undecided women voters who might provide a winning margin for him in a close election, Kerry needed to talk about "domestic issues" like the minimum wage, health care, and equal pay. However, in a campaign environment where the events of the day and the news often focused on the war in Iraq and homeland security, domestic issues did not receive much attention or news coverage. Kerry's advisors were divided over whether they should emphasize domestic issues more, as Kerry did on the campaign stump in Milwaukee on October 22, or instead focus on countering the continual attack from the Bush campaign implying that Kerry would not be a strong and decisive leader on the war on terror or the war in Iraq. The final result of the election, a narrow victory for George W. Bush, suggests that for whatever reason – the need to respond to developments in the

war on terrorism and in Iraq, the success of the Bush campaign in keeping voters focused on national security where Bush was perceived as the
stronger candidate, or miscalculation by Kerry and his advisers – Kerry
was not successful in convincing enough women voters that he would be
the more effective leader.

Kerry did win a majority of the votes cast by women (51 percent,
compared to only 44 percent of the votes cast by men) according to the
nationwide exit polls conducted by Edison Media Research and Mitofsky
International. However, he fell short of the 54 percent of women's votes
that Democrat Al Gore received in 2000 when Gore won the popular
vote nationwide but narrowly lost the election to George W. Bush in the
Electoral College. In winning a close, but decisive, victory in the 2004
election, Bush increased the proportion of women's votes he received
from 43 percent in 2000 to 48 percent in 2004.

The fact that women voters received considerable attention from the
presidential candidates in 2004 was due largely to the difference between
women and men in their political preferences, a phenomenon commonly
referred to as the "gender gap." Statistically, a gender gap can be defined as
the difference in the proportion of women and the proportion of men who
support a particular politician, party, or policy position. In the 2004 election, Bush received 48 percent of women's votes compared with 55 percent
of men's, resulting in a gender gap of seven percentage points.

Prior to the 1980 election, it was widely believed that women and
men took similar positions on most issues, had similar political preferences, and voted in much the same ways. In other words, the assumption
before 1980 was that gender did not matter much in voting. Today the
assumption is exactly the opposite – that gender does matter for politics
and that women and men, in the aggregate, have different positions on
many issues and tend to vary in their party identification and support for
political candidates. The "gender gap" is now viewed as an enduring part
of the political landscape, and candidates, parties, and politicians must pay
specific attention to women voters if they want to win elections.

This chapter traces the origins of and explores possible explanations for
the gender gap. It also examines the strategies candidates have employed
in attempting to appeal to women voters. The gender gap has led to
increased political influence for women, although that influence has been
somewhat tempered by the fact that candidates have often used symbolic
appeals, rather than strictly issue-based appeals, to respond to the growing
influence of women voters.

## THE ORIGINS OF THE GENDER GAP

In her chapter in this volume, Susan A. MacManus describes the suffrage movement that led to the addition of the Nineteenth Amendment to the Constitution in 1920, granting women the right to vote. Over the course of the several decades that it took to win the right to vote, suffragists used a variety of arguments in order to win support from different segments of the all-male electorate and political structure. Some approaches stressed fundamental similarities between women and men and demanded the vote for women as a matter of simple justice. Suffragists observed that women were human beings just as men were, and therefore women, like men, were created equal and had an inalienable right to political equality and thus the vote.

However, suffragists also used arguments that focused on how women were different from men and would use their votes to help make the world a better place. Suffragists claimed that women's experiences, especially their experiences as mothers and care-givers, gave them special values and perspectives that would be readily apparent in their voting decisions. They argued that women would use their votes to stop wars, promote peace, clean up government, ban the sale of liquor, and bring justice to a corrupt world.

The use of such arguments led some people to eagerly anticipate and others to greatly fear the consequences of women's enfranchisement. Many observers at the time expected women to go to the polls in large numbers and thought their distinctive impact on politics would be immediately apparent. However, the right to vote, in and of itself, proved insufficient to bring about a distinctive women's vote. Rather, a women's vote would only emerge decades later after other changes in society and women's perceptions of themselves took place. In the elections immediately following women's enfranchisement in 1920, women voted in much lower numbers than men, and there were few signs that women were voting much differently then men or using their votes to express a distinctive perspective.

As the decades passed after 1920, it seemed that the "women's vote," feared by some and longed for by others, was never going to materialize. However, by the early 1980s a sufficient number of women finally achieved the social and psychological independence necessary to bring about a divergence in the voting patterns of women and men. In the decades since 1980, the women's vote promised by the suffragists has finally arrived, although with underlying issues and dynamics somewhat different from those anticipated during the suffrage era.

In the decades between 1920 and 1980, the vast majority of women, particularly white women,[3] remained economically dependent on men, not necessarily by choice but because society offered them few options. As a result, women's political interests were very intertwined with, even inseparable from, the political interests of men, and for the most part women did not make political decisions that differed from those made by men. However, since the 1960s and 1970s, women's dependence on men has begun to unravel, and as this unraveling has taken place, women have started making political choices that are more independent of men's wishes and their interests.

At least three critical developments over the past several decades have contributed to the increased independence of women from men and made possible the emergence of a distinctive women's vote. The first is the fact that for a variety of reasons, including higher divorce rates and longer life spans, more women are living apart from men, often heading households on their own. The second development is that more women have achieved professional and managerial positions which, even when they live with men, provide them with sufficient incomes to support themselves and allow them a substantial degree of financial independence from men. The third critical development that has contributed to the increased independence of women from men is the contemporary women's movement, which began with the founding of the National Organization for Women in 1966 and the development of women's liberation groups around the country in 1967 and 1968. Although even today a majority of women in American society do not call themselves feminists, the women's movement has changed the way most women in the United States see themselves and their life options. Most women now recognize that they have concerns and interests that are not always identical to those of the men in their lives, and they are aware that these concerns can be relevant to their political choices.

Brief glimpses of gender differences in voting had been apparent from time to time before 1980. For example, women were slightly more likely than men to vote for Dwight Eisenhower, the victorious Republican candidate, in the 1952 and 1956 elections. However, these pre-1980 gender differences in voting were not persistent, nor were they accompanied by consistent gender differences in evaluations of presidential performance, party identification, or voting for offices other than president. In fact, a textbook on public opinion commonly used in political science courses, published just before the 1980 election, summed up the conventional thinking about gender differences at that time. This 324-page textbook devoted only one-half of a page to women and gender, concluding, "Differences in the political attitudes of men and women are so slight that they deserve only brief mention.... In political attitudes and voting, people are seldom different because of their sex."[4]

Even though women had achieved a substantial degree of independence from men and their attitudes about themselves were changing throughout the 1970s, it was not until 1980 that a political candidate came along who could crystalize political differences between women and men into a gender gap. Ronald Reagan, the Republican who was elected President in 1980 and re-elected in 1984, proved to be the catalyst for the gender gap. Unlike the 1976 presidential campaign, where most positions taken by the Republican and Democratic candidates were not starkly different, the 1980 presidential campaign presented voters with clear alternatives. Candidate Ronald Reagan offered policy proposals that contrasted sharply with the policies of then-incumbent President Jimmy Carter. Reagan promised to cut back on the size of the federal government, greatly reduce government spending, increase the strength of the U.S. military, and get tough with the Soviet Union. When offered such clear-cut alternatives, the differences in preferences between women and men became apparent.

Although Ronald Reagan defeated Jimmy Carter in 1980 and was elected President, he received notably less support from women than from men. Exit polls, conducted by the major television networks with voters leaving the voting booth on the day of the election, showed that women were 6 to 9 percentage points less likely than men to vote for Ronald Reagan. For example, an exit poll conducted jointly by CBS and the *New York Times* showed that only 46 percent of women, compared to 54 percent of men, voted for Ronald Reagan, resulting in a gender gap of 8 percentage points. Clearly, women were less attracted to the candidacy and policies of Ronald Reagan than men were. (Or alternatively, looking at the gender gap from the flip side, the policies and candidacy of Ronald Reagan resonated more with men than with women.)

Many commentators in the early 1980s thought this gender gap in presidential voting might be short-lived and disappear in subsequent presidential elections, much as any earlier glimpses of gender differences (such as those in the presidential elections of the 1950s) had done, but this time the gender gap was here to stay. As Table 3.1 shows, in every presidential election since 1980, differences have been apparent in the proportions of

TABLE 3.1: A gender gap in voting has been evident in every presidential election since 1980

| Election year | Winning presidential candidate | % Women voting for winner | % Men voting for winner | Gender gap (in percentage pts.) |
|---|---|---|---|---|
| 2004 | George W. Bush (R) | 48 | 55 | 7 |
| 2000 | George W. Bush (R) | 43 | 53 | 10 |
| 1996 | Bill Clinton (D) | 54 | 43 | 11 |
| 1992 | Bill Clinton (D) | 45 | 41 | 4 |
| 1988 | George H. W. Bush (R) | 50 | 57 | 7 |
| 1984 | Ronald Reagan (R) | 56 | 62 | 6 |
| 1980 | Ronald Reagan (R) | 46 | 54 | 8 |

Source: Data are from exit polls conducted by CBS/New York Times, 1980, 1984, 1988; Voter News Service, 1992, 1996, 2000; Edison Media Research and Mitofsky International, 2004.

women and men who voted for the winning candidate, ranging from a low of 4 percentage points in 1992 to a high of 11 percentage points in 1996. In each of these elections, women have been more likely than men to support the Democratic candidate for President.

If the suffragists who had worked so hard to achieve voting rights for women were able to return today to see the results of their efforts, they would surely say, "I told you so." It may have taken sixty years to arrive, but the women's vote that the suffragists anticipated is now clearly evident and has been influencing the dynamics of presidential elections for more than two decades.

## THE BREADTH AND PERSISTENCE OF THE GENDER GAP

The gender gap has become an enduring feature of American politics that is evident across a wide variety of political attitudes, preferences, and behaviors. Since 1980 the gender gap has been apparent not only in voting in presidential elections, but also in voting at other levels of office, in party identification, and in the performance ratings of various presidents.

The exit polls conducted on each election day have asked voters not only about their voting in the presidential contest, but also about their voting choices in U.S. House, U.S. Senate, and gubernatorial elections. In every election since 1982, women have been more likely than men to vote for Democrats in races for the U.S. House of Representatives. For example, according to exit polls conducted by Edison Media Research and Mitofsky International, a majority, 52 percent, of women, compared with a minority, 45 percent, of men voted for the Democratic candidate for Congress in their district in 2004, resulting in a gender gap of seven percentage points. In contrast, a majority of men, 53 percent, but only a minority of women, 46 percent, voted for the Republican candidate for the U.S. House seat in their district.

Gender gaps have also been evident in a majority of races for U.S. Senate and gubernatorial seats in recent elections. Thirty-three of the 100 seats in the U.S. Senate were up for election in 2004, and eleven of the fifty states elected governors. Women and men did not vote differently in all of these contests, but they did have significantly different preferences in about three-fourths of them. In twenty-five, or 75.8 percent, of the races for the thirty-three U.S. Senate seats that were up for election, gender gaps ranging from 4 to 12 percentage points were evident according to exit polls conducted by Edison Media Research and Mitofsky International. In eight, or 72.8 percent, of the eleven gubernatorial races, there were gender gaps of 4 to 10 percentage points. In each of the U.S. Senate and gubernatorial elections where a notable gender gap was present, women were more likely than men to vote for the Democratic candidate.

Women not only are more likely than men to vote for Democratic candidates, but they also are more likely than men to identify with the Democratic party. When asked whether they think of themselves as Democrats, Republicans, or Independents, more women than men call themselves Democrats. For example, a poll conducted by CBS News and the *New York Times* in June 2004 found that 39 percent of women but only 31 percent of men considered themselves to be Democrats (a gender gap of 8 percentage points). Moreover, men had no clear preference for one party over the other. They divided themselves about evenly between the two parties; 31 percent of men were Democrats and 30 percent of men were Republicans (with the rest calling themselves Independents). However, women showed a clear preference for the Democratic party over the Republican party, with 39 percent of women identifying as Democrats and only 28 percent calling themselves Republicans (with the rest Independents).

Some observers have argued that the gender gap is the result of changes in men's, not women's, political behavior, and the data on party identification offer the strongest evidence in support of this point of view. In the 1970s both women and men were more likely to identify as Democrats than Republicans, and no significant gender gap in party identification was apparent. However, that pattern changed, beginning in the early 1980s following the election of Ronald Reagan. Men shifted in the direction of the Republican party, becoming more likely to identify as Republicans and less likely to identify as Democrats than in the 1970s. In contrast, women's party identification remained more stable, showing less dramatic changes since the 1970s. Women were more likely to identify as Democrats than as Republicans in the 1970s, and they remain more likely to be Democrats in 2005.

Although the gender gap in party identification apparent today is largely the result of changes among men, this does not necessarily mean that the gender gap in party identification is the result of men's behavior alone. The behavior of women has been critical in producing this gap. Prior to 1980, when shifts occurred in the political environment, women and men generally responded similarly. But with the increasing independence of women from men, the politics of the 1980s produced a different result. When men chose to shift their party identification, women chose not to follow them.

Just as a gender gap has been evident in party identification, a gender gap also has been apparent in evaluations of the performance of presidents who have served since 1980. On surveys it conducts throughout the year, the Gallup Poll asks whether people approve or disapprove of the way the incumbent is handling his job as president. Some presidents have had higher approval ratings than others, and the ratings for each president have varied across his tenure in office. For example, George W. Bush's ratings were much higher in the months following September 11, 2001, when the World Trade Center was attacked and the American people rallied behind their leader, than they were in the weeks and months after Bush was re-elected by a small margin in 2004. Nevertheless, across most of Bush's tenure in office, women have differed from men in their evaluations of his performance. A Gallup Poll conducted March 7–10, 2005, for example, found that only 47 percent of women, compared with 57 percent of men, approved of the way Bush was handling his job as president (a 10 percentage-point gender gap).

Gender gaps have been apparent in the performance ratings of all other recent presidents as well. Women have been more critical than men of Republican presidents, and more approving than men of the lone Democrat who has served as president since 1980. Thus, women were less likely than men to approve of how Republicans Ronald Reagan and George H. W. Bush handled their jobs as president, but more likely than men to evaluate favorably Democrat Bill Clinton's performance.

## THE GENDER GAP AND WOMEN CANDIDATES

As other chapters in this volume document, the number of women running for public office has increased over the past several decades. Every
election year, some of the candidates who run for the U.S. House, U.S.
Senate, and governor are women. What happens to the gender gap when
one (or both) of the candidates in an election is a woman?

Unfortunately, there is no straightforward, easy answer to this question. It depends on whether the woman candidate is a Democrat or a
Republican, and if she is a Republican, how moderate or conservative she
is. The answer may also depend on the state or district where she runs
and the larger context of the election.

Years ago voter prejudice may have been a major problem for the
few women who were brave enough to seek public office. However, bias
against women candidates has declined significantly. Since 1937, pollsters
have asked voters if they would be willing to vote for a "qualified" woman
for President. In 1937, only about one-third of voters said that they would
vote for a woman. In contrast, by the begir.ning of the twenty-first century,
about nine of every ten Americans reported that they would vote for a
woman for the nation's highest office (although there is some evidence
that this high level of support dipped in the aftermath of the attack on
the World Trade Center in 2001).[5] Thus, voter prejudice against women
candidates, even for the most powerful office in the United States, has
declined considerably although it has not completely disappeared.

But if there still are voters who are predisposed to vote against women
candidates, there also are voters who are predisposed to cast affirmative
votes for women candidates. Moreover, research has shown that women
are more likely than men to be predisposed to support women candidates.[6]
This predisposition on the part of some voters to vote for or against a
woman candidate, all other things being equal, becomes an additional
factor that can increase or decrease the size of the gender gap when women
run for office.

In general, women candidates who are Democrats tend to have gender
gaps (with women voters more likely than men to vote *for* them) that are
similar in size to or sometimes larger than those for male Democratic
candidates. In contrast, women candidates who are Republicans tend to
have gender gaps (with women voters more likely than men to vote *against*
them) that are similar in size to or sometimes smaller than those for male
Republican candidates. An analysis of U.S. House races in three elections
in the early 1990s found that the gender gap was, on average, larger in

**TABLE 3.2:** A gender gap in voting was evident in the races of all women who won election to offices of U.S. Senator and Governor in 2004

|  | % Women voting for winner | % Men voting for winner | Gender gap (in percentage pts.) |
|---|---|---|---|
| **U.S. Senate Winners** | | | |
| Barbara Boxer (D-CA) | 65 | 53 | 12 |
| Blanche Lincoln (D-AR) | 59 | 52 | 7 |
| Barbara Mikulski (D-MD) | 68 | 61 | 7 |
| Patty Murray (D-WA) | 59 | 50 | 9 |
| Lisa Murkowski (R-AK) | 45 | 57 | 12 |
| **U.S. Governor Winners** | | | |
| Christine Gregoire (D-WA) | 53 | 45 | 8 |
| Ruth Ann Minner (D-DE) | 54 | 48 | 6 |

*Source:* Edison Media Research and Mitofsky International Exit Polls, 2004.

races where the Democratic candidate was a woman candidate than in races where a Democratic man ran against a Republican man. Similarly, on average, the gender gap was smaller in races where the Republican candidate was a woman than in races where a Republican man ran against a Democratic man.[7]

Table 3.2 shows the gender gap in races won by the five women elected to the U.S. Senate and the two women elected as governors in the 2004 elections. Four of the women senators and both women governors are Democrats, and the generalizations presented above hold up well for them. The average gender gap for the eight gubernatorial and twenty-three U.S. Senate races in 2004 where both candidates were men was 6 percentage points, with female voters more likely than male voters to vote for the Democratic candidate. As Table 3.2 shows, all four of the Democratic women senators and one of the Democratic women governors, Christine Gregoire, exceeded this norm and had gender gaps larger than the average for races involving two male candidates. The other Democratic woman governor was elected with a gender gap of average size – 6 percentage points. In 2004 as in previous elections, female Democratic candidates seem to have done as well as, and often better than, male Democratic candidates in winning support from women voters.

However, the lone Republican woman elected to the U.S. Senate in 2004, Alaska's Lisa Murkowski, had an unusually large 12 percentage-point gender gap in her race, with women less likely than men to have cast their votes for her. This sizable gender gap certainly defies the generalization above that the gender gap is often smaller when the Republican candidate is a woman and illustrates that ideology and the context of the election can influence the size of the gender gap in any given race. When Lisa Murkowski's father was elected governor of Alaska in 2002, he appointed her to serve the two years remaining in his U.S. Senate term. She was widely recognized as a moderate who had cast pro-choice votes in the three terms she had served in the Alaska state legislature, and consequently her appointment as U.S. Senator angered the more conservative wing of the Alaska Republican party, who did not want a moderate representing them in Washington, D.C. Recognizing that she would have to run in a primary against more conservative opponents in 2004, Murkowski adopted a much more conservative and pro-life posture after she became a U.S. Senator. She voted with the conservative Eagle Forum 100 percent of the time, the Christian Coalition 83 percent of the time, and the National Right to Life Committee 82 percent of the time on issues of concern to those organizations in 2004.[8] Her movement away from more moderate issue positions may have cost her support among moderate and independent women voters, helping to account for the large gender gap in her 2004 race.

But if Murkowski illustrates that a conservative record can lead to reduced support among women voters, one of Murkowski's fellow Republican women senators, Olympia Snowe from Maine, illustrates the opposite and shows the variability in the gender gap that can occur with Republican women candidates. Although Olympia Snowe's seat was not up for re-election in 2004, she was re-elected to the U.S. Senate in 2000. Whereas Murkowski had a very large gender gap with much less support from women than men, no gender gap was apparent in Snowe's race. Snowe was re-elected with 69 percent of the votes of women and 69 percent of the votes of men in her state. In contrast to Murkowski's conservative voting record, Snowe has a much more moderate, pro-choice voting record in the U.S. Senate and has been a champion for women during the years she served in both the Senate and U.S. House. Although Snowe voted with the Christian Coalition 50 percent of the time in 2004, no other Republican in the U.S. Senate more often voted in opposition to the positions favored by this conservative group. Moreover, Snowe voted for the positions advocated by the pro-choice National Abortion Reproductive Rights Action League 100 percent of the time in 2004.[9] Perhaps largely because of her moderate, pro-choice voting record and her advocacy on behalf of women, Snowe has been able to effectively neutralize the gender gap, eliminating the deficit that Republican candidates usually experience with women voters.

**TABLE 3.3:** A gender gap in voting was evident across a wide range of demographic groups in the 2004 presidential election

| Demographic group | % Women voting for Bush | % Men voting for Bush | Gender gap (in percentage pts.) |
|---|---|---|---|
| Race | | | |
|   White | 55 | 61 | 6 |
|   African American | 10 | 13 | 3 |
| Age | | | |
|   18–29 | 43 | 47 | 4 |
|   30–44 | 50 | 56 | 6 |
|   45–59 | 49 | 54 | 5 |
|   60 and older | 49 | 60 | 11 |
| Marital Status | | | |
|   Married | 55 | 60 | 5 |
|   Unmarried | 37 | 45 | 8 |
| Education | | | |
|   No college | 49 | 55 | 6 |
|   Some college | 51 | 57 | 6 |
|   College graduate | 45 | 54 | 9 |

*Source:* Edison Media Research and Mitofsky International Exit Polls, 2004.

## EXPLANATIONS FOR THE GENDER GAP

One observation about the gender gap can be made with a high degree of certainty – that the gender gap is not limited to one or even a few demographic subgroups. In an attempt to undermine women's voting power, political commentators have sometimes claimed that the gender gap is not a broad-based phenomenon, but rather one that can be fully explained by the voting behavior of some particular subgroup of women in the electorate – for example, women of color or unmarried voters. Table 3.3 reveals the obvious problem with such claims. When compared with men who shared their demographic characteristics, women of different races, ages, marital status, and levels of education less often than men voted for George W. Bush (and more often voted for John Kerry). In fact, voting differences between women and men are found in virtually every subgroup of the electorate. Consequently, no single demographic category of voters is responsible for the gender gap. Rather, the gender gap is clearly a phenomenon evident across all the various subgroups that comprise the American electorate.

Of course, to say that the gender gap is apparent across many different subgroups does not mean that gender differences are of equal magnitude across all demographic categories. As Table 3.3 also shows, the gender gap is smaller or larger for some demographic groups than for others. Perhaps because African Americans are so overwhelmingly Democratic in their voting choices, the gender gap in 2004 was smaller among African Americans than among whites. Similarly, whereas younger voters were the most pro-Kerry of all age groups, the difference between women and men in their presidential preferences was smaller among those age eighteen to twenty-nine than among older cohorts of voters. Finally, the gender gap was larger among unmarried voters and those who were college graduates than among voters who were married and those who had less education.

Beyond the fact that the gender gap is not limited to one particular subgroup but rather widespread across the electorate, definitive statements about the gender gap are difficult to make. Indeed, the gender gap appears to be a rather complex phenomenon. Nevertheless, a number of different explanations have been put forward to account for the gender gap in voting. None of these explanations seems sufficient by itself. Moreover, the explanations are not mutually exclusive; in fact, they are somewhat overlapping. However, several of the explanations offered by academic and political analysts do seem to have some validity and are useful in helping to account for the fact that women and men make somewhat different voting choices. Four of the most common explanations – compassion, feminism, economics, and the role of government – are reviewed briefly here.

The compassion explanation focuses on women's roles as mothers and care-givers. Despite recent changes in gender roles, women still bear disproportionate responsibility for the care of children and the elderly in their families and in the larger society. Mothers are still called more often than fathers when children become ill at school, and women are still a large majority of health care workers, teachers, child care providers, and social workers. Women's roles as care-givers may lead them to be more sympathetic toward those in need and more concerned with the safety and security of others. Women's care-giving responsibilities may also lead them to put greater emphasis than men on issues such as education and health care.

Consistent with this compassion explanation, in the 2000 presidential election which focused largely on domestic politics rather than foreign affairs, two of the top issues were education and health care. Polls showed that these issues were of greater concern to women voters in the election than they were to men, and both candidates spent a great deal of time talking about these issues. In an obvious attempt to appeal to women voters, the Bush campaign suggested that George W. Bush was not an old-style conservative, but rather a "compassionate conservative" who genuinely cared about the well being of Americans.

Also consistent with the compassion explanation is women's greater reluctance, relative to men's, to use military force to resolve foreign conflicts. In 1980 when the gender gap first became apparent, Americans were being held hostage in Iran, tensions were running high with the Soviet Union, and foreign policy became a central issue in the presidential campaign. Women reacted more negatively than men to Ronald Reagan's tough posture in dealing with other nations, and women had greater fears than men that Ronald Reagan might get the country involved in a war. These gender differences were important in explaining why Reagan received stronger support from men than from women.[10] Similarly, in 2004, which was the first presidential election since 1980 where foreign policy was central, a gender difference was evident in women's and men's attitudes toward the war in Iraq. Polls have consistently shown a gender gap, with women having more reservations than men about U.S. involvement in Iraq. In fact, one of the most persistent and longstanding political differences between women and men is in their attitudes toward the use of military force. For as far back as we have public opinion polling data, women have been significantly more likely than men to oppose the use of force to resolve international conflicts.

As a second explanation for the gender gap some observers have suggested that the gender gap is a product of the feminist movement. The discovery of the contemporary gender gap in voting in the aftermath of the 1980 presidential election coincided with intensive efforts by women's organizations, especially the National Organization for Women (NOW), to have the Equal Rights Amendment (ERA) ratified in the necessary thirty-eight states before the June 30, 1982, deadline. NOW also undertook an intensive effort to publicize the gender gap and women's lesser support, relative to men's, for Ronald Reagan. As a result, the ERA and the gender gap became associated in many people's minds, and there was speculation that women were less supportive than men of Ronald Reagan because he opposed the Equal Rights Amendment. However, scholarly analyses of voting and public opinion data have consistently shown that so-called women's issues – those issues most closely associated with the organized women's movement such as the ERA and abortion – do not appear to be central to the gender gap. In part, this may be because women and men in the general electorate have very similar attitudes on these issues, and in part this may be because candidates for president and other offices seldom choose to campaign on these issues.

However, the fact that women's issues such as the ERA or abortion are not central to the gender gap does not mean that feminism plays no role. As explained earlier in this chapter, the contemporary women's movement has altered the way most women in the United States see themselves and their life options. The movement has provided women with more awareness about their political interests and greater self-confidence about expressing their differences with men. Compelling empirical evidence suggests that women who identify with feminism are more distinctive from men in their political values than are other women, and that for women a feminist identity may, in fact, foster the expression of the "compassion" differences described previously. Women influenced by feminism appear to be more likely than either men or other women to express attitudes sympathetic to those who are disadvantaged and in need in our society and consequently to be more predisposed to support the Democratic party.[11]

Other explanations for the gender gap have focused on economic factors. More women than men live below the poverty line, and women earn only 76 cents for every dollar men earn. Because women on average are poorer than men, they are more dependent on government social services and more vulnerable to cuts in these services. Similarly, women are disproportionately employed in jobs that involve the delivery of human services (health, education, and welfare). Although most of these women in human services jobs are not directly employed by the government, their employers often receive substantial government funding and thus their jobs are to varying degrees dependent on the continuation of government subsidies. As the principal providers of social welfare services, women are more likely than men to suffer loss of employment when these programs are cut.

Beginning with Ronald Reagan and continuing through the 1990s with the Republican Congress's Contract with America, Republicans at the national level have argued that government (with the exception of defense) has grown too large and that cutbacks in domestic spending are necessary. When candidates and politicians propose to cut back on big government or the welfare state, the cuts they propose fall heavily on women who are disproportionately both the providers and recipients of government-funded services. Consequently, economic self-interest could lead women to favor the Democrats more than the Republicans.

However, women's economic concerns do not appear to be merely self-interested. Evidence shows that women are less likely than men to vote on the basis of economic considerations, but when they do, they are less likely than men to vote on the basis of their own self-interest and more likely to vote on the basis of how well off they perceive the country to be financially.[12] Thus, women are more likely than men to think not just of their own financial situation, but also about the economic situation others are facing. In an election like 2004 when polls showed women were worried about the state of the nation's economy, economic considerations tend to work to the disadvantage of the incumbent president, regardless of his party, among women voters. (This is one of the reasons the Bush campaign in 2004 was so intent in keeping voters focused on the issue of national security where polls showed he had an advantage, rather than talking about the economy.)

The final explanation for the gender gap, focusing on the role of government, is clearly related to the economic explanation but extends beyond economic considerations. In recent years, some of the most consistent and important gender differences in public opinion have shown up on questions about the role that government should play in our lives. Both women and men agree that government, especially the federal government, is not working as effectively as they would like. Beyond that, however, their attitudes are quite different. Men are more likely than women to see government as the problem rather than the solution, and they are considerably more likely than women to favor serious cutbacks in federal government programs and federal spending on non-defense-related programs. Men more than women prefer private-sector solutions to societal problems. In contrast, women are more likely to want to fix government rather than abandon it. Women are more worried than men that government cutbacks may go too far; they are more concerned than men about preserving the social safety net for the people who are most in need in this country. The Republican party, which receives greater support from men, is commonly perceived as the party that wants to scale back the size of government, whereas the Democratic party, which has more women among its supporters, is more commonly perceived as the party that defends government programs and works to preserve the social safety net. If the Kerry campaign had given greater attention to the constructive role the federal government could play in dealing with the health care crisis and in helping women and their families make ends meet economically, he might well have received stronger support from women voters in 2004.

Importantly, gender differences in views about the role of government are not limited to economics. There is a moral dimension as well, which offers strong possibilities for Republicans to make inroads with women voters. Women are not only more likely than men to believe that government should help those who are in economic need, but they also are more likely than men to believe that government should play a role in promoting traditional values. In the 1996 presidential election when the incumbent Democratic candidate, Bill Clinton, won a convincing victory, his campaign spent considerable time talking about moral values, focusing on issues and proposals related to violence in the media, personal responsibility, teen smoking, and drugs. In the 2004 campaign, there was little discussion by John Kerry and his campaign of proposals to promote moral values, and most political observers agreed that the Republicans gave more far more attention than did the Democrats to values in their campaign. This lack of attention to moral concerns, which the 1996 Clinton campaign showed need not be the province of Republican candidates only, may be one of many reasons why the Kerry campaign did not fare better with women voters in 2004. In fact, according to the exit polls conducted by Edison Media Research and Mitofsky International, almost one quarter of women voters in 2004 said that the issue that mattered most in their choice for president was moral values, and of these women, four out of five voted for George W. Bush.

## POLITICAL STRATEGIES FOR DEALING WITH THE GENDER GAP AND APPEALING TO WOMEN VOTERS

Given the explanations above for the gender gap, it would appear that the best way for candidates and parties to appeal to women voters would be by talking very specifically, concretely, and frequently about issues, whether they be compassion issues (such as peace, health care, and education), economic concerns, or moral issues. However, presidential candidates and campaigns often use symbolic appeals in addition to, and sometimes in lieu of, issue-based appeals to win support from women voters.

One of the ways candidates and campaigns have attempted to appeal to women voters symbolically is by showcasing prominent women. For example, when John Kerry appeared before voters in Milwaukee, Wisconsin, on October 22, 2004, as described at the beginning of this chapter, he was accompanied by Caroline Kennedy Schlossberg. John Kerry did talk substantively about issues in that campaign appearance in an effort to appeal to women voters, but he also attempted to appeal to them more symbolically by showing that a widely admired woman like Caroline Kennedy Schlossberg supported him. Kerry also campaigned with a host of other well-known women at his side, including Dana Reeve, widow of actor Christopher Reeve, and Kristen Breitweiser, one of the widows of 9-11 who lobbied for the creation of the presidential commission to examine the intelligence failures preceding the attack on the World Trade Center. Other prominent women such as Rosie O'Donnell, Hillary Clinton, Gloria Steinem, and Ann Richards appeared at pro-Kerry rallies and campaign events. Similarly, the Bush campaign frequently used appearances by Bush's wife, Laura, and his twin daughters, Jenna and Barbara, in an attempt to appeal to women voters, both older and younger. And as Barbara Burrell notes in her chapter in this volume, both political parties featured prominent women at their 2004 presidential nominating conventions.

The Bush campaign, in particular, cleverly used other symbolic, as opposed to issue-based, appeals to woo women voters. In the 2004 campaign and especially the 2000 campaign, the Bush campaign employed a new term, describing their candidate as a "compassionate conservative." Bush himself suggested, "I am a compassionate conservative, because I know my philosophy is full of hope for every American."[13] Although ambiguous as to what concrete policy proposals might flow from this philosophy, the use of the term "compassionate conservative" clearly invoked the image of a candidate who cared about people, and the term undoubtedly was coined, entirely or in part, as a strategy to appeal to women voters. However, the most clever symbolic strategy of all may have been the name that the Bush campaign chose for its organized effort to win women voters. At Bush campaign events across the country, signs appeared with the slogan, "W Stands for Women," a double entendre suggesting that Bush's middle initial and his nickname, "W," was an indicator of his supportive posture toward women.

Another use of symbolic appeals in recent campaigns has focused on the targeting of specific groups of women (and occasionally groups of men, such as NASCAR dads) to the exclusion of large numbers of other women voters. Two examples are the targeting of "soccer moms" in the 1996, and to a lesser extent the 2000, elections and "security moms" in the 2004 elections. Both "soccer moms" and "security moms" were social constructions – a combination of demographic characteristics, given a catchy name by political consultants, which at the time did not refer to an existing, self-identified group with any organizational base. When consultants and the media first started referring to "soccer moms" in 1996, women did not identify themselves as such, but the term has subsequently entered into popular usage and some women now refer to themselves this way. Similarly, women did not self-identify as "security moms" before this term was introduced in the context of the 2004 elections.

Although the definition of a soccer mom varied somewhat, she was generally considered to be a white, married woman with children (presumably of soccer-playing age), living in the suburbs. She also was often described in media coverage as stressed out and driving a mini-van. The soccer mom was considered important politically because she was viewed as a swing voter – a voter whose demographics had traditionally led her to vote Republican but who could be persuaded to vote Democratic. One of the most important characteristics of the soccer mom was that she was not primarily concerned about her own self-interest, but rather about her family, and most importantly her children. As Kellyanne Fitzpatrick, a Republican pollster, noted, "If you are a soccer mom, the world according to you is seen through the needs of your children."[14]

The "security mom," who became a focus of attention during the last several weeks of the 2004 presidential campaign, shared many of the demographic characteristics of the "soccer mom." Like the soccer mom, she was considered to be white and married, with young children. Also like the soccer mom, the security mom did not put her own needs first, but rather those of her family and children. She was repeatedly described as preoccupied with keeping her family safe from terrorism. The Republican presidential campaign, in particular, openly campaigned for the votes of these women in 2004. For example, on October 10, 2004, on CNN's Late Edition with Wolf Blitzer, Vice President Dick Cheney's daughter, Liz, urged women to vote for the Republican ticket, explaining, "You know, I'm a security mom. I've got four little kids. And what I care about in this election cycle is electing a guy who is going to be a commander-in-chief, who will do whatever it takes to keep those kids safe."[15] Similarly, in his campaign stop in Wilkes-Barre, Pennsylvania, described at the beginning of this chapter, George W. Bush was clearly targeting his remarks to mothers concerned with the safety of their families.

The intensive campaign and media attention devoted to "soccer moms" in 1996 and 2000 and to "security moms" in 2004 deflected attention away from the concerns of many other subgroups of women, including feminists, college-age women, older women, women on welfare, women of color, and professional women. Ironically, it even deflected attention away from the concerns of white, middle-class, women themselves except in their role as moms. Both the campaigns and the media were able to appear to be responsive to the concerns of women voters by talking about soccer moms and security moms while actually ignoring the vast majority of women. As a result, Clinton was reelected in 1996 and Bush was twice elected to the presidency in 2000 and 2004 without campaigning aggressively on (or, in some cases, even seriously addressing) many of the issues of greatest importance to the majority of women in this country who are not white, middle-class mothers of young children.

## CONCLUSION: WHY THE GENDER GAP MATTERS AND A LOOK TOWARD 2008

The gender gap has given women voters increased political influence in recent years. Candidates now must pay attention to women voters to win elections. As Susan A. MacManus observes in her chapter in this volume, in recent elections women have voted at slightly higher rates than men. Women also are a larger proportion of the population. These two facts combined mean that there have been many more female than male voters in recent elections. In the 2004 election, for example, about 8.8 million more women than men voted. The fact that there are so many more female voters than male voters adds power to the so-called women's vote, and clearly the more women who turn out to vote, the more clout women are likely to have.

Despite the existence of the gender gap and the larger number of female than male voters, the potential for women voters to influence politics has not yet been fully realized. In large part this is because candidates in recent presidential elections have so frequently relied upon symbolic, rather than issue-based, appeals to women voters. In particular, in focusing on specific groups of women such as "soccer moms" or "security moms," Presidents Clinton and Bush have been able to win elections without addressing in a serious and sustained way the issue-based concerns of greatest importance to the many women who do not fit the demographic profile of the soccer and security moms.

The more candidates downplay the concerns of various subgroups of women voters (e.g., college-age women, less affluent women, women of color), the more tempting it is for those women to remain uninvolved in politics and to stay away from the polls. However, this is a Catch-22 situation. The more uninvolved certain subgroups of women are, the more likely their interests will be overlooked in the political process. In fact, women whose concerns are not being addressed by candidates need to become more involved in the future and to insist that candidates respond to their concerns. Only then will the full potential power of the gender gap be realized.

In the first few months following the 2004 elections, Hillary Rodham Clinton emerged as the frontrunner for the Democratic nomination for president in 2008. A study released by the Gallup Poll in February 2004 alluded to one of the ways women voters may have a potential influence in 2008:

> New York Sen. Hillary Clinton has a substantially more favorable image among women than among men – a gender advantage that persists even among Republicans and independents. This suggests that Clinton has the potential to draw the votes of women who might ordinarily not consider voting for a Democratic candidate in the 2008 election.[16]

Gallup found an overall gender gap of 10 percentage points, with 58 percent of women but only 48 percent of men expressing a favorable opinion of Senator Clinton and with gender differences particularly evident among those who identified as Independents and Republicans. Younger voters (ages nineteen to twenty-nine) were more favorable toward Clinton than any other age group, but among these younger voters, an unusually large gender gap of 20 percentage points was evident, with 71 percent of young women compared with 51 percent of young men giving her a favorable evaluation.

Obviously, much can change in the many months until a successor to George W. Bush is elected. Hillary Clinton may ultimately choose not to run for president in 2008, and other candidates will certainly enter the race and try to chip away at her support among women voters if she does. But this early peek at support for the frontrunner on the Democratic side suggests that the gender gap will be alive, well, and interesting in the next presidential race. Meet you at the gender gap in 2008!

## NOTES

1. David M. Halbfinger. October 23, 2004. Kerry Vows Fight for Equal Pay for Women and a $7 Wage. New York Times.
2. PFA Voter Fund. Ashley's Story. <http:www.pfavoterfund.com> 2005, March 21.
3. This account applies largely to white women who constituted a large majority of women in the United States throughout these decades. The situation for African American women and other women of color was somewhat different. African American women were less likely than white women to be

economically dependent on men because they more often worked outside the home (although usually in low paying jobs). However, the political interests of African American women and men still were generally intertwined because society offered limited options for African Americans of either gender.

4. Robert S. Erikson, Norman R. Luttbeg, and Kent L. Tedin. 1980. *American Public Opinion: Its Origins, Content, and Impact*, 2nd edition New York: John Wiley & Sons, 186.

5. Jennifer L. Lawless. 2004. Women, War, and Winning Elections: Gender Stereotyping in the Post September 11th Era. *Political Research Quarterly* 53(3): 479–90.

6. Kira Sanbonmatsu. 2002. Gender Stereotypes and Vote Choice. *American Journal of Political Science* 46: 20–34.

7. Elizabeth Adell Cook. 1998. Voter Reaction to Women Candidates. *In Women and Elective Office: Past, Present, and Future*, eds. Sue Thomas and Clyde Wilcox. New York: Oxford University Press.

8. Project Vote Smart. 2004. <http://www.vote-smart.org/issue_rating_category.php?can_id=CAK67328> 2005, March 21.

9. Project Vote Smart. 2004. 2004<http://www.vote-smart.org/issue_rating_category.php?can_id=H1630103> 2005, March 21.

10. Frankovic, Kathleen A. 1982. Sex and Politics: New Alignments, Old Issues. *PS* 15(Summer): 439–48.

11. Pamela Johnston Conover. 1988. Feminists and the Gender Gap. *Journal of Politics* 50(November): 985–1010.

12. Susan J. Welch and John Hibbing. 1992. Financial Conditions, Gender, and Voting in American National Elections. *Journal of Politics* 54(February): 197–213.

13. Joe Conason. September 15, 2003. Where's the Compassion? The Nation.

14. Neil MacFarquhar. October 20, 1996. Don't Forget Soccer Dads; What's a Soccer Mom Anyway? New York Times.

15. CNN. October 10, 2004. Late Edition with Wolf Blitzer. <http://cnnstudentnews.cnn.com/TRANSCRIPTS/0410/10/le.01.html> 2005, March 21.

16. Gallup Poll News Service. February 24, 2005. Hillary Clinton's Gender Advantage.

# 4 Congressional Elections

## Where Are We on the Road to Gender Parity?

Republican House candidate Melissa Brown successfully worked the small crowd at Beauty Worx Day Spa in Philadelphia. After meeting Brown, one beautician declared: "I want to support a woman." Another followed with: "Girl Power!" Brown quickly cut in, telling the group: "I am actually running against a woman."[1] Indeed, the 2004 contest in Pennsylvania's 13th congressional district was one of eleven House races nationwide where women squared off against each other. Three of these races were open seats vacated by men, promising at least minor gains in the number of women serving in the House. Melissa Brown, however, was not one of the gains for women. Her opponent, Democratic state senator Allyson Schwartz, ultimately won the race.

Several states away, in Illinois, Democratic challenger Melissa Bean startled the political world by knocking off incumbent Philip Crane, the longest serving Republican member of the House of Representatives. Bean, a businesswoman whose only prior electoral experience was running against and losing to Crane two years earlier, devoted two years to campaigning in the district after her initial loss. She successfully portrayed Crane as lazy and out of touch, labeling him the "junket king" of Congress. Bean was one of only two Democratic challengers in 2004 able to unseat Republican incumbents. University of Chicago public policy professor Christopher Berry called Bean's victory one of the few "bright spots" for Democrats nationally.[2]

Across the country in Washington state's 5th congressional district, Republican Cathy McMorris ran against well-connected and self-financed Spokane businessman Don Barbieri. Both attempted to replace George Nethercutt, a five-term Republican incumbent who chose not to seek re-election. McMorris represented a new breed of young, politically ambitious women. Only thirty-five years old, she had ten years of state legislative experience under her belt, including serving as the minority leader in the state House. In the Republican primary, she handily defeated two experienced and well-regarded male challengers. And in the general election, she cruised to easy victory, defeating Barbieri, who was assisted by the national Democratic party, by more than 20 percentage points.[3]

Even further west, in Alaska, incumbent Republican U.S. Senator Lisa Murkowski found herself embroiled in a bitter and hotly contested race with former Democratic governor Tony Knowles. Murkowski had been appointed to the seat by her father, Frank Murkowski, who was a sitting U.S. Senator when he sought and won the governorship in 2002. Many Alaska voters expressed considerable anger when the newly elected governor bypassed more experienced candidates and chose instead to appoint his daughter to fill the Senate vacancy. Democrats attempted to capitalize on voters' anger, but despite early polls that showed Knowles in the lead, Lisa Murkowski ultimately held on to her seat with a three-point victory.[4]

As these examples illustrate, there are many routes that women can now take to Congress in the twenty-first century – women are beating women, knocking off incumbents, succeeding as career politicians, and being elevated to political office by influential family members. The different paths open to women seeking election to Congress are a new phenomenon. For most of U.S. history, political opportunities for women were severely limited.

This chapter examines the evolution of women's candidacies for Congress and the role gender plays in the electoral process. Ultimately, I focus on one fundamental question: Why are there still so few women serving in the House and Senate? In exploring the persistence of gender as a factor in congressional elections, I divide the chapter into three sections. In the first section I offer a brief historical overview of the role of gender in congressional elections. The second section compares male and female candidates' electoral performance and success in House and Senate elections from 1992–2004. The results of this analysis confirm that the electoral playing field, when considered in the aggregate, has become largely gender neutral. In the final section of the chapter, I begin to provide some answers as to why so few women are in Congress. Here, I turn to the more subtle ways that gender continues to affect congressional elections. Gendered geographic trends, women's presence in different types of congressional races, and the gender gap in political ambition combine to suggest that declarations of gender neutrality in the electoral process are premature.

**TABLE 4.1:** Over time more Democratic women than Republican women
have emerged as House candidates and winners

|  | 1970 | 1980 | 1990 | 1992 | 2000 | 2002 | 2004 |
|---|---|---|---|---|---|---|---|
| **General Election Candidates** | | | | | | | |
| Democratic Women | 15 | 27 | 39 | 70 | 80 | 78 | 88 |
| Republican Women | 10 | 25 | 30 | 36 | 42 | 46 | 53 |
| Total Women House Candidates | 25 | 52 | 69 | 106 | 122 | 124 | 141 |
| **General Election Winners** | | | | | | | |
| Democrat Women | 10 | 11 | 19 | 35 | 41 | 38 | 43 |
| % of all Democratic Winners | 3.9 | 4.5 | 7.1 | 13.6 | 19.4 | 18.6 | 21.4 |
| Republican Women | 3 | 10 | 9 | 12 | 18 | 21 | 23 |
| % of all Republican Winners | 1.7 | 5.2 | 5.4 | 6.8 | 8.1 | 9.2 | 9.9 |

*Notes:* Entries represent the raw number of women candidates and winners for each
year. The 2004 general election winner total for Democrats includes Representative Doris
Matsui who was elected in a special election in March, 2005 to take the seat of her late
husband.
*Source:* Center for American Women and Politics (CAWP), 2005 Fact Sheets.

## THE HISTORICAL EVOLUTION OF WOMEN'S CANDIDACIES FOR CONGRESS

Throughout the 1990s, women made significant strides competing for and
winning seats in the United States Congress. The 1992 elections, often
referred to as the "Year of the Woman," resulted not only in an historic
increase in the number of women in both the House and the Senate, but
also in the promise of movement toward some semblance of gender parity
in our political institutions (see Table 4.1). After all, in the history of the
U.S. Congress, there have been more than 11,500 male representatives,
but only 224 female representatives (see Figure 4.1). Only thirty-three
women have ever served in the U.S. Senate, eighteen of whom were either
appointed or won special elections. The gains of 1992 were not repeated
at a steady pace. Currently, 86 percent of the members of the U.S. Senate
and 85 percent of the members of the U.S. House are male. This places
the United States fifty-seventh worldwide in terms of the proportion of
women serving in the national legislature, a ranking far behind many
other democratic governments.[5] Further, the overwhelming majority of
the women elected to Congress have been white. Currently, of the sixty-
five (out of 435) women elected to the U.S. House in the 2004 election,
there are twelve African Americans, seven Latinas, and one Asian Pacific
Islander. There are currently no women of color serving in the U.S. Senate.

Figure 4.1: **Historic Gender Disparities in Congressional Representation.**

Since 1789, only 2% of members
of Congress have been women.

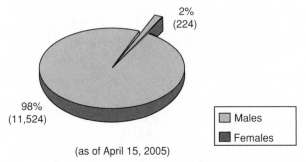

2%
(224)

98%
(11,524)

☐ Males
■ Females

(as of April 15, 2005)

*Note:* Figures include both House and Senate members.
*Source:* Center for American Women and Politics (CAWP), 2005 Fact Sheet.

The continued dearth of women in Congress suggests that a "mas-culine" ethos still dominates the congressional electoral environment. A host of interrelated factors – money, familiarity with power brokers, polit-ical experience, and support from the political parties – all contribute to a winning campaign. Traditional candidates are members of the political or economic elite. Most emerge from lower-level elected offices or work in their communities, typically in law or business. They tend to receive encouragement to run for office from influential members of the com-munity, party officials, or outgoing incumbents. And these same elites who encourage candidacies also contribute money to campaigns and hold fundraisers. This process has been in place for most of the recent history of congressional candidacies.

For obvious reasons, the manner in which congressional candidates emerge serves men well and women very poorly. Because they have been excluded from their communities' economic and political elites through-out much of the twentieth century, women's paths to Congress often take different forms. Widows of congressmen who died in office dominated the first wave of successful female candidates. Between 1916 and 1964, twenty-eight of the thirty-two widows nominated to fill their husbands' seats won their elections, for a victory rate of 88 percent. Across the same time period, only thirty-two of the 199 non-widows who garnered their parties' nominations were elected (a 14 percent victory rate).[6]

The 1960s and 1970s marked the emergence of a second type of woman candidate – one who turned her attention from civic volunteerism to politics. A few women involved in grassroots community politics rode their activism to Washington. Notable figures who pursued this path include Patsy Mink in Hawaii, elected in 1964; Shirley Chisholm in New York, elected in 1968; Bella Abzug in New York, elected in 1970; and Pat Schroeder in Colorado and Barbara Jordan in Texas, both elected in 1972.

We are currently in the third and possibly final stage of the evolution of women's candidacies. The prevailing model of running for Congress is far less rigid. Political parties' decreased power, coupled with growing media influence, facilitates the emergence of a more diverse array of candidates competing successfully for their parties' nominations. Converging with this less rigid path is an increase in the number of women who now fit the profile of a "traditional candidate." Women's presence in the fields of business and law has dramatically increased. Further, the number of women serving in state legislatures, a springboard to Congress, has increased almost six-fold since 1970 (although it is important to note that women's presence in the state legislatures has stalled in recent elections; for more on this, see Kira Sanbonmatsu's chapter in this volume). Together, these developments indicate that the eligibility pool of prospective women candidates grew substantially throughout the 1990s.

Despite the growth in the number of eligible women who could run for Congress, the most recent congressional election cycles indicate that women's progress may be beginning to stagnate. The 2002 elections marked the first time since 1994 that women did not increase their presence in Congress (see Table 4.1). In 2004, there were modest gains, with five new women sent to the House, though none to the Senate. Perhaps more importantly, there has been almost no increase in the number of women candidates since 1992. In 2002 and 2004, fewer than 200 women filed to run for the U.S. House of Representatives; more women sought office in the 1992, 1994, and 1996 House elections. Similar patterns exist for U.S. Senate races. Table 4.1 presents the number of women candidates who won their party nominations and ran in House general elections from 1970 through 2004. Although there has been steady, albeit slow, growth in the number of women running in general election races over the last thirty years, the only dramatic single-year jump occurred in 1992. The 2004 election did set a record, with 141 women candidates winning their party nominations for House seats. But to put this number into perspective, it is helpful to recognize that more than 675 male candidates garnered their parties' nominations. In the Senate, ten women received major party nominations, compared to fifty-six men.

Clearly, the historical evolution of women's candidacies demonstrates that we are in a period of increasing opportunities for women candidates.

Still, a critical question persists: Why aren't more women serving in Congress?

## MEN AND WOMEN RUNNING FOR CONGRESS: THE GENERAL INDICATORS

In assessing why so few women serve in Congress, most researchers turn to key election statistics and compare female and male congressional candidates. Turning first to overt voter bias against women candidates, the research is mixed. In a series of experimental studies in which participants are presented with a hypothetical match-up between men and women candidates, researchers have identified bias against women.[7] But studies that focus on actual vote totals fail to uncover evidence of bias.[8] Barbara Burrell, a contributor to this volume, concluded in an earlier study that candidate sex accounts for less than 1 percent of the variation in the vote for House candidates from 1968 to 1992. Kathy Dolan, who carried out a comprehensive 2004 study of patterns in gender and voting, concluded that candidate sex is a relevant factor only in rare electoral circumstances.[9]

If we turn to the performance of men and women in House elections in 2004, we arrive at a similar conclusion. The data presented in Table 4.2 confirm that there is no widespread voter bias in favor of or against women candidates. In the most recent House races, women and men fared similarly in terms of raw vote totals. In the Senate, with no more than eleven female general election candidates running in any year, and as few as six in some elections (such as 1996), statistical comparisons are not useful. The general trends, however, reveal no obvious bias for or against women Senate candidates from 2004.

Turning to the second most important indicator of electoral success – fundraising – we see similar results. In the 1970s and 1980s, because so few women ran for office, many scholars assumed that women in electoral politics simply could not raise the amount of money necessary to mount a competitive campaign. Indeed, older research that focused mostly on anecdotal studies concluded that women ran campaigns with lower levels of funding than did men. More systematic examinations of campaign receipts, however, have uncovered little evidence of sex differences in fundraising for similarly situated candidates. An early study of congressional candidates from 1972 to 1982 found only a "very weak" relationship between gender and the ability to raise campaign funds.[10] More recent research indicates that, by the 1988 House elections, the disparity between men and women in campaign fundraising had completely disappeared.[11]

**TABLE 4.2:** Women and men House candidates fared similarly with voters in 2004

| | 2004 | |
| --- | --- | --- |
| | Women<br>% | Men<br>% |
| **Democrats** | | |
| Incumbents | 69 | 67 |
| | (29) | (129) |
| Challengers | 37 | 34 |
| | (39) | (139) |
| Open Seats | 48 | 48 |
| | (9) | (19) |
| **Republicans** | | |
| Incumbents | 60 | 64 |
| | (19) | (56) |
| Challengers | 31 | 31 |
| | (22) | (135) |
| Open Seats | 44 | 54 |
| | (9) | (19) |

*Notes:* Candidates running unopposed are omitted from these results. Entries indicate mean vote share won. Parentheses indicate the total number of candidates for each category. No comparisons between men and women are statistically significant.

*Source:* Compiled from *New York Times* listing of election results.

In cases where women raised less money than men, the differences were accounted for by incumbency status: male incumbents generally held positions of greater political power and thus attracted larger contributions.[12]

If we examine fundraising totals of male and female general election House candidates in 2004, we see few gender differences (see Table 4.3). In fact, the discrepancies that do exist actually reveal an advantage for women candidates in several instances. Again, the number of women Senate candidates is too small for meaningful statistical comparisons with men. In the two most competitive 2004 Senate races with woman candidates, however, women and their opponents raised comparable amounts of money. In Alaska, Republican incumbent Lisa Murkowski raised $5,691,426 compared to Democratic challenger Tony Knowles' $5,834,694. In the hotly contested race for Florida's open Senate seat, Republican winner Mel Martinez outspent his Democratic opponent Betty Castor $12,391,521 to $11,313,570. In a race decided by less than one percent of the vote,

**TABLE 4.3:** Women and men House candidates fared similarly in raising money in 2004

|  | 2004 | |
|---|---|---|
|  | Women | Men |
| **Democrats** | | |
| Incumbents | $936,011 | $1,104,680 |
|  | (29) | (129) |
| Challengers | 494,506** | 231,078 |
|  | (39) | (139) |
| Open Seats | 939,031 | 1,004,461 |
|  | (9) | (19) |
| **Republicans** | | |
| Incumbents | 1,601,891** | 1,207,823 |
|  | (19) | (156) |
| Challengers | 446,425* | 238,426 |
|  | (22) | (135) |
| Open Seats | 1,263,547 | 1,131,510 |
|  | (9) | (19) |

*Notes:* Candidates running unopposed are omitted from these results. Entries indicate total money raised. Parentheses indicate the total number of candidates in each category. Significance levels: ** $p < .05$; * $p < .10$ in difference of means test.
*Source:* Compiled from 2004 Federal Election Commission (FEC) reports.

Martinez's edge may have made a difference. Overall, though, no clear gender differences emerge in congressional competition for funds.

Based on general indicators, we see what appears to be a gender-neutral electoral environment. Women are slowly increasing their numbers in Congress, and men and women perform similarly in terms of vote totals and fundraising. The data certainly suggest that men have lost their stranglehold over the congressional election process and that women now can find excellent political opportunities. But these broad statistical comparisons tell only part of the story.

## ARE WOMEN MAKING GAINS EVERYWHERE? STATE AND REGIONAL VARIATION

When moderate Democrat Judy McCain-Belk attempted to unseat first-term incumbent congressman, Jo Bonnor, in Alabama's 1st congressional district in the 2004, she was pursuing a quest to make history. No woman in Alabama had ever been elected to the U.S. House or Senate for a full term. The three women from Alabama who have served in Congress were all appointed or won special elections (two replaced their late husbands; the third was appointed to serve by her husband, the governor). The most recent of the three was Maryon Pittman Allen, who served in the Senate for less than five months in 1978. Certainly, Judy McCain-Belk, a Democrat in a Republican-leaning district, faced an uphill battle. But she was a successful businesswoman who had previously won election to the Mobile County School Board. She also raised more money than any other challenger in Alabama in 2004. In the end, Jo Bonnor defeated Judy McCain-Belk by a substantial margin (60 percent to 37 percent). While her story is similar to many congressional challengers facing long odds for victory, a number of commentators observed a gendered undercurrent in the race. Lieutenant Governor Lucy Baxley noted that women have done better in local elections in Alabama and that "there has been a line" drawn at federal office. University of Alabama political science professor William H. Stewart simply observed, "A good conservative man is the ideal candidate for that seat."[13]

As the story of Judy McCain-Belk suggests, women may face certain disadvantages when running for office in some parts of the United States. If we examine the prevalence of male and female House candidates by region and state, we see that the broader inclusion of women in high-level politics has not extended to all regions of the country equally. Table 4.4 tracks women's electoral success in House races since 1970 but breaks the data down by four geographic regions. Before 1990, the Northeast saw two and three times as many women candidates as any other region in the country. The situation changed dramatically with the "Year of the Woman" elections in 1992. The number of women winning election to Congress from Western states more than doubled; and in the South, the number more than tripled. Gains were much more modest in the Midwest and Northeast. Since the late 1990s, only the West continues to show clear gains for women. This geographic breakdown puts the 1992 elections, as well as the modest increases of women's elections to Congress since that time, into perspective. The 1992 "Year of the Woman" gains were largely in the West and South.

More specific than region, there are also several striking differences among individual states. Consider, for example, that heading into the 2004 elections, nineteen states had no women representatives in Washington. Further, twenty-eight states had never been represented by a woman in

**TABLE 4.4:** Sharp regional differences exist in the proportion of U.S. Representatives who are women

|  | West % | South % | Midwest % | Northeast % |
|---|---|---|---|---|
| 1970 | 3.9 | 0.0 | 2.5 | 4.9 |
| 1980 | 2.6 | 1.6 | 3.3 | 8.1 |
| 1990 | 8.2 | 2.3 | 6.2 | 9.6 |
| 1992 | 17.2 | 7.9 | 6.7 | 12.4 |
| 2000 | 25.8 | 9.2 | 10.9 | 11.3 |
| 2002 | 25.5 | 8.7 | 11.5 | 9.8 |
| 2004 | 26.5 | 11.0 | 14.0 | 10.9 |
| Net Change (1970 to 2004) | +22.6 | +11.0 | +11.5 | +6.0 |

*Notes:* Percentages reflect the proportion of House Members who are women. The ratio for the West region is heavily skewed by California; without California the percentage for the West delegation after the 2004 elections is 14% women.

*Source:* Compiled by author from Center for American Women and Politics (CAWP), 2005 Fact Sheets.

the U.S. Senate. Table 4.5 designates the states with the best and worst records in sending women to serve in the House of Representatives following the 2004 elections. Surprisingly, several states with relatively large House delegations, such as New Jersey (thirteen members), Massachusetts (ten members), and Maryland and Arizona (eight members each), sent no women to the House.[14] Only two of Pennsylvania's nineteen members are women, and only three of the thirty-two members from Texas are women.

Table 4.5 also demonstrates that women congressional candidates have succeeded in a number of high-population states, like California, Florida, and New York. Why have women done well in these states and not others? California, New York, and Florida are among those states with the biggest delegations, so perhaps we can assume that more political opportunities for women drive the candidacies. But this would not explain women's lack of success in the large states like Texas and Pennsylvania. Moreover, what explains women's success in states like Missouri, where, for much of the 1990s, three of the state's nine House members were women? Missouri borders Iowa, which has never elected a woman House candidate, and Oklahoma, which elected its only woman House member (to one term) in 1921. By the same token, why has Connecticut elected so many more women than neighboring Massachusetts?

Some political scientists argue that state political culture serves as an important determinant of women's ability to win elective office.

**TABLE 4.5:** Almost half of the states have no women serving in the U.S. House of Representatives in 2005

| States with no women representatives | States with high percentage of women representatives | |
|---|---|---|
| | | % |
| New Jersey (13) | Connecticut (5) | 40 |
| Massachusetts (10) | California (53) | 36 |
| Arizona (8) | Nevada (3) | 33 |
| Maryland (8) | New Mexico (3) | 33 |
| Alabama (7) | West Virginia (3) | 33 |
| Louisiana (7) | Colorado (7) | 29 |
| South Carolina (6) | Wisconsin (8) | 25 |
| Iowa (5)* | New York (29) | 24 |
| Oklahoma (5) | Florida (25) | 19 |
| Arkansas (4) | Virginia (11) | 18 |
| Kansas (4) | Ohio (18) | 17 |
| Mississippi (4)* | | |
| Nebraska (3) | | |
| Utah (3) | | |
| Hawaii (2) | | |
| Idaho (2) | | |
| New Hampshire (2)* | | |
| Maine (2) | | |
| Rhode Island (2) | | |
| Alaska (1) | | |
| Delaware (1)* | | |
| Montana (1) | | |
| North Dakota (1) | | |
| Vermont (1)* | | |

*Notes:* Five states – Alaska, Arkansas, Louisiana, Maine, and Maryland – that have no women House members, do have women serving in the U.S. Senate. Two states, each with only one House seat, Wyoming and South Dakota, both have a woman serving. * Indicates states that have never sent a woman to either the House or Senate. Number in parentheses is the number of House seats in the state as of 2004.

*Source:* Compiled by author from Center for American Women and Politics (CAWP), 2005 Fact Sheets.

Researchers Barbara Norrander and Clyde Wilcox have found considerable disparities in the progress of women's election to state legislatures across various states and regions. They explain the disparities by pointing to differences in state ideology and state culture.[15] States with a conservative ideology, and a "traditionalist or moralist" culture, are less likely to elect women.[16] A strong correlation between the percentage of women in the state legislature and the number of women in Congress, however, does not always exist. New Hampshire and Massachusetts, for example, are above average in terms of the number of women serving in the state legislature, yet each has a very poor record of electing women to the House of Representatives. Diagnosing the specific causes of regional and state differences in electing women House members is beyond the scope of this chapter. These findings, however, suggest that the manner in which gender manifests itself in the political systems and environments of individual states is an important part of the explanation for why so few women are in Congress.

## ARE WOMEN RUNNING FOR BOTH PARTIES AND UNDER THE BEST CIRCUMSTANCES?

Like most congressional election cycles, 2004 was dominated by hopeless challengers running against safely entrenched incumbents. Reporters for *Congressional Quarterly* completed an analysis of all 435 U.S. House races in June, five months before the 2004 elections, and concluded that only twenty-one (out of 404) races with incumbents running were competitive.[17] Consider, for instance, the candidacy of California Republican challenger Jennifer Depalma. A libertarian Republican, Depalma challenged long-time Democratic Congresswoman and House Minority Leader Nancy Pelosi. DePalma, who graduated from Princeton University and the University of Chicago Law School, had an impressive resume as a lawyer and policy expert. She entered the race because, as she stated in an interview, "Competitive elections encourage our elected officials to be accountable to us."[18] Ultimately, she managed to raise little money and garnered little media coverage. Her lofty goal seemed futile when Pelosi defeated Depalma by a margin of 85 percent to 12 percent.

Or consider Democrat Katherine Fox Carr, a long-time community activist, who challenged incumbent Republican Dan Burton of Indiana. Burton became popular among conservatives throughout the country as an outspoken critic of President Bill Clinton during the impeachment proceedings of the late 1990s. Over the course of the election, Carr received literally no media coverage in mainstream Indiana newspapers. She also failed to generate substantial campaign contributions; Burton raised $756,305, compared to Carr's $9,289. Burton also had a million more dollars in the bank at his disposal, should the need to campaign vigorously arise. The outcome was never in doubt. Burton defeated Carr

72 percent to 26 percent. Most congressional elections with challengers running against incumbents resembled these lopsided "contests."

Expectedly, political scientists often identify the incumbency advantage as one of the leading explanations for women's slow entry into electoral politics. Low turnover, a direct result of incumbency, provides few opportunities for women to increase their numbers in male-dominated legislative bodies. Between 1946 and 2002, only 8 percent of all challengers have defeated incumbent members of the U.S. House of Representatives.[19] In most races, the incumbent cruised to reelection with well over 60 percent of the vote. Accordingly, as congressional elections scholars Ronald Kieth Gaddie and Charles Bullock state, "Open seats, not the defeat of incumbents, are the portal through which most legislators enter Congress."[20]

In the 2004 general elections, only thirty-five of the 435 seats in the House of Representatives did not have an incumbent running. Of the thirty-four seats up for re-election in the Senate, only eight were open. Ninety-eight percent of the 400 House incumbents who ran in the general election won their races. Democrat Tom Daschle of South Dakota was the only incumbent Senator who was defeated. Moreover, because open seat races tend to attract the largest number of qualified and experienced candidates, particularly those with experience serving in local and state government offices, they also tend to be better funded. The average winning open seat candidate's receipts in the 2004 election even exceeded the average winning incumbent's receipts, and the average challenger's by roughly $750,000.

In order to begin to assess whether women are as likely as men to take advantage of the dynamics associated with an open seat race, we can examine the presence and performance of women in open-seat House contests. Table 4.6 compares women's presence in House elections by time period, party affiliation, and type of seat. In this analysis, I divided the data into three time periods to more clearly examine the evolution of women's candidates. As expected, women were significantly more likely to run for office in the later eras (1992–2000, 2004), although the increase in women candidates is not constant across parties. Between the first and second time period, the number of women Democrats running in all types of races more than doubled, whereas the increases among Republicans were much smaller. Regardless of party, however, in the second and third time periods, the highest ratio of women candidates sought open seats. And in 2004, the proportion of Republican women seeking open seats more than doubled that of prior periods.

**TABLE 4.6:** In 2004 in races for the U.S. House, a greater proportion of open seats were contested by women candidates than ever before

| Type of Seat | 1980–1990 | | 1992–2000 | | 2004 | |
|---|---|---|---|---|---|---|
| | Democrat % | Republican % | Democrat % | Republican % | Democrat % | Republican % |
| Open Seat | 11 (24) | 8 (16) | 23 (61) | 12 (30) | 29 (10) | 23 (9) |
| Challengers | 10 (80) | 9 (98) | 20 (157) | 10 (92) | 23 (41) | 15 (24) |
| Incumbents | 4 (59) | 5 (52) | 12 (149) | 7 (64) | 20 (37) | 10 (20) |

*Note:* Entries indicate the percentage of all candidates for that electoral category who were women. The number of candidates for each category is in parentheses.

*Source:* Compiled by author from Center for American Women and Politics (CAWP), 2005 Fact Sheets and *New York Times* listing of election results.

Aside from open seat races in 2004, where the parties were closer to even, the Democrats have been much more likely than the Republicans to nominate women to run for all seats (see also Table 4.1). This carries serious long-term implications for the number of women serving in Congress. For women to achieve full parity in U.S. political institutions, women must be represented fully in both parties, especially if the Republicans continue to constitute a majority in Congress. Researchers must focus more on what the parties do to recruit and promote women's candidacies not only for Congress, but also at the state and local levels.

## ARE MEN AND WOMEN EQUALLY AMBITIOUS TO RUN FOR CONGRESS?

The decision to run for office and ultimately seek a seat in Congress is a critical area of inquiry for those interested in the role of gender in electoral politics. As at least one example from the 2004 elections suggests, this is not always an easy decision for women. Following months of lobbying by hopeful supporters, Democrat Michelle Nunn, the daughter of popular former U.S. Senator Sam Nunn, withdrew her name from consideration for an open U.S. Senate seat in Georgia. Nunn was an attractive potential candidate not only because she would have greatly benefited from her father's name recognition, but also because of her political experience as the founding director of Hands On Atlanta, one of the largest urban volunteer organizations in the country.[21] Most of the other prominent Democrats in Georgia had already stepped aside to clear the path for her to win the Democratic primary. In a prepared statement, though, Nunn acknowledged that she had been presented with a unique political opportunity, but concluded that the timing was not right for her.[22]

Until recently, very little empirical research explored the decision to run for office. But if the general election playing field is largely gender neutral, then gender differences in political ambition likely provide a crucial explanation for women's under-representation in Congress. In 2002, Jennifer Lawless and I conducted a national survey of women and men working in the three professions most likely to precede a career in Congress. Some of the results of the survey, entitled the *Citizen Political Ambition Study*, are shown in Table 4.7. On the critical question of interest in running for office, the results of the study highlighted a substantial gender gap in political ambition.[23] Even though women who run for office are just as likely as men to emerge victorious, a much smaller ratio of women than men ever emerge as candidates. This is the case because women are

**TABLE 4.7:** Among potential candidates, women are less interested than men in seeking elective office

|  | Women % | Men % |
|---|---|---|
| Has Thought About Running for Office | 36 | 55 |
| Discussed Running with Party Leaders | 4 | 8 |
| Discussed Running with Friends and Family | 17 | 29 |
| Discussed Running with Community Leaders | 6 | 12 |
| Solicited or Discussed Financial Contributions with Potential Supporters | 2 | 4 |
| Investigated How to Place Your Name on the Ballot | 4 | 10 |
| Sample Size | 1,248 | 1,454 |

*Notes:* Sample is composed of lawyers, business leaders and executives, and educators. Entries indicate percent responding "yes." All differences between women and men are significant at p < .05 level.

*Source:* Adapted from the Citizen Political Ambition Study. See Richard L. Fox and Jennifer L. Lawless, "Entering the Arena: Gender and the Decision to Run for Office," *American Journal of Political Science,* 2004, 48(2): 264–280.

far less likely than men to consider running for office. They are also significantly less likely to engage in the key activities that typically precede a campaign.

Further, when we consider male and female potential candidates' interest in running for Congress, the gender gap in political ambition is amplified. Table 4.8 shows the interest of potential candidates in running for the U.S. House and Senate. Potential candidates were asked to identify what offices they would be most likely to seek first. They were also asked to identify which offices they might ever be interested in running for. Table 4.8 only shows the results for Congress. For both questions, men were significantly more likely than women to demonstrate an interest in running for Congress. Men were twice as likely as women to name the U.S. House and U.S. Senate as the first office they would run for.

We concluded that three critical factors explain the gender gap in political ambition. First, women are significantly less likely than men to receive encouragement to run for office. This difference is very important since potential candidates are twice as likely to think about running for office when a party leader, elected official, or political activist attempts to recruit them as candidates. Second, women are significantly less likely than men to view themselves as qualified to run for office. In other words, women, even in the top tier of professional accomplishment, tend not to consider

**TABLE 4.8:** Among potential candidates, women are less interested than men in running for the U.S. House or Senate

|  | Women % | Men % |
|---|---|---|
| **First Office you would likely run for . . .** | | |
| U.S. House of Representatives | 5 | 10 |
| U.S. Senate | 2 | 4 |
| **Interested in someday running for . . .** | | |
| U.S. House of Representatives | 15 | 27 |
| U.S. Senate | 13 | 20 |
| Sample Size | 816 | 1022 |

*Notes:* Sample is composed of lawyers, business leaders and executives, and educators who indicated some degree of interest in running for office. Entries indicate percent responding "yes." All differences between women and men are significant at p < .05 level.

*Source:* Adapted from the Citizen Political Ambition Study. See Richard L. Fox and Jennifer L. Lawless, "Entering the Arena: Gender and the Decision to Run for Office," *American Journal of Political Science*, 2004, 48(2): 264–280.

themselves qualified to run for political office, even when they have the same objective credentials and experiences as men. The problem is further compounded, because women are also less likely to have people suggest to them that they run for office. The suggestion to run, especially by a party official or someone already in elected office, often makes potential candidates believe they are qualified to run for office. Third, even among this group of professionals, women were much more likely to state that they were responsible for the majority of child care and household duties. Even though many of the women in the study had blazed trails in the formerly male professions of law and business, they were still serving as the primary caretakers of their homes. As a result, many women noted that they simply did not have the time to even think about running for office.

## CONCLUSION AND DISCUSSION

When researchers and political scientists in the late 1970s and early 1980s began to study the role of gender in electoral politics, concerns about basic fairness and political representation motivated many of their investigations. For many scholars, the notion of governing bodies overwhelmingly dominated by men offends ours sense of "simple justice." In this vein, some researchers argue that the reality of a male-dominated government may suggest to women citizens that the political system is not fully open to them. These concerns are as pertinent today as they were in the past. As Susan J. Carroll and I noted in the introduction to this volume, a growing body of empirical research finds that a political system that does not allow for women's full inclusion in positions of political power increases the possibility that gender-salient issues will be over-looked. Evidence based on the behavior of public officials clearly demon-strates that women are more likely than men to promote legislation geared to ameliorate women's economic and social status, especially concerning issues of health care, poverty, education, and gender equity.[24] Despite the substantive and symbolic importance of women's full inclusion in the elec-toral arena, the number of women serving in elected bodies remains low. This chapter's overview of women's performance in congressional elec-tions makes it clear that we need to adopt a more nuanced approach if we are to understand gender's evolving role in the electoral arena.

As to answering the central question of the chapter, "Why are there still so few women in Congress?," two broad findings emerge from the analysis. First, on a more optimistic note, women now compete in U.S. House and Senate races more successfully than at any previous time in history. There are almost no gender differences in terms of the major indicators of electoral success – vote totals and fundraising. The evidence presented in this chapter continues to show that women and men general election candidates performed similarly in the 2004 elections. Based on these facts, I confirm what a number of analysts have speculated, that when considered this way, the electoral environment is gender neutral.

The second broad finding to emerge from this chapter, however, is that gender continues to play an important role in the electoral arena and in some cases works to keep the number of women running for Congress low. Notably, there are sharp state and regional differences in electing men and women to Congress. Women cannot emerge in greater numbers until the candidacies of women are embraced throughout the entire United States. Also, women's candidacies must be embraced by both parties. Women's full inclusion will not be possible if the overwhelming majority of women candidates continue to identify with the Democratic party. Further, the almost impenetrable incumbency advantage and the dearth of open seat opportunities make the prospect for any sharp increase in the number of women serving in Congress unlikely. Finally, and perhaps most impor-tantly, gender differences in political ambition – particularly to run for the U.S. Congress – suggest that gender may be exerting its strongest impact at the earliest stages of the electoral process. Many women who would make ideal candidates never actually consider running for office. The notion of entering politics still appears not to be a socialized norm for women. As these findings suggest, gender permeates the electoral environment in subtle and nuanced ways. Broad empirical analyses tend to overlook these dynamics, yet the reality is that these dynamics help explain why so few women occupy positions on Capitol Hill.

## NOTES

1. This story is recounted by AP reporter Lara Jakes Jordan, September 30, 2004. Pa. House Race is Nation's Most Competitive between Women. The Associated Press State & Local Wire.
2. Donna Leinwand, Cesar G. Soriano, and Joe Eaton. November 4, 2004. Election 2004: Regional Roundup. USA Today.
3. Nicholas K. Geranios. November 2, 2004. McMorris Wins 5th District, Reichert Leading 8th. The Associated Press State & Local Wire.
4. Matt Volz. October 16, 2004. Oil Money Flows One Way in Alaska Senate Race. The Associated Press State & Local Wire.
5. Women in National Parliaments. 2005. Inter-Parliamentary Union. <http://www.ipu.org/wmn-e/classif.htm> 2005, January 6.
6. Irwin Gertzog. 1984. *Congressional Women*. New York: Praeger, 18.
7. For examples of experimental designs that identify voter bias, see Leonie, Huddy and Nadya Terkildsen. 1993. Gender Stereotypes and the Perception of Male Female Candidates. *American Journal of Political Science* 37: 119–47; Leonie Huddy and Nadya Terkildsen. 1993. The Consequences of Gender Stereotypes for Women Candidates at Different Levels and Types of Office. *Political Research Quarterly* 46: 503–25; and Richard L. Fox and Eric R. A. N. Smith. 1998. The Role of Candidate Sex in Voter Decision-Making. *Political Psychology* 19: 405–19.
8. For a comprehensive examination of vote totals through the mid-1990s, see Richard A. Seltzer, Jody Newman, and M. Voorhees Leighton. 1997. *Sex as a Political Variable*. Boulder, CO: Lynne Reinner.
9. Kathleen A. Dolan. 2004. *Voting for Women*. Boulder, CO: Westview.
10. Barbara Burrell. 1985. Women and Men's Campaigns for the U.S. House of Representatives, 1972–1982: A Finance Gap? *American Political Quarterly* 13: 251–72.
11. Barbara Burrell. 1994. *A Woman's Place Is in the House*. Ann Arbor: The University of Michigan Press, 105.
12. Carole Jean Uhlaner and Kay Lehman Schlozman. 1986. Candidate Gender and Congressional Campaign Receipts. *Journal of Politics* 52: 391–409.
13. Lauren Shepherd. February 18, 2004. Belk Hoping to Break through Glass Ceiling in Conservative Ala. The Hill.
14. This is not to suggest that these states have always had problems electing women. In Maryland, for example, in the early 1990s four of the eight-member delegation were women.

15. Barbara Norrander and Clyde Wilcox. 1998. The Geography of Gender Power: Women in State Legislatures. In *Women and Elective Office*, ed. by Sue Thomas and Clyde Wilcox. New York: Oxford University Press.
16. Kira Sanbonmatsu. 2002. Political Parties and the Recruitment of Women to State Legislatures. *Journal of Politics* 64(3): 791–809.
17. Republicans Maintain a Clear Edge in House Contests. June 4, 2004. CQ Weekly.
18. Sfist Interview: Jennifer Depalma. October 25, 2004, Sfist. <http://www.sfist.com/archives/2004/10/25/sfist_interview_jennifer_depalma.php> 2005, January 9.
19. Gary C. Jacobsen. 2004. *The Politics of Congressional Elections*, 6th edition. New York: Longman, 23.
20. Ronald Keith Gaddie and Charles S. Bullock. 2000. *Elections to Open Seats in the U.S. House*. Lanham: Rowman and Littlefield, 1.
21. Maria Saporta. August 6, 2003. Michelle Nunn May Run for Senate; Her Father Held the Job for Decades. Atlanta Journal-Constitution.
22. Rhonda Cook. October 25, 2003. Michelle Nunn Decides Not to Run for Senate. Atlanta Journal-Constitution.
23. Richard L. Fox and Jennifer L. Lawless. 2004. Entering the Arena: Gender and the Decision to Run for Office. *American Journal of Political Science* 48(2): 264–80.
24. For one of the most recent analyses of on how women in Congress address different policy issues than men, see Michele L. Swers, 2002. *The Difference Women Make*. Chicago: University of Chicago.

# 5 African American Women and Electoral Politics

## Journeying from the Shadows to the Spotlight

Flashing her trademark warm, full, inviting smile and exuding her usual charisma, Carol Moseley Braun ended a campaign speech by making the signature statement of her campaign. Moseley Braun shared with the crowd the most important reason to choose her as the Democratic nominee for the 2004 elections, stating with a flourish, "I don't look like [George W. Bush]. I don't talk like him. I don't think like him. And I certainly don't act like him." The crowd roared to their feet. After her speech, she dazzled the crowd, holding conversations with many between handshakes and hugs.

But for all the photo snapshots and autographs requested from those attending, the voters sensed the truth. Carol Moseley Braun was not a "real" presidential candidate. She had once again left voters with two distinct conclusions: first, that she is a dynamic candidate and should become the next president, and second, that unfortunately, she will never become president.

As the second African American woman to make a serious bid for the White House, Carol Moseley Braun ran as the "African American," "the woman," and perhaps most importantly, the "anti-Bush candidate." At every campaign stop, she pointed to the ways in which she differed from not only President Bush, but also the entire field of Democratic contenders. Indeed, as Moseley Braun points out, she was unique among the nine candidates seeking the Democratic Party's nomination for the White House. With such notable differences, we might expect that the media would be overcome by her story and that political pundits would be struck with curiosity. Counter to such predictions, she received mostly minor mentions in the press and was an afterthought in most media coverage.

"Laboring in the shadows," as Carol Moseley Braun did, is an apt description of African American women's participation in electoral politics throughout their history in the United States. In declaring her presidential candidacy, Carol Moseley Braun continued an established legacy of African American women seeking political empowerment by running for political offices. Her bid for the White House certainly reflects the progression of African American women in mainstream politics over their history in this country. It also reflects the barriers African American women face when seeking high-profile elected offices. As with Shirley Chisholm's run for the presidency more than thirty years ago, Carol Moseley Braun was never considered a viable presidential candidate during the 2004 election. Despite her considerable political experience, she remained a second-string candidate in a field of varsity players. Analysis of the 2004 election offers an opportunity to examine the state of African American women in electoral politics, bringing greater visibility to their critical – albeit often overlooked – political participation.

Traditional measures and indicators of political participation suggest that African American women would be among the least likely to participate, yet they are heavily engaged in a range of political activities. In this chapter, I trace African American women's participation in formal electoral politics from Shirley Chisholm's 1972 campaign to Carol Moseley Braun's 2004 presidential candidacy. Examining the candidacies of African American women during this period illustrates the extent to which they are engaged in electoral politics.

The 2004 elections reflect African American women's ongoing journey from the shadows to the spotlight in American politics. African American women are still experiencing a number of "firsts" in electoral politics, signifying that their journey is not yet complete. The 2004 election cycle makes visible the considerable challenges African American women continue to face to simply be considered as viable candidates. In response to these barriers to political advancement, African American women are organizing and exploring new strategies to ensure their future leadership in American politics. By focusing on African American women's experiences, we have an opportunity to examine the extent of America's progress toward political inclusiveness along both race and gender lines.

## AFRICAN AMERICAN WOMEN AND THE PARADOX OF PARTICIPATION

Political participation has consistently been a part of African American women's experiences in America despite formidable barriers to their participation in formal electoral politics such as voting and running for political office. At its inception in 1787, the U.S. Constitution limited the citizenship rights of African American women, as well as African American men, regarding each one as only three-fifths of a person. Later, as Mamie Locke argues, African American women would move from three-fifths of a person under the Constitution to total exclusion from constitutional protections with the passage of the Fifteenth Amendment in 1870, which extended the right to vote to black men only.[1] When women earned the right to vote in 1920 with the passage of the Nineteenth Amendment, large numbers of African American women remained restricted from the franchise through the cultural norms of the Jim Crow South. African Americans, both men and women, were disenfranchised through literacy tests, poll taxes, grandfather clauses, and all-white primaries. It was not until the passage of the Voting Rights Act of 1965 that African American women secured the right to freely practice the franchise.

The impact of the Voting Rights Act was keenly apparent in the states of the Deep South. Black voter registration in Mississippi, for example, increased from 6.7 percent in 1964 to 64 percent in 1980.[2] The Voting Rights Act of 1965 was arguably the single most important piece of legislation in securing the franchise for African American voters and realizing black political empowerment. The rapid growth in the numbers of black elected officials is further evidence of its impact. At the time the Voting Rights Act passed, fewer than 500 black elected officials held office nationwide. Today the number of black elected officials has grown to more than 9,000.[3]

Studies of American politics have defined political participation narrowly in terms of electoral participation. As Cathy Cohen argues, such a limited definition of political participation has hindered the development of research on African American women's political activism because political participation among women of color tends to extend beyond electoral politics to community organizing and civic engagement.[4] Because the arena of electoral politics was effectively closed to African American women until the passage of the Voting Rights Act of 1965, we have developed a limited understanding of African American women as political actors. Because African American women were excluded from participation in formal politics, first by the condition of their enslavement and then by equally oppressive systems of exclusion, their nontraditional political activism developed outside the electoral system and was informed by their political, economic, and social conditions.[5]

Defining political participation beyond the narrow framework of voting and holding elected office allows us to see the consistent levels of

African American women's political participation across history. With new questions and an awareness of the nontraditional spaces of women's activism such as churches, private women's clubs, and volunteer organizations, feminist historians have uncovered countless activities of women of color involved in social movements. African American women have been central to every effort toward greater political empowerment for both African Americans and women. As historian Paula Giddings attests, African American women were the linchpin in struggles against racism and sexism. African American women understood that the fates of women's rights and black rights were inextricably linked and that one would be meaningless without the other.[6]

In spite of such a rich legacy of activism, African American women's political participation represents a puzzle of sorts. African American women appear to be overrepresented in elective office while simultaneously holding the characteristics that would make them least likely to be politically engaged. African American women are a larger proportion of black elected officials than white women are of white elected officials.[7] In the 109th Congress, 29 percent of African Americans in the House are women compared to only 15 percent of all members of the House who are women. Further, as Figure 5.1 illustrates, since the early 1990s there has been a steady increase in the number African American women elected officials, which is not the case for African American men. In fact, over the last decade all of the growth in the number of black elected officials is attributed to African American women. This reverses the trends of the 1970s immediately following the passage of the Voting Rights Act when 82 percent of the growth in black elected officials was attributed to African American men.[8]

Scholars who study the intersection of race and gender argue that African American women suffer from a "double disadvantage" in politics in that they are forced to overcome the ills of both sexism and racism.[9] Darcy and Hadley, however, concluded that African American women defied expectations in that they proved more politically ambitious than their white counterparts, enjoying greater success in election to mayoral, state legislative, and congressional office by comparison with their white female counterparts throughout the 1970s and 1980s. These authors linked the puzzle of African American women's achievement to their activism in the civil rights movement and the skills developed during the movement, which they quickly translated into formal politics once opportunities became available after the passage of the Voting Rights Act.[10]

**Figure 5.1: The Number of African American Women Elected Officials Has Increased in Recent Elections While the Number of African American Men Has Leveled Off.**

Number of African-American Elected Officials, by Gender

1972-2001

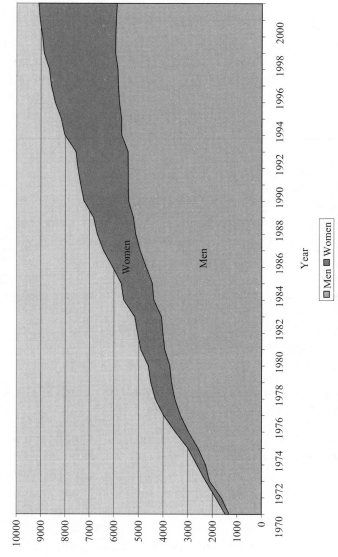

Women

Men

Year

■ Men ■ Women

*Source:* Compiled by author from David Bositis, "Black Elected Officials: A Statistical Summary," Washington, DC: Joint Center for Political and Economic Studies, 2001.

This high level of officeholding is in contrast to the material conditions of African American women's lives, which suggest that they would be far less politically active. As of the 2000 U.S. Census, 43 percent of black families were headed by a single mother, and the poverty rate among African American women was more than twice that of non-Hispanic white women.[11] Studies of political participation have consistently concluded that the affluent and the educated are more likely to participate in politics at higher rates.[12] However, for African American women, the usual determinants of political participation – education and income – are not strong predictors of their participation.[13]

Regardless of their socioeconomic status, African American women are far more likely than African American men to engage in both traditional forms of political participation (including voting and holding office) and nontraditional forms of participation (such as belonging to organizations and clubs, attending church, and talking to people about politics). Given these inconsistencies, African American women's political participation is perhaps one of the phenomena least understood by social scientists.[14] The 2004 elections present an opportunity to better understand African American women's political participation by focusing on their experiences as candidates for elected office.

## FROM CHISHOLM TO MOSELEY BRAUN: AFRICAN AMERICAN WOMEN AND THE PRESIDENCY

African American female elected officials are enduring symbols of the long fight African American women have waged for political inclusion. Though the legal barriers preventing their participation in politics have been removed, African American women continue to confront considerable barriers when seeking political office. The higher profile the office, the more formidable barriers they face to being considered viable candidates.

In 1972, Congresswoman Shirley Chisholm broke barriers as the first African American woman to make a serious bid for the presidency.[15] Chisholm was well positioned to run for president, with political experience at the community, state, and national levels. She served in the New York General Assembly before becoming the first African American woman elected to Congress. As the lone African American woman in Congress, she joined her twelve African American male colleagues in founding the Congressional Black Caucus (CBC).[16]

After two terms in the House of Representatives, Chisholm decided to run for president. Her run came at point when the civil rights leadership was calling for greater political engagement and the women's movement was at its height. In running for president, Chisholm hoped to bring the concerns of these communities to the forefront of national politics. She spoke out for the rights of African Americans, women, and gays. She was quickly dismissed as a serious candidate.

Chisholm faced a 1970s America that was just becoming accustomed to women in the workforce and in politics. She challenged notions of women's proper place. On the campaign trail, she routinely encountered hecklers who were happy to tell her the proper place for a woman. She told the story of a man at a campaign stop who questioned whether she had "cleaned her house" and "cared for her husband" before coming there.[17] Chisholm often faced such blatant sexism and, in other encounters, racism in her campaign, but she continued to press toward the Democratic national convention.

Though Chisholm fashioned herself as both the "black candidate" and the "woman candidate," she found herself shunned by both the black leaders in Congress and the feminist community. Far from supporting her, members of the CBC, an organization she had helped to found, charged that her run was detrimental to the black community, dividing it along gender lines at a time when the black community could not afford such divisive politics. Chisholm, a founder of the National Organization for Women (NOW), was dealt an equally devastating blow when prominent feminists such as the co-founder of NOW, Gloria Steinem, and fellow U.S. Congresswoman Bella Abzug decided not to endorse her candidacy publicly. Instead, they opted to protect their political leverage by supporting Senator George McGovern, who was considered at that time the more viable candidate of the Democratic contenders and the candidate most capable of defeating then-President Nixon.[18]

Deserted by both the leaders of the CBC and the feminist community, Chisholm survived the primaries and was voted on by the delegates at the Democratic national convention. She received 151 of the delegate votes on the first ballot at the convention, far short of the roughly 2,000 needed to secure the nomination. In the end, Chisholm acknowledged that her bid for the White House was less about winning and more about demanding full inclusion for African Americans and women. By waging a national presidential campaign, her candidacy had shown the world what was possible for women and men of color with increased access to political empowerment in a more democratized America.

More than three decades later, there is no doubt that Carol Moseley Braun benefited from Chisholm's trailblazing candidacy. The differences between the two experiences signify some progress for African American women as high profile candidates, even as they bring to light enduring problems African American women face in achieving greater political empowerment.

Carol Moseley Braun's treatment in the 2004 election cycle symbolizes some progress from the blatant, overt sexism and racism that Shirley Chisholm encountered in 1972. Moseley Braun experienced a more subversive, structurally embedded sexism and racism that are more difficult to recognize. Her experiences reflect the extent to which the office of the president is consistently associated with white men, a pattern Georgia Duerst-Lahti documented in her chapter in this volume. There is an understanding that the President of the United States will be a man and white, and this sentiment has dominated thinking about the presidency.[19] Since Moseley Braun was neither a man nor white, she struggled constantly to convince the public that her candidacy was, in fact, viable. The doubts surrounding the feasibility of her candidacy affected all aspects of her campaign, but were most devastating to her fundraising efforts. The negligible and trivializing media coverage she received reinforced doubts and further stymied her campaign. Such struggles are reflective of the remaining institutional racism and sexism that continue to impede qualified candidates who differ from societal expectations about who should serve as president. Moseley Braun campaigned promising to "take the 'men only' sign off the White House door," but this seemed to be a challenge America was not ready to accept.

By objective measures, Moseley Braun was well positioned to run for the presidency. Once questioned as to why she was running, Moseley Braun quickly responded, "Why not?" adding, "If I were not a woman – if I were a guy – with my credentials and my experience and what I bring to the table, there would be no reason why I wouldn't think about running for president."[20] In the field of Democratic contenders, Moseley Braun's political record was among the most stellar. She was the only candidate to have experience at the local, state, national, and international levels of government.

Moseley Braun officially announced her run for the presidency on January 15, 2003, to a crowd of students at her alma mater, the University of Illinois, with those in attendance cheering, "We Want Carol!" and interrupting her speech with overwhelming applause. She continued her campaign kick-off by touring historically black colleges and universities and women's colleges. At each stop, she swayed the audience with her well delivered statements on Iraq, the budget deficit, and the absence of quality health care.

Despite energetic responses from the crowds at each campaign stop, the political pundits remained dismissive of her campaign. According to Moseley Braun, this was nothing new, "Nobody ever expected me to get elected to anything. For one thing, I'm black, I'm a woman and I'm out of the working class. So the notion that someone from my background would have anything to say about the leadership of this country is challenging to some."[21]

As soon as she announced her candidacy, she faced speculation that her entrance into the race was simply an attempt on the part of Democratic elites to undercut the campaign of Reverend Al Sharpton by splitting the black vote. Others reasoned that her candidacy was a public effort to clear her name of alleged financial misdealings lingering from her 1998 senatorial campaign. Like Shirley Chisholm, she also faced charges of running a purely symbolic campaign to establish that women are capable of running for the country's top executive office.

Women's groups stood firmly behind Moseley Braun, as did many in the African American community. She received critical endorsements from the National Women's Political Caucus (NWPC) and NOW, two of the leading feminist organizations. As her campaign dollars declined, she received a boost with the endorsement of EMILY's List, a donor network supporting pro-choice women candidates. Patricia Ireland, former president of NOW, took over as her campaign manager, which meant even more connections to the established women's community. Notable white feminists, including the legendary Gloria Steinem and Marie Wilson, director of the White House Project, a non-profit organization dedicated to getting a woman into the White House, publicly supported the campaign. Black women's organizations, including the National Political Congress of Black Women, invested in Moseley Braun's campaign, and she enjoyed public endorsements from notable African American women from Coretta Scott King to Dr. Dorothy Height, president emerita of the National Council of Negro Women. From this perspective, her bid represents progress over Shirley Chisholm's candidacy, which struggled to win such support.

Campaign fundraising remained a problem for Moseley Braun, and her efforts continuously lagged behind most other candidates even after she gained these impressive endorsements. During the first three quarters of 2003, Moseley Braun reportedly raised approximately $342,000,

placing her eighth in the field of candidates according to fundraising esti-
mates. During this same period, Howard Dean raised $25 million dol-
lars while John Kerry raised $17 million dollars. Even long-shot candi-
date Dennis Kucinich raised $3.4 million. Political scientist Paula McClain
argues that Moseley Braun was disadvantaged from the onset in crafting a
name for herself in this campaign, given the Democratic Party leadership's
preference that candidates forego more leftist politics. As she argues,
Moseley Braun's identity as an African American woman positioned her
clearly as a "left-of-center candidate" and subsequently constrained her
ability to establish an alternative identity as a candidate in the minds of
voters.[22]

Garnering media attention proved to be an equally challenging problem for Moseley Braun's campaign, creating a circular effect; without
media visibility, her capacity to raise funds was limited, and with mini-
mal funding, her campaign drew less media attention. She had extreme
difficulty getting her message to the voters. When she received any coverage at all, it most often referred to her as "improbable," "non-viable," a
"long shot" candidate, or at worst an "also-ran." Her campaign was dealt
a devastating media blow in December of 2003, when the major television networks decided to stop traveling with Moseley Braun and the
other so-called second-tier Democratic candidates, Dennis Kucinich and
Al Sharpton, opting instead to cover their campaigns by phone. Moseley
Braun and Sharpton responded angrily. Moseley Braun was quick to link
the networks' decisions to the amount of money the campaigns had raised.
She fought back, arguing that the networks were allowing fundraising
dollars to control the democratic process yet again. As she stated, "It's a
terrible commentary on the state of the media if their idea of democracy is
only relating to those candidates who have the most money." In effect, she
argued, the media were positioning themselves, rather than the voters, to
make critical decisions about the candidates.

The impact of limited funding showed throughout her campaign.
While other candidates arrived at campaign functions in chauffeured
cars, accompanied by numerous campaign staffers, Moseley Braun often
drove herself, and she traveled on commercial flights with only one
staffer. Her campaign did not set up headquarters in the critical early
primary states of New Hampshire and Iowa, or even South Carolina,
where she had a chance of securing a significant number of votes from
the large African American population. Her campaign operated from a
single streamlined office in Chicago, the result of extreme funding limita-
tions. Moseley Braun's campaign failed on several occasions to qualify for

federal matching dollars, having missed the deadlines. Some argue that the missed deadlines were a result of staff disorganization and high turnover of personnel.

Whatever its challenges, Moseley Braun's campaign was certainly not confronted with the overt sexism and racism Chisholm had experienced. Instead, a much more subtle, indirect brand of racism and sexism plagued her campaign, characterized by the outright dismissal of her candidacy as a serious bid for the White House. Consistent slights affected all facets of her campaign. The failure to garner media attention, along with fundraising challenges, forced Carol Moseley Braun to formally pull out of the race on January 15, 2004, almost one year after she first announced her candidacy.

Since she withdrew even before the first primary, we can only speculate about how well she would have fared with voters. In a Newsweek poll released on November 8, 2003, Moseley Braun received the support of 7 percent of likely voters, similar to John Kerry's and John Edwards' polling numbers at that time. While the numbers turned around for Kerry and Edwards, Moseley Braun never got to that point.

David Bositis of the Joint Center for Political and Economic Studies may have best captured her predicament when he argued that, "Part of Carol Moseley Braun's problem is that she is a black woman." Bositis observed that Democratic voters were looking for a candidate who could beat George W. Bush, and unfortunately, she was not perceived as a candidate who could do that.[23]

## MOSELEY BRAUN AND SHARPTON: NEW POSSIBILITIES FOR BLACK LEADERSHIP?

To fully understand the complexities of Moseley Braun's treatment during the 2004 election, her coverage must be compared to that of her fellow second-tier candidate, the only other African American in the race, Al Sharpton. This election marked the first time in history that two African American candidates sought the Democratic Party's presidential nomination. The 2004 election offers a unique opportunity to examine persistent historical conflicts within the African American community on questions of gender and leadership in the context of an election where voters could choose between an African American man and an African American woman.

Sharpton's campaign received attention and media coverage from the outset. Some speculated that he could emerge as the next broker of the black vote, assuming a role similar to that of Jesse Jackson following his 1984 and 1988 presidential campaigns. Other pundits were more doubtful, questioning the idea that Al Sharpton could fill the so-called leadership vacuum in the African American community. Though Sharpton received mixed reviews in terms of his fitness to serve as the spokesperson and political leader for black America, he was nevertheless given considera-tion, a luxury that Moseley Braun quite strikingly never received. The difference in coverage is difficult to explain, since both carried their own share of political baggage, and neither rallied black America by increasing voter registration or turnout. Further, on the measure that most separates the candidates – prior political experience – Moseley Braun's credentials were stronger since Sharpton had never held an elected or appointed office.

Both Sharpton and Moseley Braun faced the challenges of overcoming public scandals. Moseley Braun's past was plagued by charges of mishan-dling campaign funds, though she was later cleared of these accusations by the Internal Revenue Service and the Federal Election Commission. Sharpton's record of public scandals includes a 1983 FBI tape released by HBO Sports, in which Sharpton is depicted as engaging in a money-laundering scheme with a supposed drug dealer who was an undercover FBI agent. Sharpton was never charged in the incident and sued HBO for defamation of character.

Neither the Sharpton nor Moseley Braun campaign achieved success comparable to either of Jesse Jackson's campaigns. Both fell woefully behind Jackson's performances in 1984 and 1988 on a number of mea-sures. Jackson is credited with dramatically increasing black voter registra-tion and black voter turnout in the primaries and the general elections. He built the Rainbow Push Coalition, a grassroots organization that mobilized many first-time voters with amazing results. In 1984, Jackson placed third in the race for the Democratic Party's nomination, garnering 3.5 million voters. With increased mobilization in 1988, he placed second, winning 7 million votes nationally and more than 1,200 delegates at the Democratic national convention.[24]

Neither Moseley Braun nor Sharpton built this type of grassroots orga-nization, and the outcomes of their races were quite different from Jack-son's campaigns. The failures of Sharpton and Moseley Braun to deliver black voter turnout in the primaries or even to increase dramatically black voter registration precluded both from leveraging their bids to attain Jackson-like power within the Democratic Party. However, Sharpton was able to maintain a presence well after the primaries, securing a coveted prime-time speaking slot for his nomination address at the Democratic

Party convention and operating as one of the party's pundits through the general election. In contrast, Moseley Braun largely drifted into the shadows, with the exception of her appearance during the Democratic convention, when she delivered a short nominating address scheduled outside of primetime network coverage.

Given equally lackluster campaigns, what accounts for Sharpton's political celebrity and his consideration as the next potential leader of the African American community while Moseley Braun faded from view? Some would argue that Shapton's charismatic style and ostentatious oratory landed him in this position. While this may partially explain the difference in treatment of these candidates, the masculine gender assumptions that construct leadership ideals in the African American community offer a more compelling explanation.

Scholars of black politics and journalists regularly debate the absence of leadership in the African American community.[25] A far less recognized and widely contentious topic is the set of masculine assumptions surrounding leadership in the black community. Johnetta Cole and Beverly Guy-Sheftall highlight the historical absence of women's pastoral leadership in the black church, a pillar institution of the African American community. They argue that the exclusion of African American women from one of the most highly regarded leadership positions in the black community is a lingering artifact of a patriarchal system in which black men possessed control over and adamantly protected the only independent institution of the black community. Though heavily resisted by black feminist men and women inside the church, women's exclusion from leadership remains a common practice in African American communities.[26]

Throughout the history of racial liberation politics, African American women worked diligently beside their male counterparts, yet because of their exclusion from traditional leadership posts, their contributions were largely overlooked in historical accounts.[27] African American women's leadership in the civil rights movement, as Belinda Robnett argues, existed outside the realm of the charismatic, formal organizational leadership structure which was dominated by men. Instead, African American women acted as bridge leaders who did not occupy the spotlight, but worked to link members of the community to the movement organizers.[28]

These gender-based contentions about who qualifies as a leader informed the 2004 elections and are important to understanding Moseley Braun's positioning in the race, particularly in comparison to Sharpton's. When black leadership appeared up for grabs, traditional views about the intersection of race and gender in the African American community surfaced, with both leaders and likely leaders conceptualized as male.

## AFRICAN AMERICAN WOMEN AND ELECTED OFFICE

Carol Moseley Braun's presidential candidacy compels us to ask whether there are additional African American women poised to run for the presidency in future elections. Are African American women securing offices at the local, state, and national levels in preparation for the highest political offices? African American women's engagement in electoral politics as a means of securing greater political empowerment and placing their concerns on the political agenda has produced mixed results. On the one hand, they are gaining increased access to political office, now outpacing African American men in winning elections. Yet they continue to face considerable obstacles to securing high-profile offices at the state and national levels.

## AFRICAN AMERICAN WOMEN IN STATE AND LOCAL POLITICS

Of the more than 3,000 African American women elected officials, most are elected to sub-state level offices such as regional offices, county boards, city councils, judicial offices, and local school boards. African American women have gained increasing access to leadership positions at the local level. As of 2004, forty-two African American mayors led cities with populations of 50,000 or more and eight of those were women.[29] (See Table 5.1.) Shirley Franklin, mayor of Atlanta, Georgia, leads one of the largest cities. Still, few scholars have devoted attention to women of color in sub-state level offices, largely because variations among localities make comparisons difficult.

As African American women move beyond the local level, they face greater challenges in winning office. Statewide offices are more difficult for African American candidates to secure, especially for African American women. No state has ever elected an African American woman as governor, and today, only two African American women are holding statewide office. In Ohio, Republican Jennette Bradley made history as the first African American woman elected to the office of lieutenant governor as the running mate of Governor Bob Taft. In January of 2005, she was appointed by Governor Taft to the office of state treasurer, replacing Joseph Deters, who vacated the office. Democrat Denise Nappier of Connecticut made history in 1998 as the first African American woman elected as state treasurer, and in 2005 she continues to serve in that capacity.

In running for statewide offices, African American candidates do not have the benefit of African American majorities and must depend on the

**TABLE 5.1:** Eight African American women were mayors of cities with populations over 50,000 in 2005

| Mayor | City | Population |
|---|---|---|
| Irma Anderson | Richmond, California | 99,216 |
| Gwendolyn A. Faison | Camden, New Jersey | 79,904 |
| Shirley Franklin | Atlanta, Georgia | 416,474 |
| Shirley Gibson | Miami Gardens, Florida | 100,809 |
| Wilmer Jones Ham | Saginaw, Michigan | 61,799 |
| Brenda L. Lawrence | Southfield, Michigan | 78,296 |
| Rhine McLin | Dayton, Ohio | 166,179 |
| Lorraine H. Morton | Evanston, Illinois | 74,239 |

*Source:* Compiled by author from National Conference of Black Mayors, www.ncbm.org.

support of white majorities for election. Because African Americans are significantly more supportive of African American candidates than are whites, attracting white voters is a significant challenge. African American candidates, who must depend on racially tolerant whites in order to win,[30] face the dual challenge of offering strong crossover appeal for white voters while maintaining a connection to communities of color to ensure their high voter turnout.

In state legislatures, African American women are steadily increasing their numbers, yet their gains still appear minuscule. This is perhaps most clear when examining the numbers of African American women in state legislatures relative to the number of available legislative offices. As of late 2004, there were 7,382 state legislators, of whom only 314 were women of color. African American women led women of color in holding state legislative seats with 215, followed by sixty-seven Latinas, twenty-three Asian American Pacific Islander women, and nine Native American women.[31] Although the numbers of women of color in state legislatures remain small, they have increased steadily while the overall numbers of women in state legislatures, as reported in Kira Sanbonmatsu's chapter in this volume, seems to have reached a plateau. In 1998, for example, only 168 African American women served as state legislators. By 2004 their numbers grew by forty-seven, a 28 percent increase.[32] Similar trends hold for Asian American/Pacific Islander, Latina, and Native American women.

African American women's influence in state legislatures is concentrated in a limited number of states. (See Table 5.2.) Only thirty-nine state legislatures have African American women currently serving. Georgia and

**TABLE 5.2:** The proportion of African American women among state legislators varies across the states

| | No African American women in state legislature | 0.1%–4 % African American women in state legislature | >4% African American women in state legislature |
|---|---|---|---|
| States with African American population under 5% | Nebraska<br>Hawaii<br>Utah<br>Wyoming<br>North Dakota<br>South Dakota<br>Maine<br>Vermont<br>Idaho<br>Montana | Rhode Island<br>Alaska<br>Minnesota<br>Washington<br>West Virginia<br>Arizona<br>Iowa<br>New Mexico<br>New Hampshire<br>Colorado<br>Oregon | |
| States with African American population 5–15% | Kentucky | New Jersey<br>Texas<br>Pennsylvania<br>Connecticut<br>Oklahoma<br>Nevada<br>California<br>Wisconsin<br>Indiana<br>Kansas<br>Massachusetts | Florida<br>Michigan<br>Ohio<br>Missouri |
| States with African American population 15.1–20% | | Delaware | Virginia<br>Tennessee<br>New York<br>Arkansas<br>Illinois |
| States with African American population greater than 20% | | South Carolina | Mississippi<br>Louisiana<br>Georgia<br>Maryland*<br>Alabama<br>North Carolina |

*Notes:* Within each cell, states are listed in descending order by African American population. * Maryland has the highest proportion of African American women in its state legislature (9.6 %), followed by Georgia (7.6%), Illinois (7.3%), and Louisiana (6.9%).

*Sources:* Center for American Women and Politics (CAWP), 2005 Fact Sheets. State percentage of African Americans population is drawn from 2000 U.S Census data.

Maryland lead the states, with eighteen African American women serving in each, followed by Illinois (thirteen), Missouri (twelve), New York (eleven), and Mississippi (ten). Overall, women have traditionally fared poorly in southern and border state legislatures; yet the trend is different for African American women who have experienced some of their greatest successes in these states, where there is a significant concentration of African American voters.

## AFRICAN AMERICAN WOMEN IN NATIONAL POLITICS

In the aftermath of the 2004 elections, the 109th Congress opened with thirteen African American women members. The 2004 elections produced two "firsts" for African American women at the national level – the first African American U.S. Senate candidate from Georgia, Denise Majette, and the election of the first African American congresswoman from the state of Wisconsin, Gwen Moore. These two firsts symbolized the growing possibilities for African American women in national politics. (See Table 5.3).

In Georgia, Congresswoman Denise Majette made an historic bid for the U.S. Senate. She became the first African American and the first woman to be nominated to the U.S. Senate by either major party in Georgia. Over the course of her candidacy, she shifted from a long shot to a viable candidate. Her ultimate loss resulted largely from the sheer difficulty of an African American woman running in a statewide race as discussed earlier, combined with partisan changes in Georgia politics and a well-funded opponent.

Much like other Deep South states, Georgia has experienced a major shift from Democratic to Republican control. Offices once held largely by conservative Democrats are now held by Republicans, including the governor's office. Two years ago, Georgia elected its first Republican governor in over 100 years.

Once Democratic U.S. Senator Zell Miller announced his plans to retire from the Senate, the Democrats understood that they would have a fight to retain his seat. Upon Miller's announcement in 2002, three-term Republican Congressman Johnny Isakson immediately announced his candidacy for the seat. From that point forward, Isakson was considered the frontrunner, easily securing the Republican nomination. Among Democrats, a frontrunner was slower to emerge. The party attempted to recruit its most notable leaders in hopes that their prominence would

**TABLE 5.3:** Thirteen African American women served in the U.S. House of Representatives in 2005

| Congresswoman | Party | District | Major city in the district | Year first elected to congress |
|---|---|---|---|---|
| Rep. Corrine Brown | D | 3<sup>rd</sup> | Jacksonville, FL | 1992 |
| Rep. Julia M. Carson | D | 7<sup>th</sup> | Indianapolis, IN | 1992 |
| Rep. Stephanie Tubbs Jones | D | 11<sup>th</sup> | Cleveland, OH | 1998 |
| Rep. Eddie Bernice Johnson | D | 30<sup>th</sup> | Dallas, TX | 1992 |
| Rep. Carolyn Cheeks Kilpatrick | D | 15<sup>th</sup> | Detroit, MI | 1996 |
| Rep. Barbara Lee | D | 9<sup>th</sup> | Oakland, CA | 1997 |
| Rep. Shelia Jackson Lee | D | 18<sup>th</sup> | Houston, TX | 1994 |
| Rep. Cynthia McKinney | D | 4<sup>th</sup> | Decatur, GA | 1992 2004 re-elected |
| Rep. Juanita Millender-McDonald | D | 37<sup>th</sup> | Compton, CA | 1996 |
| Rep. Gwen Moore | D | 4<sup>th</sup> | Milwaukee, WI | 2004 |
| Del. Eleanor Holmes Norton | D | * | Washington, D.C. | 1991 |
| Rep. Maxine Waters | D | 35<sup>th</sup> | Los Angeles, CA | 1990 |
| Rep. Diane E. Watson | D | 32<sup>nd</sup> | Los Angeles, CA | 2000 |

*Note:* * Eleanor Holmes Norton is a non-voting delegate representing the District of Columbia.
*Source:* Compiled by author from Center for American Woman and Politics (CAWP), 2005 Fact Sheets, and David Bositis, "Black Elected Officials A Statistical Summary," Washington, D.C.: Joint Center for Political and Economic Studies, 2001.

increase the chances of retaining the seat. This proved a tough sell for sitting officeholders since Georgia's "resign to run" law requires elected officials to vacate one office before seeking another. However, after serving only one term in the House, Majette, much to the dismay of many of her original supporters and major funders, decided to vacate her seat in the House to run for the open Senate seat. She maintained that she was led by God to run, telling an Atlanta paper, "It was a leap of faith for me, another step in my spiritual journey, and it has been a wonderful step in that journey."[33] She entered the race just four months before the primary and defeated the field of Democratic contenders.

Majette, a former state court judge, had entered national politics in 2002 after defeating five-term incumbent Congresswoman Cynthia

McKinney, also an African American, in a hotly contested primary. McKinney, an outspoken critic of President Bush and Israel's treatment of the Palestinians, had made several controversial statements that arguably cost her re-election. McKinney's political enemies, many outside of Georgia, funded her defeat, making way for Majette's rise.

Majette entered the 2004 senate race with heavy-hitting television campaign ads criticizing Isakson's record and his relationships with special interest groups. Even with extensive television ads, Isakson raised more money and subsequently outspent Majette. By the last quarter of the campaign, Isakson had raised $7.52 million while Majette had raised only $1.76 million.[34] Despite the considerable difference in funding, Majette ran a savvy campaign, including fundraising house parties and an email campaign to attract national donors. Fellow members of the Congressional Black Caucus campaigned for her and endorsed fundraising efforts. Her campaign focused on securing additional funding and benefits for the nation's veterans, including an extension of education and health benefits. Building on the success of Georgia's education lottery, Majette called for a national education lottery to raise funds that would be used to reduce class size and improve test scores.

What began as a long shot became considerably less so as the campaign progressed. Majette released polling data midway through the campaign indicating that despite Isakson's considerable fundraising edge, she was within a 5-point striking distance with voters.[35] Releasing this poll data provided a temporary boost for Majette but was not enough to secure a win. Ultimately, Isakson triumphed by 58 percent to 40 percent.

Despite Majette's defeat in the U.S. Senate race, the seat she vacated in the House is still held by an African American woman. Adopting a more diplomatic, reserved persona, Cynthia McKinney launched a successful candidacy and regained the House seat she held from 1993 to 2003.

The 2004 elections produced another historic first for African American women when Gwen Moore became not only the first African American woman, but also the first African American elected to Congress from Wisconsin. Elected from the 4th Congressional District, which includes the city of Milwaukee, Moore ran on a traditional Democratic Party agenda of job creation, health care, and education. Her victory demonstrates how African American women can strategize effectively to win seats in Congress.

Moore's election to Congress illustrates the importance of state legislative seats as stepping stones for African American women and other women of color. Moore, the first African American woman elected to the state senate in Wisconsin, served sixteen years in the Wisconsin legislature, which allowed her to establish a substantial legislative record. She crafted a reputation for promoting women's issues and poverty issues, including authoring legislation to extend Medicaid coverage to women diagnosed with cervical and breast cancers.

Moore's successful bid was also notable for her strategic decision to run for the open seat created by the retirement of Representative Gerald Kleczka. Her successful congressional bid and prior service in the state legislature place her among the growing number of strategic politicians in the House whose political ambition may lead them to seek even higher office. African American women in the House are displacing the long-held assumption that women serving in Congress are by and large widows of congressmen or come from prominent or wealthy families.[36]

Moore was a sure favorite to win in the mostly Democratic district. Though she lagged behind her most formidable opponent in fundraising early in the primary, her fortunes quickly changed once she received the critical endorsement from EMILY's List. This support solidified her fundraising efforts, and she won the Democratic primary having raised four times the amount of her closest opponent, Matt Flynn. Beyond ensuring critical campaign funds, the endorsement also bolstered her claim that she was invested in building a coalition among African Americans, women, and progressives. Moore received support from an array of sources within the African American community and the women's community, including campaign endorsements from the NOW Political Action Committee and the newly formed Future PAC, which seeks to increase the numbers of African American women elected to office. In addition, Moore secured financial backing from five major unions, ranging from "teachers to truckers."[37]

Moore's victory is notable because her district is majority white, with only one-third African Americans. Moore may very well symbolize the new realities for African American candidates. Her win differs from the traditional road to Congress for African Americans, who are usually elected from districts in which African Americans are in the majority. Majority-minority districts resulted from provisions in the Voting Rights Act of 1965 and its subsequent challenges, which allowed for the formation of new districts where African Americans consisted of a plurality or majority of the electorate. In these new districts, African Americans could run for open seats, which not only alleviated the incumbency advantage but also freed them from dependence on white voters. As many scholars have conceded, historically it has been nearly impossible for African American candidates to win in districts without black majorities since some whites continue to resist voting for African American candidates.[38]

The number of African American women serving in Congress today is largely a result of the creation of majority-minority districts. Although 1992 was widely proclaimed the "Year of the Woman" in politics, reflecting the phenomenal success of women candidates for Congress, for African American women, 1992 was also the "Year of Redistricting." A number of open seats were created nationally as a result of redistricting following the 1990 Census, and most were majority-minority districts. Five African American women won seats in the U.S. House of Representatives in 1992, more than doubling their numbers.[39] Four of the five African American women won in newly created majority-minority districts. Although the fifth African American woman elected in 1992, Eva Clayton of North Carolina, won a special election following the death of Representative Walter Jones, this district had also been redrawn as a majority-minority district.

While majority-minority districts have helped to secure African American women a place in Congress, these districts have been debated before the U.S. Supreme Court as a means of increasing black representation. As a result of a string of cases in the 1990s from Georgia, Louisiana, North Carolina, and Texas, the future of majority-minority districts is now in question.

Many scholars insist that African Americans' continued success in winning elective office, particularly congressional seats, is dependent upon the preservation of majority-minority districts. Although Gwen Moore's win in a majority-white district might prompt some scholars to revisit these conclusions, inferring from Moore's victory that majority-minority districts are no longer necessary to produce black elected officials is not warranted. The key to Moore's success was not only her positioning in Milwaukee politics, but also the national attention her campaign garnered, which ensured her crossover appeal for white voters. The funds generated by her national visibility provided for television, radio, and print ads that allowed her personal story and her message to enter the homes of white voters, increasing her appeal. At the same time, she was able to maintain her connections with African American and Latino voters. National Democratic Party notables such as Jesse Jackson, members of the Congressional Black Caucus, and several Hollywood actors appeared in her district at "get out the vote rallies." This allowed Moore to build a diverse coalition of African Americans, women, and progressives that extended beyond her district. These resources added to the uniqueness of Moore's campaign, and such resources might not be as readily available for other African American candidates.

Nevertheless, Gwen Moore's election strategies may become the standard for African American candidates if majority-minority districts continue to fall under attack. Due to the precarious future of such districts, the number of African American women elected to Congress is likely to grow at a considerably slower pace than it did in the 1990s. To the extent that the number of African American women does grow in future years, the increase in their numbers will likely come largely at the expense of African American men who must compete with African American women for the limited number of seats available in majority-minority districts.[40]

## THE FUTURE OF AFRICAN AMERICAN WOMEN IN POLITICS

In light of the formidable challenges facing African American women as they seek higher-profile offices, African American women are not leaving their political futures to chance. They are forming political action committees to address serious barriers to fundraising. One group, Women Building for the Future (Future PAC), formed in 2002 to capitalize on the growing voting power of African American women. Future PAC's major objective is to increase the numbers of African American women elected at every level of government by financially supporting candidates and identifying women to run for office. In describing the purpose of the group, Donna Brazile, a strategist for the Democratic Party, argues that African American women face three major hurdles in seeking office: lack of name recognition; the tendency of the "old-boy network" to endorse other men; and garnering financial support. Brazile adds, "Our objective is to try to help women overcome one of the major barriers – financial – which will hopefully break down the other two."[41] Future PAC endorses African American women who have proven records in their communities and who support a range of issues from education to health care.[42]

This type of organizing is essential if African American women are to continue overcoming the considerable barriers to increasing their representation. Such organizing efforts hold the promise of translating African American women's high voting rates into increased officeholding.

Other national groups such as the Black Women's Roundtable, a group established by the National Coalition on Black Civic Participation, are also working to increase political participation by mobilizing African American organizations, such as Greek letter fraternities and sororities and other influential community organizations, around voter education and civic empowerment.[43] These groups are invested in the important work of empowering citizens, mobilizing voters, and identifying likely candidates.

The most difficult work, however, remains in transforming American society to fully embrace African American women as political leaders. This is an issue that has to be addressed both inside the African American community and in the larger American society. Not until such core cultural issues are addressed will the journey begun by Shirley Chisholm and Carol Moseley Braun be completed and an African American woman be considered a contender for the highest office in the country.

## NOTES

1. Mamie Locke. 1997. From Three Fifths to Zero. In *Women Transforming Politics*, eds. Cathy Cohen, Kathleen B. Jones, and Joan Tronto. New York: New York University Press.
2. Frank R. Parker. 1990. *Black Votes: Count Political Empowerment in Mississippi after 1965*. Chapel Hill: The University of North Carolina Press.
3. Linda F. Williams. 2001. The Civil Rights-Black Power Legacy: Black Women Elected Officials at the Local, State, and National Levels. In *Sisters in the Struggle: African American Women in the Civil Rights-Black Power Movement*, eds. Bettye Collier-Thomas and V. P. Franklin. New York: New York University Press.
4. Cathy J. Cohen. 2003. A Portrait of Continuing Marginality: The Study of Women of Color in American Politics. In *Women and American Politics: New Questions, New Directions*, ed. Susan J. Carroll. New York: Oxford University Press.
5. See Paula Giddings. 1984. *When and Where I Enter: The Impact of Black Women on Race and Sex in America*. New York: Bantam Books; Darlene Clark Hine and Kathleen Thompson. 1998. *A Shining Thread of Hope: The History of Black Women in America*. New York: Broadway Books; Dorothy Sterling. 1997. *We Are Your Sisters: Black Women in the Nineteenth Century*. New York: W.W. Norton.
6. Giddings 1984.
7. Williams 2001.
8. David A. Bositis. 2001. Black Elected Officials: A Statistical Summary 2001. Washington, D.C.: Joint Center for Political and Economic Studies.

9. See Robert Darcy and Charles Hadley. 1988. Black Women in Politics: The Puzzle of Success. *Social Science Quarterly* 77: 888–98; Gary Moncrief, Joel Thompson, and Robert Schuhmann. 1991. Gender, Race and the Double Disadvantage Hypothesis. *Social Science Journal* 28: 481–7.

10. Darcy and Hadley 1988.

11. United States Census. 2003. The Black Population in the United States. <http://www.census.gov/prod/2003pubs/pg20-541.pdf> 2005, February 23.

12. See Andrea Y. Simpson. 1999. Taking Over or Taking a Back Seat? Political Activism of African American Women. Paper Delivered at the Annual Meeting of the American Political Science Association, Atlanta, GA, September 1–5. For an extensive discussion of political participation see Sidney Verba, Kay Lehman Scholzman, and Henry E. Brady. 1995. *Voice and Equality: Civic Volunteerism in American Politics*. Cambridge: Harvard University Press.

13. Sandra Baxter and Marjorie Lansing. 1980. *Women and Politics: The Invisible Majority*. Ann Arbor: University of Michigan Press.

14. Simpson 1999.

15. Although Shirley Chisholm's 1972 run for the White House is most often cited, there is a long legacy of African American is running for the presidency, largely as third-party candidates. For example, Lenora Fulani ran for the presidency in both 1988 and 1992. For a full discussion, see Hanes Walton, Jr. 1994. Black Female Presidential Candidates: Bass, Mitchell, Chisholm, Wright, Reid, Davis, and Fulani. In *Black Politics and Black Political Behavior: A Linkage Analysis*, ed. Hanes Walton Jr. Westport: Praeger.

16. Katherine Tate. 2003. *Black Faces in the Mirror: African Americans and Their Representatives in the U.S. Congress*. Princeton: Princeton University Press.

17. Shirley Chisholm. 1973. *The Good Fight*. New York: Harper & Row.

18. For a more elaborate discussion of Chisholm's supporters and detractors during the 1972 presidential campaign, view "Chisholm '72 Unbought and Unbossed," a documentary by filmmaker Shola Lynch.

19. Georgia Duerst-Lahti and Rita Mae Kelly, eds. 1995. *Gender Power, Leadership, and Governance*. Michigan: University of Michigan Press.

20. Monica Davey. December 18, 2003. In Seeking Presidency, Braun Could Win Back Reputation. The New York Times.

21. Nedra Pickler. May 2, 2003. Washington Today: Braun Appears with the Presidential Candidates, but Isn't Running Like One. Associated Press State & Local Wire.

22. Paula McClain. 2004. Gender and Black Presidential Politics: From Chisholm to Moseley Braun Revisited. Comments made at Roundtable on Black and Presidential Politics, American Political Science Association Meeting, September 1–5, Chicago, IL.

23. Adam Reilly. December 12–18, 2003. Hitting with Her Best Shot. The Portland Phoenix. <www.portlandphoenix.com> 2005, March 15.

24. Robert C. Smith. 1996. *We Have No Leaders: African Americans in Post-Civil Rights Era*. Albany: State University of New York Press.

25. Among academics with this question, see Smith 1996; Ronald W. Walters and Robert C. Smith. 1999. *African American Leadership*. Albany: State University of New York Press. For journalistic accounts of this question, see Alexandra Starr, Paul Magnusson, and Richard S. Dunham. April 12, 2004. After Sharpton: The Great Black Hopes. Business Week.

26. Johnetta Betsch Cole and Beverly Guy-Sheftall. 2004. *Gender Talk: The Struggles for Women's Equality in African American Communities*. New York: Ballantine Books One World.

27. Wendy G. Smooth and Tamelyn Tucker. 1999. Behind But Not Forgotten: Women and the Behind the Scenes Organizing of the Million Man March. In *Still Lifting, Still Climbing African American Women's Contemporary Activism*, ed. Kimberly Springer. New York: New York University Press.

28. Belinda Robnett. 1997. *How Long: How Long? African American Women in the Struggle for Civil Rights*. New York: Oxford University Press.

29. For a complete listing go to the webpage of the National Conference of Black Mayors, www.ncbm.org.

30. See Lee Sigelman and Susan Welch. 1984. Race, Gender, and Opinion Toward Black and Female Candidates. *Public Opinion Quarterly* 48: 467–75; Ruth Ann Strickland and Marcia Lynn Whicker. 1992. Comparing the Wilder and Gantt Campaigns: A Model of Black Candidate Success in Statewide Elections. *PS: Political Science and Politics* 25: 204–12.

31. Center for American Women and Politics, 2005. Fact Sheet. Women of Color in Elective Office 2005.

32. See Center for American Women and Politics, Women of Color in Elected Office Fact Sheets for 1998 and 2005.

33. Anna Varela. November 4, 2004. Election 2004: Isakson's Romp Beats Expectations; 18 Point Margin Laid to Turnout, High Profile. Atlanta Journal Constitution.

34. Anna Varela. October 21, 2004. Election 2004: Majette Gets Cash Boost, but Isakson Keeps Lead. Atlanta Journal Constitution.

35. Anna Varela. September 16, 2004. Election 2004: Majette Poll Puts Democrat 5 Points Back; Isakson Lead Much Bigger, Campaign Says. Atlanta Journal Constitution.

36. Irwin N. Gertzog. 2002. Women's Changing Pathways to the U.S. House of Representatives: Widows, Elites, and Strategic Politicians. In *Women Transforming Congress*, ed. Cindy Simon Rosenthal. Oklahoma: Oklahoma University Press.

37. Larry Sandler. September 4, 2004. Moore Nears Lead in Fundraising; Candidates Close in on $2 Million in Spending. Milwaukee Journal Sentinel.

38. Bernard Grofman and Chandler Davidson, eds. 1992. *Controversies in Minority Voting: The Voting Rights Act*. New York: Cambridge University Press.

39. Tate 2003.

40. Gertzog 2002.

41. Joyce Jones. January 2004. The Future PAC. Black Enterprise.

42. Robin M. Bennefield. Jul/Aug 2004. Women Join Forces to Support Black Female Politicians. *Crisis* (The New).

43. See the Black Women's Roundtable (BWR) a part of The National Coalition on Black Civic Participation at <http://www.bigvote.org/bwr.htm>. 2005, February 20.

# 6 Political Parties and Women's Organizations

## Bringing Women into the Electoral Arena

Woman-versus-woman races have grown increasingly common in congressional elections, but it is still rare in a highly competitive open seat for the U.S. House of Representatives that both parties would have female nominees. So when both the Democrats and the Republicans nominated women to run for the House from Pennsylvania's 13th Congressional district, it was not because the party organizations intentionally tapped women for the race. To get their party nominations, both Democrat Allyson Schwartz and Republican Melissa Brown had to defeat other would-be nominees in primary races. Schwartz beat her primary opponent 52 percent to 48 percent. Brown reached the general election by earning 39 percent of the primary vote, while her opponents obtained 35 percent and 26 percent, respectively. Both women saw their political parties' national campaign committees pour money into the race in the general election, but not before they had fended off tough intra-party opposition.

Schwartz, a state senator, had prominent supporters in the primary. The chair of the Montgomery County Democratic Party, along with the Philadelphia controller, a major political figure in the area, endorsed Schwartz when she announced her candidacy. She also received the support of EMILY's List, a Democratic group that recruits and trains pro-choice women candidates and provides resources to their campaigns. Donations from EMILY's List members helped Schwartz lead all primary candidates in fundraising by October 2003, a year before the general election. EMILY's List reported providing over $175,000 in expenditures on her behalf in the primary as well as sending its "Women Vote" grassroots turnout operation into her district.

At the same time, Schwartz's Democratic primary opponent, Joe Torsella, had the political network of Governor Ed Rendell supporting his nomination. Torsella had never run for office before, but had worked for Rendell. (The governor himself remained officially neutral in the race, endorsing neither candidate.)

On the Republican side, the Philadelphia Republican Committee voted unanimously to back Melissa Brown's primary election effort, and the Republican Pennsylvania state house speaker endorsed her over her two opponents. In the general election, WISH List, the Republican counterpart to EMILY's List, endorsed Brown, providing her with financial backing.

This high-profile, high-cost race illustrates the kinds of resources women need to undertake viable campaigns and increase their representation in elective positions. Political parties and interest groups are key sources of such campaign support for candidates in U.S. elections. Party leaders can play significant roles in steering women candidates to ultimate victory. And women's organizations can bring critical resources to women pursuing public office. In fact, the presence and support of women's organizations has been shown to help women candidates emerge and win public office. With the advent of the second wave of the women's rights movement in the United States in the 1960s, equality for women in political leadership became a central goal of many activists.

The National Women's Political Caucus, for example, was formed in 1971 to "help elect women and also men who declare themselves ready to fight for the needs and rights of women and all underrepresented groups." Its statement of purpose pledged to oppose sexism, racism, institutional violence, and poverty through the election and appointment of women to political office; to reform political party structures to give women an equal voice in decision making and the selection of candidates; to support women's issues and feminist candidates across party lines; and to work in coalition with other oppressed groups.

The women's movement in the United States has increasingly centered on electoral and partisan politics to promote its goal of equality, with the election of women to public office the main strategy to achieve this end. An extensive network of organizations and political action committees (PACs) supply money to political campaigns with the purpose of electing more women to public office. These groups have pressured the political parties to advance women as candidates, formed groups within the parties to recruit women and provide resources for their candidacies, and worked independently to elect women.

This chapter explores the changing dynamic in American elections with regard to the interplay between political parties and women's organizations in promoting and facilitating the election of women to public office. The chapter is divided into five sections. The first section provides a brief overview of the historical relationship of women to the major political party organizations and then describes how their 2004 national conventions served as centers of activity for showcasing women candidates, as arenas for promoting women's candidacies, and as forums for the candidates themselves to promote their campaigns. The second section assesses party organizational activities to advance women's candidacies and the growth of women's leadership within party campaign organizations. The third section addresses the development of women's groups organized to elect women to public office. The fourth and fifth sections look at the financial support parties and women's groups provided to women running for the U.S. House of Representatives in 2004. I conclude with a reflection on how these organizations contribute to increasing parity for women in elective office and identify questions for further research regarding how the organizations address the critical issue of recruitment of women candidates.

## AN HISTORICAL LOOK AT WOMEN AND THE PARTIES

Beginning with the suffragists, women have a long and complex history of working within party organizations to become voters, attain political influence, and help other women to win electoral office. Suffragists lobbied party organizations to include planks supporting the women's vote in their platforms. By their account, they undertook 277 such campaigns in the seventy-two-year effort to secure the right to vote.[1] In the years immediately preceding the passage of the Nineteenth Amendment to the United States Constitution, party leaders feared the entrance of women onto the voter rolls. The major political parties worried that women, armed with the vote, might form their own parties and act independently in the political process, undermining the capacity of major parties to control elections and the spoils of victory. Historian William Chafe notes that parties were concerned about the creation of a "petticoat hierarchy which may at will upset all orderly slates and commit undreamed of executions at the polls"[2] and viewed the formation of the non-partisan League of Women Voters as threatening.

For these reasons, as gender politics scholar Kristi Andersen notes, "The national party organizations, sensitive to the demands and the potential influence of a new element in the electorate, responded to the imminent granting of suffrage with organizational changes designed to give women nominally equal roles in the party hierarchy and to allow for the efficient mobilization of women voters by women leaders."[3] Fearing the independence of women voters, the parties undertook a dual effort, establishing distinct organizations led by women to work with women voters and making efforts to integrate women into their leadership committees through expansion of those organizations.

The Democratic Party acted first, creating in 1916 a Women's Bureau to mobilize women voters in the western states where they had already gained the right to vote. In 1917, the Democratic National Committee (DNC), the main governing body of the party, created a women's version of itself, staffed by appointed female members from the states that had already granted women full suffrage.[4] In 1919, they adopted a plan for an Associate National Committee of Women. The DNC also agreed that year to appoint a woman associate member from each state based on the nomination of the state committeeman. In addition, the DNC recommended that Democratic state committees provide women with similar representation at the state and local levels and equal representation of men and women on the executive committee. At their 1920 national convention, delegates voted to double the size of their national committee and stated that "one man and one woman hereafter should be selected from each state."[5]

In 1918, the Republicans created a Republican Women's National Executive Committee. The next year, they adopted a plan calling for state chairmen to appoint "a State Executive Committee of women numbering from five to fifteen members to act with the State Central Committee"[6] and established a women's division. But in 1920, they rejected equal representation for women on the Republican National Committee (RNC) although eight women were appointed to its twenty-one-member Executive Committee. In 1924, Republican leaders agreed to the enlargement of the RNC and the election of male and female members from each state.

Women came to represent about 10 to 15 percent of the delegates to the parties' national conventions in the years after they won the vote. Although they gained some measure of formal equality in the party organizations in those days, women activists struggled for many years to gain respect and influence within the parties, in part because women did not vote differently from men or in large numbers, as Susan MacManus explains in her chapter in this volume.

By the latter part of the 1960s, women were still only marginally represented within the ranks of party leadership. Party organizations had not made any particular effort to promote women as candidates for public office, and women were encouraged to run primarily in situations where the party had little chance of winning.

As the second women's rights movement took off, however, activists adopted the strategy of engaging in partisan politics. The fledgling National Women's Political Caucus (NWPC), formed in 1971, pressured both parties to increase their representation of women as national convention delegates in 1972. The Caucus created Democratic and Republican party task forces and challenged both parties to help women achieve positions of public leadership.

The Democratic Party undertook a reform effort in the wake of the debacle of its 1968 national convention and its subsequent loss in the presidential election, establishing the McGovern-Fraser Commission to spearhead the changes. The commission included in its 1971 report a recommendation that racial minorities, youth, and women be represented in state delegations "in reasonable relationship to their presence in the population of the state." The NWPC pushed the Democratic Party to interpret "reasonable representation" as meaning matching the proportions in a state's population. As a result, they were successful in substantially increasing the percentage of women as convention delegates. Prior to the reform effort, at the 1968 Democratic national convention, only 13 percent of the delegates had been women; in 1972, women constituted 40 percent of the delegates. The push for greater representation of women among delegates continued throughout the 1970s, and since 1980, Democratic Party rules have mandated gender equity within all state delegations to its national conventions.

While the Republicans have not followed the Democrats in mandating equal numbers of men and women in convention delegations, in the 1970s the GOP, under pressure from the NWPC, adopted affirmative steps to encourage state parties to elect more women as convention delegates. The percentage of female Republican delegates increased from 17 percent in 1968 to 30 percent in 1972 and has continued to rise since then.

By 2004, one-half of the delegates to the Democratic National Convention and approximately 40 percent of the delegates to the Republican National Convention were women. Table 6.1 presents a chronology of important dates in the history of parties, women's organizations, and women's candidacies for public office from suffrage to the contemporary period.

Jo Freeman, one of the founders of the women's liberation movement in the United States and an astute observer of U.S. political parties, describes the parties as having become completely polarized around feminism and their reaction to it. In her view, "On feminist issues and concerns the parties are not following the traditional pattern of presenting different versions of the same thing, or following each other's lead into new

**TABLE 6.1:** Important dates in the history of parties, women's organizations, and women's candidacies for public office

1918   Republican Women's National Executive Committee established.

1919   Democratic National Committee passes a resolution recommending that the Democratic State Committees "take such practical action as will provide the women of their respective states with representation, both as officers and as members thereof;" also passes a resolution calling for equal representation of the sexes on the Executive Committee of the Democratic National Committee.

Republican National Committee urges state and country committees to select "one man and one woman member" as "the principle of representation."

1920   Delegates to the Democratic National Convention vote to double the size of their national committee and "one man and one woman hereafter should be selected from each state."

1924   Republican National Committee votes for one male and one female representative from each state.

1940   The Republican party endorses an Equal Rights Amendment to the Constitution in their party platform for the first time.

1944   The Democratic party includes a plank endorsing the Equal Rights Amendment in their platform for the first time.

1966   The National Organization for Women (NOW) is founded.

1971   The National Women's Political Caucus is founded with the major aim of increasing the number of women in public office.

1972   U.S. Representative Shirley Chisholm seeks the Democratic nomination for president.

Frances "Sissy" Farenthold's name is placed in nomination for vice president at the Democratic National Convention. She receives 420 votes.

Jean Westwood is appointed chair of the Democratic National Committee.

1974   The Women's Campaign Fund is founded, the first women's PAC. Mary Louise Smith is appointed chair of the Republican National Committee.

1975   NOW forms a Political Action Committee to fund feminist candidates.

1976   Democrats mandate equal division between men and women in their national convention delegations, effective in 1980.

1977   The National Women's Political Caucus (NWPC) forms a PAC, the Campaign Support Committee.

1979   The NWPC forms a second PAC, the Victory Fund.

1980   Republican Party removes support for the Equal Rights Amendment from its platform.

1984    Democrats nominate U.S. Representative Geraldine Ferraro for vice-president.

National Political Congress of Black Women founded.

1985    EMILY's List is founded on the principle that "Early Money Is Like Yeast – it makes the dough rise."

1991    Clarence Thomas, a nominee for associate justice of the U.S. Supreme Court, is accused of sexual harassment by a former staffer, Anita Hill. Many women are disturbed by the absence of women senators and the dismissive attitude toward Hill during Thomas's confirmation hearings, and one result is a record number of women seeking office.

1992    The WISH List is founded.

The NWPC sponsors a "Showcase of Pro-Choice Republican Women Candidates" at the Republican convention with 13 GOP candidates.

The National Organization for Women (NOW) adopts an Elect Women for a Change campaign and raises about $500,000 for women candidates.

NOW also initiates the formation of a national third party, the 21st Century Party.

1999    Elizabeth Dole enters the Republican race for president but drops out before the first caucuses and primaries.

2003    Former U.S Senator Carol Moseley Braun enters the Democratic race for president but drops out before the first caucuses and primaries.

*Source:* Compiled by author.

territory. They are presenting two different and conflicting visions of how Americans should engage in everyday life."[7] The Republican Party has become more hospitable to anti-feminism while the Democratic Party is perceived to be the more pro-feminist party.

But both parties want to appear to promote women in political leadership positions. Thus, as Freeman observes, the 1992 national conventions, for example, emphasized showcasing women candidates and raising money to elect more women far more than discussing polarizing issues. The 2004 national conventions took this showcasing of women in political leadership to new heights.

## THE 2004 NATIONAL PARTY CONVENTIONS AND WOMEN CANDIDATES

Where once they were occasions for political power struggles and ideological battles with uncertain outcomes fought before the public on television, national party conventions have changed dramatically in the past few decades becoming staged media events to showcase candidates and promote a favorable impression of the party among the general public. Party platforms and party nominees have already been decided before the convention convenes, requiring only formal ratification. In this new style of convention, one function is to highlight party support for women in political leadership positions, presumably to attract the support of women voters.

Women in political and public leadership positions were prominently featured at both the Democratic and Republican 2004 national conventions. The conventions provided many opportunities for women candidates in the 2004 election to increase their visibility. On the first night of the Democratic convention in Boston, the nine Democratic female U.S. Senators gathered on stage, led by Senator Barbara Mikulski of Maryland, the senior woman in the Senate. Representative Louise Slaughter of New York brought a delegation of congresswomen on stage Thursday night, prior to Senator John Kerry's speech accepting the presidential nomination. The Democrats also sponsored a Women for Kerry lunch. A few weeks later, over a thousand Republican women gathered in the grand ballroom of New York City's Waldorf-Astoria Hotel to hear from three generations of the Bush family women and the female members of the Vice President's family.

Women's groups worked the conventions. Approximately 350 women attended the luncheon at the Republican convention sponsored by WISH List, the pro-choice Republican women's PAC. EMILY's List, the Democratic pro-choice women's PAC, held a luncheon for 2000 donors featuring the leading women of the Democratic party, including U.S. Senator Hillary Clinton and former Secretary of State Madeleine Albright. At the Democratic convention there was the Stand Up For Choice meeting, the Boston "She" Party and the Revolutionary Women rally. The Women's Campaign Fund, the oldest bipartisan pro-choice women's PAC sponsored a Breakfast of Champions at the Republican National Convention and held a Cool Summer Luncheon at the Democratic National Convention.

Convention showcasing has been an especially visible aspect of party efforts to promote greater parity for women in public leadership. The next section explores party recruitment of and support for women as candidates and the role of women's groups in prodding that process.

## THE PARTIES AND WOMEN'S CANDIDACIES FOR PUBLIC OFFICE

Several steps are required to increase the number of women in elective office. Women willing to run in winnable districts must be identified;

some will initiate the process themselves, while others may need encouragement and training. Candidates may require assistance in securing resources to win their party's nomination and in financing their campaigns once they become nominees.

The Democratic party's distinct culture made it the site of early action.[8] Feminists, as an accepted organized group within the party, had the attention of leadership and gained a sympathetic ear within the party's liberal wing. As early as 1974, the Democratic party sponsored a Campaign Conference for Democratic Women aimed at electing more women to political office.[9] The 1,200 women who attended the workshop passed resolutions urging their party to do more for potential women candidates. Most of the female members of the U.S. House of Representatives in the 1970s were Democrats, including a number who won their seats not because they were championed within their local party organizations, but because they challenged local party structures and beat them.

The Republican Party did not begin to hold similar conferences until nearly a decade later. This later start by the Republicans does not mean that their party has been less receptive to female candidacies, however. Indeed, feminist leaders Eleanor Smeal, former chair of the National Organization for Women (NOW), and former Congresswoman Bella Abzug have argued just the opposite.[10] Republican women have tended to credit men for bringing them into the organization.[11]

Wanting to appear supportive of women in the face of an emerging gender gap among voters in the 1980s, as described by Susan J. Carroll in her chapter in this volume, the parties saw it as expedient to champion women candidates. Republican leaders, in particular, publicly acknowledged this fact. Republican Senatorial Campaign Committee (RSCC) chair Senator Richard Lugar issued a press statement in 1982 declaring that "a concerted drive by the Republican Party to stamp itself as the party of the woman elected official would serve our nation as well as it serves our own political interests. The full political participation of women is a moral imperative for our society and intelligent political goal for the Republican Party." He pledged to "commit the RSCC to the maximum legal funding and support for any Republican woman who is nominated next year, regardless of how Democratic the state or apparently formidable the Democratic candidate. I am prepared to consider direct assistance to women candidates even prior to their nomination, a sharp departure from our usual policy."[12]

The Democrats in 1984 included a section in the party platform, the major document produced by each party outlining its principles and policy positions, on "Political Empowerment for Minorities and Women." This

section stated, "We will recruit women and minorities to run for Governorships and all state and local offices. The Democratic Party (through its
campaign committees) will commit to spending maximum resources to
elect women and minority candidates and offer these candidates in-kind
services, including political organizing and strategic advice. And the bulk
of all voter registration funds will be spent on targeted efforts to register
minorities and women."

In 1988, both national party platforms included statements recommending support for women's candidacies. The Democrats endorsed "full
and equal access of women and minorities to elective office and party
endorsement," while the Republicans called for "strong support for the
efforts of women in seeking an equal role in government and [commit-
ment] to the vigorous recruitment, training and campaign support for
women candidates all levels." However, these pledges did not include any
action plans for implementation. Prior to 1990, the calls for increasing
the number of women candidates were only rhetoric, as there were few
substantive actions to insure that women were nominated in favorable
electoral circumstances.

Then, for a variety of reasons, 1992 began to develop as the "Year of
the Woman" in American politics. With the end of the Cold War, attention
was increasingly turning away from foreign policy and defense and toward
domestic issues where women were perceived to have expertise. The confirmation hearings for Clarence Thomas' nomination to the U.S. Supreme
Court shone a spotlight on the absence of women in the Senate and
upset women who thought that Anita Hill's charges of sexual harassment
against Thomas were trivialized. And the reapportionment and redistricting process resulted in more open seats than usual, creating new electoral
opportunities. All of these forces stimulated the parties to direct an even
greater share of their recruitment activity toward women than in previous
years. The leadership of both parties' congressional campaign committees
made special efforts to seek out qualified women House candidates. The
Democratic Senatorial Campaign Committee formed a women's council
that raised approximately $1.5 million for Democratic women running for
the Senate. These affirmative steps did not, however, spur the parties to
clear the field of primary competition for women or discourage anyone,
male or female, from running against women.[13]

Specific efforts by Republican women in their party to recruit and train
women as political and public leaders include the work of the National
Federation of Republican Women (NFRW) and the Republican National
Committee's Excellence in Public Service Series. The NFRW has provided

training for potential Republican women candidates. As early as 1976, it published a booklet, *Consider Yourself for Public Office: Guidelines for Women Candidates*. The Excellence in Public Service Series is a political leadership development program offered by groups of Republican women in a number of states; most of the programs are named for prominent Republicans. First was the Lugar Series in Indiana, initiated in 1989; now there are programs in a dozen additional states, with ten others considering their own versions. Typically, the year-long series of programs, with eight monthly sessions and a three-day leadership seminar in Washington, D.C., is offered to selected women willing to make a commitment to play an active role in the political arena. Classes are designed to encourage, prepare, and inspire women leaders to seek new levels of involvement in government and politics. The extra edge afforded by these programs is very much needed since research has shown that the biggest hurdle for Republican women has been winning their party's primaries.

Women have also increasingly become prominent actors within the party organizations. A woman first managed a presidential campaign in 1988, when Susan Estrich captained the campaign of Democrat Michael Dukakis. In 2000, Donna Brazile became the first African American woman to manage a presidential campaign, that of Democratic Vice-President Al Gore. In 2004 Mary Beth Cahill was campaign manager of the John Kerry quest for the presidency. In the 2004 Republican campaign, former White House assistant Karen Hughes, while not campaign manager, was a key advisor in the Bush re-election effort, the same position she held in the 2000 election. Celinda Lake and Linda DiVall are leading pollsters for the Democratic and Republican parties, respectively. Few women have headed either party's national committee, but in 2004, women chaired eight of the Democratic state committees and eleven of the Republican state committees.

## CONGRESSIONAL CAMPAIGN COMMITTEES AND WOMEN'S CANDIDACIES

The use of primary elections to nominate party candidates for public office has weakened the control of party organizations over candidate selection. But the parties still recruit those they believe will be the most viable candidates to run in competitive districts and, through the kinds of campaign organizations described in the introduction to this chapter, provide resources and expert advice to general election candidates. These organizations have become major sources of campaign money, services, and advice for congressional candidates.[14] In recent election cycles, both parties have promoted women into leadership positions within their campaign committees and established subgroups to promote the candidacies of women.

At the national level, both parties have established House and Senate campaign committees to recruit, train, and provide financial support for their candidates: the Democratic Congressional Campaign Committee (DCCC) and the National Republican Congressional Committee (NRCC) for the House, and the Democratic Senatorial Campaign Committee (DSCC) and the Republican Senatorial Campaign Committee (RSCC) for the Senate. By federal law, these groups may contribute directly to any one candidate's campaign only $5,000 for a primary race and $5,000 for the general election. Beyond these funds, these organizations can contribute much larger amounts in coordinated expenditures, such as financing a public opinion poll for several candidates, and in independent expenditures, such as buying TV ads supported by the party committee and shown "independently" of the candidates' campaigns in their districts. These party committees have become major resources for candidates in recent elections.

In the 107th Congress (2001–2002), Congresswoman Nita Lowey of New York chaired the Democratic Congressional Campaign Committee and Senator Patty Murray chaired the Democratic Senatorial Campaign Committee. In 1999, Lowey had founded Women Lead, a fundraising subsidiary of the DCCC to target women donors and contributors to women candidates. When Lowey became chair of the DCCC, she appointed Congresswoman Jan Schakowsky of Illinois to head Women Lead. In the 2001–2002 election cycle, that committee raised approximately $25 million for women candidates. Lowey had admired Schakowsky's fundraising prowess in her initial run for an open House seat in 1997. Schakowsky had approached all the female law partners in the greater Chicago area asking for donations in what she called "an untapped constituency" of women contributors. "The strategy paid off.... Schakowsky raised 57 percent of her campaign funds from women donors that year – a higher percentage than any other congressional candidate in the 1998 election cycle."[15]

Prior to being appointed to chair the DSCC, Murray had launched a similar program in 1999 called Women on the Road to the Senate, which helped elect four women senators in 2000. In 2002, the program, renamed the Women's Senate Network and now headed by Senator Debbie Stabenow of Michigan, raised $1.3 million on top of some $2 million collected through separate events early in that election cycle. Fundraising activities included $1,000-per-person issue conferences that showcased Senators Hillary Rodham Clinton, Dianne Feinstein, and other "prominent senators who happen to be women" in a series of seminar discussions on topics such as terrorism, national security, and the economy. Stabenow noted that it irked her that her female colleagues are so rarely interviewed on such topics.[16] In 2004, this group held a similar event in California, netting $200,000 for Senator Barbara Boxer's campaign for re-election.

The election of Congresswoman Nancy Pelosi to the position of House Minority Leader in 2003 may be of most significance to party recruitment efforts of women candidates. Pelosi, rather than the "old boys" network, is directing decisions about the types of people who should be recruited to run in viable districts to maintain and expand the number of seats the Democratic party holds. There is every reason to believe that she is sensitive to the importance of recruiting women candidates and proactive in that effort. The long-range impact of her leadership role for women candidates will need to be assessed in the future.

Through the 108th Congress (2003–2004), no woman had chaired a corresponding Republican campaign committee, although Representative Anne Northup of Kentucky has headed up recruitment for the National Republican Congressional Committee. However, for the 109th Congress (2005–2006), Republicans elected Senator Elizabeth Dole of North Carolina to head the National Republican Senatorial Committee (NRSC). She won the position by defeating Senator Norman Coleman of Minnesota by one vote in the Senate Republican caucus. Dole had campaigned for the presidency in the early stages of the 2000 election before winning her Senate seat in 2002. She had also served in two cabinet positions in earlier Republican presidential administrations. Described as "about as close to a rock star as the Republican Senate has," she is considered to be a celebrity within the party.[17] She helped raise over $16 million for the NRSC in the 2004 election cycle.[18] In addition, "Dole's supporters argued that she would help Republicans win over female and minority voters by putting a 'different face on the party.'"[19]

## WOMEN'S PACS AND WOMEN'S CANDIDACIES

As noted earlier, women's groups have been integral in prodding the parties to advance women's candidacies. They have also taken matters into their own hands–recruiting, training, and providing resource bases for women candidates. The formation of women's political action committees has been especially significant. Political action committees (PACs) are set up to provide financial contributions to political candidates. Women's PACs that raise money primarily or exclusively for female candidates stand "at the nexus of political change and politics as usual: bringing women into positions of power by mastering the political money game."[20] They have encouraged women to run, trained them in campaign tactics and strategy, raised vital early money to start their campaigns, and provided a network of supportive organizations that could sustain a campaign during the final weeks of the election.[21]

The activities of Linden Rhoads Amadon and Tracy Newman in Seattle, Washington, illustrate this effort. In 2001, they were angry over the defeat of Al Gore in 2000 presidential election and worried about the implications of a Bush administration for abortion rights. In their view, men had dominated Democratic fundraising events, while liberal women had not been paying attention to politics. They decided to find a way for pro-choice women to wield greater influence on politics. Recognizing that senators vote on Supreme Court nominations, they launched a women-only political committee, Washington Women for Choice, with the singular mission of supporting pro-choice U.S. Senate candidates. During the 2004 election, seventy contributors pledged at least $1,000 per year to the group. According to a *Boston Globe* article, "the movers and shakers in liberal Democratic politics quickly added this PAC to their Seattle fund-raising schedule, eager to make a connection with such a high-profile group of women."[22] Washington Women for Choice contributed $119,000 to Democratic pro-choice candidates who ran for the U.S. Senate across the country in 2004. Six female senatorial nominees each received $10,000 from the group, and one candidate received $5,000,[23] maximums allowed by federal law.

A recent fact sheet from the Center for American Women and Politics lists forty-one women's PACs or donor networks which either give money predominantly to women candidates or have a predominantly female donor base (not including issue PACs).[24] This list includes fourteen national women's PACs or donor networks and twenty-seven state or local PAC or donor networks. Donor networks are groups that collect checks from individuals written directly to a candidate and "bundle" them to present as a package to endorsed candidates, a concept originated by EMILY's List in the 1980s. Members of the organization are encouraged – and in some cases committed – to write checks directly to endorsed candidates, sending them to the PAC to pass along to the candidates. While the PACs themselves are limited to a total of $10,000 in direct contributions to candidates for national office, bundling greatly expands a PAC's clout by allowing it to deliver larger sums made up of individual contributions – a $20,000 package consisting of two hundred $100 checks, for example. This is an effective campaign tool for some PACs.

A 2004 election example illustrates the force of women's PACs in recent elections. Three candidates vying for the Democratic Party nomination for the open U.S. Senate seat in Florida were U.S. Representative Peter Deutsch, Miami-Dade County mayor Alex Penelas, and University of South Florida president Betty Castor. Deutsch, trailing in the polls but having raised $4.2 million, accused EMILY's List of trying to buy the Senate seat for Castor. EMILY's List contributors had donated more than $1 million to her campaign, and the organization was spending $800,000 on televised advertising praising her health agenda. In a televised debate, Deutsch complained that although all three candidates had the same pro-choice views, the men in the race had a problem. "No matter what we do, unless we go through a sex-change operation, we're not getting EMILY's List's endorsement," quipped Deutsch. A Deutsch supporter filed a complaint with the Federal Election Commission claiming the political organization and Castor were coordinating campaign strategy in violation of FEC rules. Castor went on to win the primary handily, but lost the general election. Male candidates complaining of discrimination because of the power of a women's group is certainly a new twist to quests for political leadership!

EMILY's List, the WISH List, the National Women's Political Caucus (NWPC), and the Women's Campaign Fund have been the most prominent national women's groups recruiting, training, and providing resources to women candidates. Table 6.2 profiles these four organizations. The NWPC is the oldest of the four groups, while the Women's Campaign Fund, founded in 1974, was the first to establish a PAC to provide resources for women candidates. These two groups are bipartisan, supporting both Democratic and Republican candidates who are pro-choice, but the vast majority of their money has gone to Democratic candidates since more of them support reproductive rights. The leadership of the NWPC in recruiting and providing resources for women candidates has faded in recent years as two intra-party groups, EMILY's List and the WISH List, have become key players. EMILY's List was established in 1985 and the WISH List was founded in 1992. EMILY's List has come to wield considerable power within Democratic circles because of its accumulated financial clout and campaign expertise. In recent elections it has led all political action committees (not just women's PACs) in the amount of money raised.

**TABLE 6.2:** Description of four major women's PACs

**National Women's Political Caucus**

Year Founded:        1971

Mission Statement:   The National Women's Political Caucus is a
                     multicultural, intergenerational, and multi-issue
                     grassroots organization dedicated to increasing
                     women's participation in the political process and
                     creating a true women's political power base to
                     achieve equality for all women. NWPC recruits, trains
                     and supports pro-choice women candidates for
                     elected and appointed offices at all levels of
                     government regardless of party affiliation. In addition
                     to financial donations, the Caucus offers campaign
                     training for candidates and campaign managers, as
                     well as technical assistance and advice. State and
                     local chapters provide support to candidates running
                     for all levels of office by helping raise money and
                     providing crucial hands-on volunteer assistance.

2004 Election        Endorsed 4 U.S. Senate and 34 U.S. House candidates
   Facts:            Raised $13,409
                     Contributed to federal candidates, $6,000

**The Women's Campaign Fund**

Year Founded:        1974

Mission Statement:   The Women's Campaign Fund strives to preserve access
                     to reproductive choice by helping to elect progressive
                     women to political office; created to provide
                     pro-choice women of all parties with the resources
                     they need to win – not just money, but strategic
                     consulting, fundraising, networking, and campaign
                     assistance.

2004 Election        Endorsed 11 U.S. Senate, 70 U.S. House, 2
   Facts:            Gubernatorial and 41 State Legislative Candidates
                     Raised $1,532,696
                     Contributed to federal candidates, $84,450

**EMILY's List**

Year Founded:        1985

Mission Statement:   EMILY's List members are dedicated to building a
                     progressive America by electing pro-choice
                     Democratic women to office.

2004 Election        Endorsed 5 U.S. Senate, 10 U.S. House, and 2
   Facts:            Gubernatorial Candidates
                     Raised $34,128,818
                     Contributed to federal candidates, $1,007,334; also
                     $8,036,363 in independent expenditures

**WISH List**

| | |
|---|---|
| Year Founded: | 1992 |
| Mission Statement: | The WISH List raises funds to identify, train and elect pro-choice Republican women at all levels of government – local, state, and national. |
| 2004 Election Facts: | Endorsed 1 U.S. Senate, 13 U.S. House, and 56 State Legislative and Local Office Candidates Raised $1,662,840 Contributed to federal candidates, $41,645 |

*Source:* Compiled by author from the Federal Election Committee, Campaign Finance Reports and Data, 2004.

Figure 6.1 shows the growth in the amount of money EMILY's List funneled to endorsed candidates, including both its direct contributions and its bundled money. Indeed, Democratic Party efforts to recruit women candidates have become virtually indistinguishable from the candidate recruitment strategies of EMILY's List.[25]

The National Organization for Women (NOW) also established a PAC (NOW-PAC) in the 1980s to support feminist candidates, both men and women. At the national level, it engages primarily in presidential elections. In 2004, it contributed to Carol Moseley Braun's race for the Democratic Party nomination for president. Most of NOW's PAC contributions for U.S. Senate and House races come through its state chapters. NOW, along with the Feminist Majority, has adopted a strategy of encouraging large numbers of women to run for political office in major party primaries regardless of the likelihood of their winning a nomination and actually getting elected. This strategy contrasts with that of EMILY's List and the WISH

**Figure 6.1: EMILY's List Contributions Increased Dramatically from 1986 to 2004.**

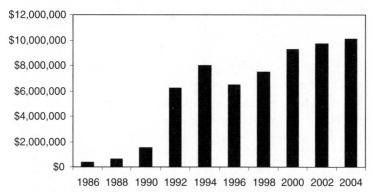

*Source:* EMILY's List, www.emilyslist.org/about/where-from.html.

List, who are more strategic in their financial aid, endorsing only "viable" candidates, those who show evidence of a well-organized campaign with a good chance of winning.

The four women's PACs described in this chapter represent groups that give money almost exclusively to women candidates, are run by women, and have a membership base made up primarily of women. Other groups also have been considered part of what might be called the women's PAC community. Organizations such as the American Nurses Association have mostly female donor bases, but contribute to both male and female candidates without insisting that candidates support positions that are necessarily feminist. Other groups, such as the Business and Professional Women's PAC, make funding decisions based on feminist issue positions (similar to NOW).

Sometimes the Susan B. Anthony List, a pro-life women's PAC, is also included in these listings of women's PACs. However, the goal of the Susan B. Anthony List is to increase the *percentage* of pro-life women in Congress and high public office. Thus, as their web site describes their goals, the List "recruits and endorses pro-life women candidates, our primary focus, endorses pro-life men challenging pro-abortion incumbent women, endorses pro-life male incumbents challenged by pro-abortion women candidates, and endorses pro-life male candidates challenging pro-abortion women candidates in open seats." This emphasis on defeating pro-choice women candidates, not just electing pro-life women candidates, makes the Susan B. Anthony List an anomaly in the women's PAC community.

## PARTY SUPPORT FOR WOMEN CANDIDATES IN 2004

Political scientist Irwin Gertzog has described contemporary women candidates as "strategic politicians...experienced, highly motivated career public servants who carefully calculate the personal and political benefits of running for higher office, assess the probability of their winning, and determine the personal and political costs of defeat before deciding to risk the positions they hold to secure a more valued office."[26] Referring to the field of women candidates in 2004, Karen White of EMILY's List, a top player in recruiting and promoting women's candidacies, described the women who were running as "tough as nails." She continued, "These are women who know how to raise the money, put together the campaign operation, and have the political and constituent bases."[27] These women would seem to be well positioned to compete for party resources and women's PAC support.

Analyses of their campaign contributions have shown that the parties in recent elections have tended to provide comparable financial support to similarly situated female and male nominees for Congress.[28] In his chapter in this volume, Richard L. Fox shows this trend continuing in 2004. This assessment is based on comparing the amount of direct contributions federal law allows the parties to donate to their candidates. But looking at the larger base of resources, including coordinated and independent expenditures, how helpful were the major parties' national campaign committees to their women candidates in 2004? In particular, how helpful were they to the women in competitive situations and to women who could expand female representation in the parties' congressional delegations by winning open seats dominated by their party?

In 2004, thirty of the 435 U.S. House of Representatives seats were open during the primary season, meaning there were no incumbents seeking re-election in those districts. Such districts represent the greatest opportunity for women to increase their presence in Congress. However, these districts represent different opportunities for Republicans and for Democrats.

When determining where to invest in campaigns, the parties look primarily to competitive situations and races where incumbents may need shoring up. Several political groups rate the competitiveness of U.S. House district races. In 2004, twelve of the thirty open-seat districts were rated by at least one of these groups as being competitive or having the potential of becoming competitive by the candidate filing deadlines, while nine districts were considered safe Republican seats and nine were rated as safe Democratic seats. An additional fifty races with incumbents were classified as competitive or potentially competitive. These races included five women incumbents.

According to Federal Election Commission records, the Democratic Congressional Campaign Committee (DCCC) raised nearly $92 million in 2004, contributed over $50 million directly to its candidates, made independent expenditures of $36 million on behalf of its candidates, and spent an additional $2 million in coordinated expenditures. The National Republican Congressional Committee (NRCC) had receipts of $175 million and contributed over $135 million directly to its candidates. It made an additional $47 million in independent expenditures and $3 million in coordinated expenditures. Table 6.3 lists the overall amounts these two committees contributed to women candidates who received more than token financial assistance from the party organizations.

The DCCC provided substantial funding, totaling nearly $10 million, to eleven women candidates, led by Stephanie Herseth, who first won a

**TABLE 6.3:** The Congressional Campaign Committees contributed significant sums of money to women running for the U.S. House in 2004

|  | Amount contributed |
|---|---|
| **Democratic Congressional Campaign Committee** | |
| Stephanie Herseth (SD-open seat, incumbent) | $3,622,580 |
| Lois Murphy (PA-challenger) | $1,462,791 |
| Virginia Schrader (PA-open seat) | $1,469,648 |
| Melissa Bean (IL-challenger) | $925,328 |
| Allyson Schwartz (PA-open seat) | $844,379 |
| Patty Wetterling (MN-challenger) | $538,757 |
| Willie Landry Mount (LA-open seat) | $382,439 |
| Patricia Keever (NC-challenger) | $350,408 |
| Jan Schneider (FL-challenger) | $139,026 |
| Diane Farrell (CT-challenger) | $103,588 |
| Darlene Hooley (OR-incumbent) | $42,736 |
| **National Republican Congressional Committee** | |
| Arlene Wohlgemuth (TX-challenger) | $1,769,985 |
| Nancy Naples (NY-open seat) | $940,244 |
| Melissa Brown (PA-open seat) | $838,778 |
| Cathy McMorris (WA-open seat) | $790,648 |
| Thelma Drake (VA-open seat) | $419,895 |
| Anne Northrup (KY-incumbent) | $143,545 |
| Heather Wilson (NM-incumbent) | $123,606 |
| Beverly Kilmer (FL-challenger) | $92,343 |
| Jeanne Patterson (MO-open seat) | $72,591 |

*Note:* Contributions include direct contributions, coordinated expenditures, independent expenditures, and expenditures against an opponent.

*Source:* Federal Elections Commission, Campaign Finance Reports and Data, 2004.

special election for the at-large seat in South Dakota in June and then successfully defended the seat in November. Both Democratic women in competitive open seat races (Allyson Schwartz and Virginia Schrader) were heavily subsidized. The NRCC funded nine women candidates with nearly $5.2 million. Their two women candidates in competitive open seat races were amply supplied with funds. Most heavily supported, however, was Arlene Wohlgemuth, who challenged Democratic incumbent Chet Edwards in Texas' 17th district. The NRCC spent a reported $1.4 million in independent expenditures against Edwards in addition to the money it funneled into the Wohlgemuth campaign.

The parties appear to substantially subsidize their most competitive candidates in the final days of the campaign. For example, the Democratic

**TEXT BOX 6.1:** A savvy contribution by an ambitious woman House candidate

Typically candidates in races for a congressional seat approach the Democratic Congressional Campaign Committee (DCCC) or its Republican counterpart, the National Republican Campaign Committee (NRCC), asking for financial aid and other resources to help them run viable campaigns. In a unique twist in 2004, Debbie Wasserman Schultz, running for an open House seat in the 20th Congressional District of Florida, donated $100,000 to the Democratic Congressional Campaign Committee. DCCC spokesperson Greg Speed said it was the first ever six-digit donation to that organization from a Democratic challenger. Schultz, endorsed by U.S. House Minority Leader Nancy Pelosi in March, faced no opposition in the Democratic primary to succeed Congressman Peter Deutsch, for whom she had worked as a legislative aide when he had been a state representative. The 20th Congressional District is a staunchly Democratic area, and Schultz was considered the overwhelming favorite to win in November against Republican Margaret Hostetter. Raising over one and a half million dollars for her campaign, Schultz did win election to Congress with 70 percent of the vote. She represents a new group of contemporary women candidates sophisticated in their electoral prowess, strategically oriented, and formidable as political actors. According to a report in *The Hill*, a Capitol Hill newsletter, she was putting herself in a position to obtain the committee seat she desired, Commerce and Energy, once she had been elected to the House. House leadership determines committee assignments that provide members with influence within the body and assets that bring benefits to their constituents.

*Source:* Peter Harrell. June 25, 2004. A Florida Democrat Poised to Succeed Her Political Mentor in the House. *New York Times.*

Congressional Campaign Committee provided challenger Melissa Bean in Illinois's 8th Congressional District with a $500,000 broadcast ad offensive in the final days of the election. She was one of the few challengers to mount a successful campaign, as noted by Fox in his chapter. Former Vice-President Al Gore and Democratic primary presidential contender retired General Wesley Clark attended fundraisers on her behalf. The DCCC also spent $500,000 on TV commercials for Virginia Schrader in the open 8th Congressional District in Pennsylvania and was reported to have purchased $1 million in television ads for Lois Murphy in her bid to defeat first-term incumbent Jim Gerlack in Pennsylvania's 6th District.[29] In the special election in the summer of 2004 for the at-large seat from South Dakota, the DCCC spent $2.4 million in independent expenditures on behalf of candidate Stephanie Herseth, while the NRCC spent $1.7 million on behalf of her opponent.[30]

## THE IMPORTANCE OF EARLY MONEY

In addition to overall amounts contributed to campaigns, the timing of contributions is important. For newcomers, the toughest hurdle is often winning the primary to get the party's nomination. At the end of the second 2004 reporting period, the DCCC reported spending nearly $5 million in coordinated expenditures, direct contributions, and in-kind contributions to its candidates. Little of that money had found its way to open seat contenders at that point in the campaign process. Only one female candidate – Allyson Schwartz, who had won the primary in Pennsylvania's 13th District – had received a contribution from the DCCC, amounting to $12,500. Leader PACs had also contributed $10,000 to her campaign. Primaries in Pennsylvania are held in April, early in the campaign season, and contributions to Schwartz came after the primary. Debbie Wasserman Schultz in Florida, who had no primary opponent, also received $5,000 from one of the leader PACs.

On the Republican side, the NRCC had contributed over $3.7 million to its candidates at the end of the second reporting period. Three open seat contenders had received a total of $39,000 by June 30, and leader PACs had given a total of $90,000 to eight open seat contenders. Melissa Brown, the Republican running against Allyson Schwartz, had received $10,000 from a Republican leader PAC.

As these small amounts show, parties generally stay out of primary elections, and women candidates have not received sufficient financial support early in the campaign process to ensure that either party can showcase women candidates in the general election. But certainly party leadership and its campaign committees have a great interest in seeing that strong candidates are fielded in competitive races. The recruitment aspect of campaigns deserves more research.

Still, as illustrated above, the campaign committees have mechanisms for substantially augmenting the funds candidates directly raise through independent expenditures on their behalf. As the end of the race nears, the parties assess the likelihood of success and the need for additional support to put a candidate into the winning column. Where women show good prospects for success, these examples would suggest that the parties do not hesitate to back them to the maximum amount allowable. But getting to that position for women has often meant extensive work on the part of women's PACs. EMILY's List, for example, was founded on the premise that what women candidates needed was "early money" to compete equally with male candidates. Indeed, EMILY stands for "Early Money Is Like Yeast – it makes the dough rise." As seen from the example in the introduction to this chapter, EMILY'S List was a major player in Allyson Schwartz's successful primary campaign for the open 13th District seat in Pennsylvania.

## WOMEN'S GROUPS' FINANCIAL SUPPORT FOR WOMEN CANDIDATES IN 2004

This section further explores the financial support of the women's PACs described above. Table 6.2 shows the number of women candidates endorsed by the four women's PACs profiled earlier and the total amount of money spent on their candidacies. Eight of the ten women nominees for the U.S. Senate were endorsed by at least one of these four groups, while sixty-four women won at least one endorsement for the House. Democratic Senate candidates Barbara Boxer, Patty Murray, Nancy Farmer, and Betty Castor were endorsed by all of the groups except the Republican WISH List. Seven House candidates received endorsements from these same three groups.

In addition, in 2004 donor networks EMILY's List and the WISH List provided $10,000,000 and $750,000, respectively, to their endorsed candidates. EMILY's List sets quite stringent criteria for candidates to obtain its endorsement. At the same time, an endorsement from EMILY's List is considered a major indication of a candidate's strength and opens up substantially greater financial backing.

The money the women's PACs and donor networks direct into women's campaigns, well over $10 million in 2004, seems to provide an advantage for a subset of women candidates, primarily those who are pro-choice Democrats. Conservative Republican women, especially those who are not pro-choice, are at a disadvantage when it comes to securing support targeted for women candidates.

## CONCLUSION

Gone are the days when women candidates won party nominations primarily as "sacrificial lambs" in districts where a party had little prospect of winning. The parties have found it to their advantage to promote women candidates, and once women become nominees, they are as likely as male candidates to have access to party resources, particularly in highly competitive races where they can often count on substantial support in the final days of the campaign. Women candidates, particularly those who are pro-choice, also have the advantage of access to women's PACs, which have become formidable players in campaigns. A continuing problem for women candidates, however, is reaching the point of being a competitive candidate, given what research has shown to be women's hesitancy to run for office and the limited opportunity structure for newcomers.

Party organizations no longer control the nomination process, and while they do involve themselves in recruiting candidates, they have seldom made it a policy to recruit women candidates and promote them over male candidates in order to increase their numbers in elective office. Members of Congress and the campaign committees' staffs do appear to encourage some prospective candidates to run. As congressional scholar Paul Herrnson has observed, "Armed with favorable polling figures and the promise of party assistance in the general election they search out local talent. Promising individuals are invited to meet with the members of Congress and party leaders in Washington and to attend campaign seminars."[31]

It is at this early stage of the campaign process that women's groups are so valuable. They recruit and train women candidates so that they will be viable candidates, and as the examples from the campaigns of Betty Castor and Allyson Schwartz illustrate, they work aggressively in primary elections and provide a substantial resource base at least for a subgroup of women candidates, those who are pro-choice regarding reproductive issues.

In the world of political campaigns, women are now strong players. As noted in this chapter, several factors have advanced women's prospects: the rise of women's PACs promoting women's candidacies for public office and funding their campaigns; the lessening of party discrimination against women candidates; and the availability of substantial support from congressional campaign committees in competitive situations. None of these positive factors, however, offsets such negative factors as the fact that women still make up a small percentage of the pool of candidates, male incumbents have great advantages, and gender still matters in political campaigns. Still, women's candidacies have indeed come a long way in terms of party support and the development of their own pool of backers and financiers.

## NOTES

1. Aileen Kraditor. 1965. *Ideas of the Woman Suffrage Movement, 1890–1920*. New York: Columbia University Press.
2. William Chafe. 1972. *The American Woman: Her Changing Social, Economic, and Political Roles, 1920–1970*. New York: Oxford University Press, 25.
3. Kristi Andersen. 1996. *After Suffrage: Women in Partisan and Electoral Politics before the New Deal*. Chicago, IL: The University of Chicago Press, 80–1.
4. Anna Harvey. 1998. *Votes Without Leverage: Women in American Electoral Politics, 1920–1970*. New York, NY: Cambridge University Press.
5. Harvey 1998, 85.
6. Harvey 1998, 113.
7. Jo Freeman. 1993. Feminism vs. Family Values: Women at the 1992 Democratic and Republican Conventions. *PS: Political Science and Politics* 26 (March): 21–7.
8. Jo Freeman. 1987. Whom You Know Versus Whom You Represent: Feminist Influence in the Democratic and Republican Parties. In *The Women's Movements of the United States and Western Europe: Consciousness, Political Opportunity, and Public Policy*, eds. Mary Fainsod Katzenstein and Carol McClurg Mueller. Philadelphia, PA: Temple University Press.
9. Austin Scott. March 31, 1974. Democratic Women See Gains in 1974. Washington Post.
10. Jo Freeman. 1989. Feminist Activities at the Republican Convention. *PS: Political Science and Politics* 22 (March): 39–47; Bella Abzug. 1984. *The Gender Gap: Bella Abzug's Guide to Political Power for American Women*. Boston, MA: Houghton Mifflin.
11. Ronna Romney and Beppie Harrison. 1988. *Momentum: Women in America Politics Now*. New York: Crown Publishers.
12. Richard Lugar. August 21, 1983. A Plan to Elect More GOP Women. Washington Post.
13. Robert Biersack and Paul S. Herrnson. 1994. Political Parties and the Year of the Woman. In *The Year of the Woman: Myths and Realities*, eds. Elizabeth Adell Cook, Sue Thomas, Clyde Wilcox. Boulder, CO: Westview Press.
14. Paul Herrnson. 1995. *Congressional Elections: Campaigning at Home and in Washington*. Washington, D.C.: CQ Press.
15. Allison Stevens. January 14, 2002. Both Parties Say Women's Wallets Ripe for Tapping. Women's E-news.
16. Sheryl Gay Stolberg. April 28, 2004. Partisan Loyalties and the Senate Women's Caucus. New York Times.
17. Jamie Dettmer. November 12, 2004. Senator Dole Is Eyeing Leadership of Key Senate Committee, GOP Post. The New York Sun.
18. David Dolan. November 18, 2004. Dole to Lead GOP Senate Efforts; N.C. Senator Will Raise Money for 2006 Campaigns, Recruit Candidates. The Herald-Sun.
19. Frederic J. Frommer. November 17, 2004. Republicans Choose Elizabeth Dole to Head 2006 Senate Campaigns. <www.sfgate.com> 2004, December 3.

20. Christine L. Day and Charles D. Hadley. 2005. *Women's PACs: Abortion and Elections.* Upper Saddle River, NJ: Pearson Prentice Hall.

21. Candice J. Nelson. 1994. Women's PACs in the Year of the Woman. In *The Year of the Woman: Myths and Realities,* eds. Elizabeth Adell Cook, Sue Thomas, Clyde Wilcox. Boulder, CO: Westview Press. See also Mark Rozell. 2000. Helping Women Run and Win: Feminist Groups, Candidate Recruitment and Training. *Women & Politics* 21(3): 101–16.

22. Jessica Kowal. 2004. Women Wield Political Power. The Boston Globe. <www.boston.com/news/politics/president/articles/2004.> 2004, October 9.

23. This PAC also contributed money to male pro-choice candidates.

24. Center for American Women and Politics. 2005. *Women's PACs and Donor Networks: A Contact List.* New Brunswick, NJ: Eagleton Institute of Politics.

25. Rosalyn Cooperman. 2001. Party Organizations and the Recruitment of Women Candidates to the U.S. House Since the "Year of the Woman." Paper presented at the Annual Meeting of the American Political Science Association, San Francisco, CA.

26. Irwin Gertzog. 1995. *Congressional Women: Their Recruitment, Integration, and Behavior,* 2nd edition. Westport, CT: Greenwood Press.

27. Gail Chaddock. October 19, 2004. The Rise of Women Candidates. Christian Science Monitor.

28. Biersack and Herrnson 1994.; Burrell, Barbara. 1994. *A Woman's Place Is in the House: Campaigning for Congress in the Feminist Era.* Ann Arbor: University of Michigan Press.

29. Peter Savodnik. October 20, 2004. Democrats Seek Beachhead in Suburban Philadelphia. The Hill.

30. Hans Nichols. June 3, 2004. Who Gets Chopped from Ag. The Hill.

31. Herrnson 1995.

# 7 Advertising, Web Sites, and Media Coverage

## Gender and Communication Along the Campaign Trail

U.S. Senator Patty Murray (D-WA), one of five women elected to the U.S. Senate in 1992's so-called "Year of the Woman," entered the 2004 campaign on the verge of making history. If she won re-election, she would be the first senator from Washington state to earn a third consecutive term since the late Henry "Scoop" Jackson.

In 1992, Murray had made a name for herself campaigning – in her televised political ads, news releases, and speeches – as the proverbial "mom in tennis shoes," referring to a remark made by a male state legislator in the early 1980s when she was lobbying against budget cuts to a preschool program where she taught. Told by the legislator that she could not make a difference because she was "just a mom in tennis shoes," Murray went on to organize 13,000 parents to save the preschool program, serve on her local school board and then in the Washington State Senate, and win election to the U.S. Senate in 1992 against a powerful Republican congressman.

While her "mom in tennis shoes" persona remained intact in 2004, Murray exhibited her political savvy in her re-election campaign, defeating Republican Congressman George Nethercutt, who was strongly backed by President Bush, by more than 345,000 votes and raising twice as much money as her opponent.

Murray's 2004 re-election campaign is an example of how a political candidate's communication – both through televised political spots and a web site – as well as media coverage can come together to create a positive, integrated message that connects with voters. In her television ads, Murray emphasized the "the need to take care of our own," including the men and women in Iraq. Murray, one of only twenty-three senators to vote against giving President Bush the authority to use force in Iraq, nonetheless emphasized her patriotism in her television ads and on her campaign web site.

For example, one of her 2004 television ads focused exclusively on her work on behalf of veterans, including her decades-ago experience as a hospital volunteer and her current service on the Senate's Veterans' Affairs Committee. Murray narrated the ad, which also included endorsements from four citizens with military backgrounds and newspaper headlines touting her work on behalf of veterans. "I learned first-hand working in a VA hospital the price our soldiers pay for our freedom," Murray says as the ad begins. A Vietnam veteran then talks of how Murray has "made a real difference" by serving on the Veterans' Affairs Committee. A retired military officer talks of how Murray "stopped the Bush administration from closing three Vets' hospitals in our state." A former Veterans of Foreign Wars commander proclaims that Murray "supported two and one-half trillion dollars in defense spending." And a woman with military service and a son in Iraq states that "Patty Murray has led the fight to get the equipment our sons and daughters need in Iraq."

Similarly, Murray's campaign web site opened with ways to "support our troops" with symbols of the American flag and yellow ribbons. Under her "accomplishments" link was a section on veterans, which stated that "Murray is the daughter of a World War II veteran and is proud to be the first woman to serve on the Senate Veterans' Affairs Committee" and that she "has challenged both Democratic and Republican Presidents for providing inadequate funding for veterans' healthcare."

The media responded positively to Murray's campaign messages in 2004. An article in the *Seattle Times* noted that Murray's "no-frills style masks her competitiveness and tenacity," stating that she has "brought record levels of transportation dollars home to the state" as a member of the Senate Appropriations Committee, "never wavered in her support of a controversial third runway at the Seattle-Tacoma International Airport," and had "no regrets" over her votes on Iraq.[1] Another *Seattle Times* article called Murray's vote against the war "a brave stand at the time" and "a hit in this anti-Bush, anti-war state," adding that she is "the everywoman, the un-politician" whom "voters seem pretty comfortable with . . . in part because she is kind of like us."[2]

This chapter focuses on the three major communication channels through which voters see candidates – their media coverage, television commercials, and web sites. In today's political campaign, the media are powerful and important sources of information, not necessarily because they influence voting behavior, although there is some evidence that they do, but because they draw attention to the candidates and their campaigns. Moreover, candidates, especially for federal and statewide elected office, have found that the media provide efficient ways to reach potential voters and, thus, focus their campaigns on getting their messages out through television ads, web sites, and newspaper coverage.

From the time a candidate contemplates her candidacy to the day of the election, she will be engaged in some aspect of communication. Analysis of female candidates' communication during political campaigns reveals their styles and strategies in running for public office and offers a comparison with male candidates. Similarly, by looking at the media coverage of female and male candidates for political office, we can see how both are presented to voters and speculate on how differences in coverage may affect their support from voters.

## MEDIA COVERAGE OF WOMEN POLITICAL CANDIDATES

Women forging new political ground often struggle to receive media coverage and legitimacy in the eyes of the media and, subsequently, the public. According to some observers, journalists often hold women politicians accountable for the actions of their husbands and children, though they rarely hold male candidates to the same standards. They ask women politicians questions they don't ask men, and they describe them in ways and with words that emphasize their traditional roles and focus on their appearance and behavior.

For example, in 1992's "Year of the Woman" campaign, in which record numbers of women – like Washington's Patty Murray – ran for and were elected to political office, news stories nonetheless commented on their hairstyles, wardrobes, weight, and physical appearance. For example, a story in the *Washington Post*, described unsuccessful U.S. Senate candidate Lynn Yeakel from Pennsylvania as a "feisty and feminine fifty-year-old with the unmistakable Dorothy Hamill wedge of gray hair . . . a congressman's daughter [with] a wardrobe befitting a first lady . . . a former full-time mother."[3]

In 1992, the *Chicago Tribune* described Carol Moseley Braun, who was elected to the U.S. Senate from Illinois, as a "den mother with a cheerleader's smile."[4] Six years later, the *Chicago Tribune* was still focusing on Moseley Braun's personality and appearance, as this story from her 1998 re-election campaign shows: "Though she boasts that her legislative record is one of the best in the Senate, it is not her votes that make many of her supporters go weak in the knees. It is her personality, featuring a signature smile that she flips on like a light switch, leaving her admirers aglow."[5] Similarly, in 1998, the *Arizona Republic* described incumbent gubernatorial candidate Governor Jane Dee Hull as a "grandmotherly redhead dressed in a sensible suit."[6]

It does not seem to make a difference – in terms of stereotypical media coverage – if two women are running against each other, rather than a male opponent, as these excerpts from stories in the *Seattle Times* covering the 1998 U.S. Senate campaigns of incumbent U.S. Senator Patty Murray and challenger U.S. Representative Linda Smith illustrate: "Murray has been airing soothing television commercials that make her look so motherly and nonthreatening, in her soft pinks and scarves, that voters might mistake her for a schoolteacher." And, Murray and Smith are different "in style as well as politics. Even the shades of their blue power suits hinted at the gap between the women. Murray's was powder blue; Smith's royal."[7]

Although there seems to have been less emphasis on the physical appearance and personality of women political candidates in the 2000, 2002, and 2004 campaigns, there were still examples of such coverage. For example, the weight, wardrobe, and hairstyles of former first lady Hillary Rodham Clinton, who successfully ran for U.S. Senate in New York in 2000, were a constant source of media comment. An article in the *Milwaukee Journal Sentinel* declared that Clinton had "whittled her figure down to a fighting size 8" by "touching little more than a lettuce leaf during fundraisers."[8] An article in the *New York Times*, reflecting on her victory, was titled "First Lady's Race for the Ages: 62 Counties and 6 Pantsuits," and referred to retiring U.S. Senator Daniel Patrick Moynihan as walking the newly elected Senator Clinton "down the road to a gauntlet of press like a father giving away the bride."[9]

In the 2002 campaign, the *St. Petersburg Times* had this to say about Katherine Harris, a Republican from Florida who was elected to the U.S. House of Representatives:

> The first thing many people mention about Katherine Harris is her size. She's much smaller than she looks on TV. Her driver's license pegs Harris as 5-foot-4-inches. Most people know her as the rigid, heavily made up woman reading statements on CNN or even a crazed floozy played by a Saturday Night Live actor.[10]

The same story described Harris as she appeared in the Sarasota Memorial Day parade, "sporting a red, white and blue lei and American eagle earrings with pearls." The story also noted that Harris had married a Swedish businessman at Notre Dame in Paris and that she had a twenty-year-old stepdaughter.

Such examples of the media's attention to the appearance of women political candidates are backed by more than twenty-five years of research by scholars from political science, journalism, and communication. Even though media coverage has improved, women and men in politics are still treated differently by the media, suggesting that gender stereotypes continue to pose problems for female politicians.

For example, women candidates who ran for election in the 1980s and 1990s were often stereotyped by newspaper coverage that not only emphasized their "feminine traits" and "feminine issues," but also questioned their viability as candidates. In an experiment where fictitious female candidates were given the same media coverage usually accorded to male incumbents, they gained viability.

In the mid-to-late 1990s, women political candidates began to receive more equitable media coverage, both in terms of quantity and quality, when compared with male candidates.

Although women political candidates running for U.S. Senate and governor in 1994 received less coverage than males in open races, they received more coverage than males in gubernatorial races and more neutral coverage than males overall. In 1998, female and male candidates for governor received about the same amount of coverage, but women received less issue-related coverage than men did.

Women running for their party nominations for U.S. Senate and governor in the 2000 primary races and general election received more coverage than men, and the quality of their coverage – slant of the story and discussion of their viability, appearance, and personality – was mostly equitable. For example, the *Detroit Free Press* treated Democratic challenger Debbie Stabenow as a viable candidate in every article printed concerning her 2000 race for the U.S. Senate in Michigan. This is notable since she was running against an entrenched incumbent, Republican Senator Spencer Abraham. Stabenow went on to win the race.[11]

Still, women candidates in 2000 were much more likely to be discussed in terms of their gender, marital status, and children, which can affect their viability with voters. However, a gradual evolution seems to be taking place within newspapers' coverage of women running for political office. While some stereotyping does exist, the playing field for female candidates is becoming more equal.

The 2000 campaign also provided a rare opportunity to analyze the media's treatment of a woman campaigning for a major political party nomination for president. During her seven-month campaign in 1999, Elizabeth Dole received less equitable coverage in terms of quality, and especially quantity, as compared to her male opponents. Polls consistently showed Dole as a distant runner-up to George W. Bush for the Republican nomination for president, but she not only received significantly less coverage than Bush, but also less coverage than Steve Forbes and John McCain, who at the time were behind her in the polls.

In terms of the quality of coverage, Dole received less issue coverage than Bush, Forbes, or McCain. However, Dole's issue coverage was balanced between such stereotypical "masculine" issues as taxes, foreign policy, and the economy and such stereotypical "feminine" issues as education, drugs, and gun control. Dole also received more personal coverage than her male opponents, including references to her appearance and, especially, personality.

However, the media coverage of women political candidates did continue to improve in the 2002 and 2004 elections, especially in terms of the number and length of stories written about their campaigns. For example, the newspaper coverage of women and men candidates running against each other for U.S. Senate and governor in 2002 was about even in terms of quantity, with 35 percent of the articles focusing on men and 34 percent on women.[12]

However, in terms of the quality of their coverage, we find that gender stereotypes still exist. For example, in 2002, the media paid significantly more attention to the backgrounds of female candidates and to the competence of male candidates. And the media continue to link some issues – particularly those that resonate with voters – with male candidates more often than female candidates. For example, male candidates were linked significantly more often with taxes in 2002. Perhaps not surprisingly, women candidates continue to be linked more often than men with so-called "women's issues," such as reproductive choice, and sometimes in a negative manner.

The newspaper coverage of the 2004 campaign of Christine Gregoire for governor of Washington reveals the gender stereotypes not only of the media, but also of voters. "I don't think in the end voters really got to know Chris Gregoire," she told the *Seattle Times* as she was sworn in as the state's 22nd governor after a closely contested election with several recounts and a 129-vote victory margin. "I'm a mom. I'm a spouse. I'm a breast cancer survivor. I came from very humble beginnings. I'm the first in my family to have gone to college. I bet that most people don't know that today."[13]

It's not that she didn't try. Gregoire's television commercials emphasized her humble roots and her success, as Washington's attorney general, in suing big tobacco companies. However, the media portrayed her differently than her roots and experiences as a woman would indicate, emphasizing her "reputation for being tough," appearing "stern," being "high-powered and full of ambition," and seeming "more lawyerly, more self-assured – and some people don't know what to make of that."[14] In the end, Gregoire said, "I'm not going to say I haven't been advised, 'In light of all this, maybe you should be a little more low-key and softer in your approach.' I have rejected that."[15]

As we approach subsequent elections in the twenty-first century, we find that the media coverage of female and male candidates is mostly equitable in terms of quantity as well as quality, e.g., assessments of their viability, positive versus negative slant, and mentions of their appearance. However, the media continue to associate male candidates more often with "masculine" issues and images and female candidates with "feminine" image traits. Also, women candidates are more often than men described by the media in terms of their sex, children, and marital status, which can affect how voters view their ability to hold political office by stirring up stereotypical images of their responsibilities as mothers and wives.

The differences that remain in the media coverage of female versus male candidates may entangle with gender biases within the electorate to create an untenable position for women candidates. By reinforcing some of the traditional stereotypes held by the public about men and women and their roles in society, the media may have an impact on the outcome of elections and, thus, upon how the nation is governed.

## TELEVISED POLITICAL ADVERTISING OF WOMEN CANDIDATES

Because women political candidates are often framed in stereotypical terms by the media, television advertising – and the control it affords candidates over campaign messages about their images and issues – may be even more important for female candidates. Over time, we find both differences and similarities in the ways in which female and male candidates use this campaign communication medium.

In the 1980s, female candidates' political ads were more likely to emphasize social issues, such as education and health care, whereas men were more likely to focus on economic issues such as taxes in their political spots. As far as image traits, women were more likely to emphasize compassion and men to stress their strength, although sometimes both sexes emphasized stereotypical "masculine" traits such as competence and leadership. In their nonverbal communication, men were more likely to dress in formal attire and women preferred "feminized" business suits and office or professional settings.

From the 1990s to the present, as more women ran for political office, we find that female and male candidates were strikingly similar in their uses of verbal, non-verbal, and film/video production techniques, though some differences were discovered.[16] In terms of their verbal communication strategies, female and male candidates were similar in the use of negative spots, employing attacks in about one-third of their total ads. Female and male candidates were increasingly similar over time in the issues discussed in their ads and, especially, in the image traits emphasized and appeal strategies used.

The similarities and differences that did emerge over the past fifteen years are interesting from a gender perspective. For example, although female and male candidates have been similar recently in their use of attacks, they differ in the purpose of the attacks and strategies employed. Both female and male candidates now use negative ads primarily to attack their opponents on the issues. However, the ads of women candidates are significantly more likely to criticize the opponent's personal character. And, although negative association was the preferred attack strategy in the ads of both women and men, the spots of women are significantly more likely to use name calling.

Attacking the opponent's character, rather than his or her stance on the issues, and calling the opponent names are seen as much more personal. Here, female candidates may be taking advantage of voter stereotypes, which portray women as more caring and compassionate. That is, female candidates may be given more latitude than male candidates to make personal attacks as they enter the race with the stereotypical advantage of being considered kinder. Of course, defying stereotypical norms also may backfire for women candidates as they may be labeled as too aggressive, rather than assertive, by the media. Male candidates, on the other hand, may feel more constrained by expectations that they treat women with some degree of chivalry by refraining from attacks on the personal characteristics of their female opponents. So, instead, they lash out significantly more often at their opponent's group affiliations, which is a more acceptable and indirect way to question their opponent's character as a member of certain organizations. Although female and male candidates are increasingly similar in the issues they discuss, image traits they emphasize, and appeal strategies they use in their ads, the differences that did emerge are interesting from a gender perspective. For example, the top issue in the ads by women candidates running for office between 1990 and 2002 – and one that was discussed significantly more often in females' spots than in the ads for male candidates – was the stereotypically "feminine" concern of education and schools.

Democrat Kathleen Sebelius, in an open seat race for governor of Kansas in 2002, typified the use of this "feminine" issue in her campaign. Sebelius frequently discussed education in her ads in an attempt, according to media accounts, to woo moderate Republicans. In one ad, titled "Dedicated," a male voiceover announced: "Kathleen Sebelius. As governor, [she will be] dedicated to our schools, lift teacher pay from fortieth in the nation, cut government waste to get more dollars into the classroom, and promote local control so parents and educators decide what's best for their schools." At the conclusion of this ad, Sebelius personally delivers her message that, "As Governor, I'll always put our children and schools first."

The ads of female candidates between 1990 and 2002 also discussed other issues considered "feminine" because they are more commonly associated with women – health care, senior citizen issues, and women's issues – significantly more often than the ads of their male opponents. As with the issue of education, women candidates may be conforming to stereotypical expectations that consider them to be experts on such concerns. However, female candidates also were more likely than male candidates to discuss the economy, which is usually associated more with men than with women and therefore can be considered a "masculine" issue.

In 2004, U.S. Senate candidate Patty Murray (D-WA) and U.S. House of Representatives candidate Katherine Harris (R-FL), both incumbents, demonstrated how "masculine" issues, like the economy, could be interwoven with "feminine" issues, such as education and health care, within the same commercial. In an ad titled "America," Murray is pictured in an orchard behind a cart of red and green apples. She narrates the ad, stating:

> I grew up and raised my family here in Washington state. It's been an honor to serve you in the U.S. Senate. But, today, I'm very concerned about the direction of our country. We need to take care of our own people. Invest in American business. Create American jobs. Improve our own local schools. Lower the cost of heath care right here at home. I'm Patty Murray, and I approved this ad because it's time to change priorities and put America first.

Harris sounded a similar tone, though from a different political perspective, in her 2004 ad titled "Promise." Harris narrates the ad, stating:

I went to Congress to restore the promise of security. Here's a report. Social Security is secure, and safe and affordable drugs are on the way. We're providing tax relief while creating a million and a half new jobs and opening the American dream to more families than ever. I'm proud of that. We're securing ports, strengthening first response, and letting our troops and veterans know we honor courage. I'm Katherine Harris, and I approved this message because we will never be free if we're not secure.

The only issues discussed significantly more often in the ads of male candidates, compared to female candidates, were crime and prisons, more "masculine" issues, and welfare, a more "feminine" issue. However, some of the male candidates discussing welfare took a hard-line approach, focusing on limiting the number of families receiving such benefits.

Even fewer differences are evident between female and male candidates in the images they emphasize and appeal strategies they use. However, the traits they choose to emphasize both defy and underscore stereotypical expectations about the roles and behaviors of women and men in today's society. The top traits emphasized in the ads by women candidates between 1990 and 2002 were aggressive/fighter, toughness/strength, past performance, leadership, and action-oriented – commonly considered "masculine" attributes – and honesty/integrity, more commonly considered a "feminine" quality. The top traits emphasized in the ads by men candidates were past performance, leadership, aggressive/fighter, action-oriented, toughness/strength, and experience in politics – all "masculine" attributes. Of these traits, women candidates were significantly more likely than men to emphasize toughness/strength, and men candidates were significantly more likely than women to discuss their experience in politics.

An ad from Kathleen Sebelius' successful run for governor of Kansas in 2002 illustrates how women candidates balance "masculine" and "feminine" image traits in their television advertising. Although she frequently discussed "feminine" issues – health care, education, and senior citizen issues – she did so within a framework of masculine traits and appeals. For example, when discussing health care, she would emphasize her past accomplishments as Kansas Insurance Commissioner and also her toughness and strength, stating that she "crack[ed] down" on HMOs and "block[ed] an out-of-state takeover" of Blue Cross/Blue Shield. In addition to portraying her strong business image, Sebelius was able to incorporate images of being sensitive in similar discussions of her past accomplishments, for example, patting a senior citizen's arm while he sat in a chair and she bent down to talk with him. When discussing education, she did so within the framework of taking strong, decisive stands, yet coupled the verbal message with a visual of a classroom and children at work while Sebelius turned to the camera, smiled, and crossed her arms.

The appeal strategies used in female and male candidate ads were closely related to the traits they emphasized and, thus, also are interesting from a gender perspective. Both female and male candidates were equally as likely to use all of the elements of "feminine style," which is characterized by an inductive structure, personal tone, addressing the audience as peers, relying on personal experiences, identifying with the experiences of others, and inviting audience participation. Male candidates did rely on statistics – a "masculine" strategy – significantly more often than female candidates, and female candidates were significantly more likely to make gender an issue in their ads, an indication that at least some women are campaigning as female candidates and not political candidates who happen to be women. The fact that both women and men candidates used elements of feminine style in similar proportions may suggest that this style works best for thirty-second spots on television.

In the nonverbal content of their television ads, it is interesting to note that female candidates were more likely to dress in businesslike, as opposed to casual, attire and to smile significantly more often than men did. Both of these nonverbal characteristics reflect gender-based norms and stereotypical expectations. For example, the choice of businesslike attire reflects the gender-based norms that society imposes on women as they face the challenge of portraying themselves as serious and legitimate candidates. In their everyday life, smiling is regarded as a nonverbal strategy that women use to gain acceptance. Perhaps women candidates are more likely than men candidates to smile in their ads for the same reason – to gain acceptance from viewers in the traditionally male political environment.

Because society's gender stereotypes more often associate women with families and children, it is interesting to note who is pictured in female and male candidate ads. Interestingly, women candidates distanced themselves from their roles as wives and/or mothers by picturing their families in only 9 percent of their ads, while male candidates showed their families in

20 percent of their ads between 1990 and 2002. In picturing their families or not, both male and female candidates are confronting societal stereotypes. Women candidates may want to show voters that they are more than wives and/or mothers and to dismiss any concerns voters may have over their abilities to serve in political office due to family obligations. Men candidates, on the other hand, may want to round out their images beyond business and politics by portraying themselves as loving husbands and/or fathers.

When female and male candidates are compared by their political party affiliation, differences also emerge in their television advertising strategies. For example, television ads tended to be more negative in races between female Democrats and male Republicans than in races between female Republicans and male Democrats. Female Democrats were more likely than other candidates to use negative advertising, to attack the opponent's personal qualities and background, and to discuss education and school issues, taxes, and health care. Male Democrats were more likely than other candidates to attack their opponents' issues stands and group affiliations; voice their dissatisfaction with government; and emphasize their experience in politics, leadership, and past performance. Female Republicans were more likely than other candidates to discuss the economy and emphasize their toughness/strength and qualifications. Male Republicans were more likely than other candidates to talk about crime/prisons and emphasize their trustworthiness.

Winning female and male candidates also use different strategies than losing female and male candidates. Specifically, female candidates who ultimately won had discussed issues more frequently – taxes, health care, senior citizen issues, and women's issues, in particular – and emphasized being aggressive/a fighter more often than other candidates. Male candidates who won had discussed crime and prison issues more frequently and emphasized their leadership and experience. Women candidates – both winning and losing – used attacks in almost half of their ads. Losing males were the most negative and winning males the least negative of all candidates in their campaigns.

Overall, it is notable that female candidates who won tended to be those who emphasized "masculine" traits and both "feminine" and "masculine" issues (although more "feminine" than "masculine" issues). Winning candidates, both female and male, used substantial issue discussion in their advertising, but this was particularly true of the ads of winning female candidates. Winning male candidates, however, incorporated a mix of "feminine" and "masculine" strategies to ensure their success.

In addition to the content of their television ads, it is interesting to look at the effects these appeals have on potential voters. At first, researchers speculated that "masculine" strategies (aggressive, career) – rather than traditional "feminine" strategies (non-aggressive, family) – worked best for women candidates in their political ads. However, it now seems that women are most effective when balancing stereotypical "feminine" and "masculine" traits. Also, neutral, as opposed to emotional, appeals for women candidates seem to trigger the greatest audience recall, especially for issue stances. Women are more effective when communicating about stereotypical "feminine" issues such as women's rights, education, and unemployment than such stereotypical "masculine" issues as crime and illegal immigration.

Based on the research, then, women candidates should be advised to emphasize both stereotypical "feminine" and "masculine" images and issues in their televisions commercials. Voters will perceive a woman candidate as more honest and trustworthy than a man, and just as intelligent and able to forge compromise and obtain consensus. However, especially in a climate of international terrorism, homeland security, and the war in Iraq, a woman candidate will need to emphasize her ability to lead the nation during a crisis and to make difficult decisions.

Issue emphasis will vary with the context of the campaign. In the 1992 through 2000 elections, the economy, education, and health care were the top issues. According to survey research, voters rate female candidates about the same as, or more favorably than, male candidates on these issues. However, women candidates are considered less able to handle such issues as law and order, foreign policy, and governmental problems. In elections like those of 2002 and 2004, when war and terrorism emerge among the top voter concerns, women candidates must demonstrate their competency on such issues. Clearly candidates like U.S. Senator Patty Murray (D-WA) and U.S. Representative. Katherine Harris (R-FL) were successful in demonstrating that they could handle these issues, though from opposite political viewpoints, in winning re-election in 2004.

## WEB SITES OF WOMEN POLITICAL CANDIDATES

In recent years, the Internet has provided political candidates and officeholders with an important means of communicating with voters and constituents, and researchers with another way to look at the political communication of female and male politicians. In the November 2002 elections, all candidates in gubernatorial races with a woman running against a man, 83 percent of candidates in mixed-gender U.S. Senate races, and 66 percent of candidates in mixed-gender U.S. House races hosted web sites.

Web sites, like television advertising, represent a form of political communication controlled by the politician, rather than interpreted by the media. When we examine web sites to compare ways that female and male politicians present themselves, we find that the strategies employed are mostly similar.[17] For example, in 2000 and 2002, both female and male candidates discussed "feminine" issues much more frequently than "masculine" issues on their web sites. Both female and male candidates were equally as likely to discuss the "feminine" issue of education. On so-called "masculine" issues, male candidates were only slightly more likely to discuss taxes, whereas female candidates were slightly more likely to discuss the economy.

Certainly, the World Trade Center and Pentagon attacks on September 11, 2001, stimulated increased discussion of international issues and homeland security on both female and male candidate web sites in the 2002 and 2004 campaigns. For example, Democrat Jeanne Shaheen, a candidate for U.S. Senate from New Hampshire in 2002, headlined "Enhancing Security" as an issue category on her web site, followed by the issue heading of "Ensuring Our Safety After September 11." The text on the site indicated that Shaheen, in her past position as governor of New Hampshire, had acted to secure the state by "stepping up patrols of our harbors and bridges and increasing inspections along our highways." Similarly, the re-election web site home page of U.S. Representative Anne Northup (R-KY) in 2004 had a link to "Operation Iraqi Freedom" with sub-links on "support our troops," "resources for military families," and "White House: Iraq information center." Overall, female and male candidates discussed mostly the same issues on their web sites as they did in their television ads, suggesting, once again, that issue emphasis is more related to the context of the particular political campaign than to the sex of the candidates.

Both female and male candidates attempted to establish similar images on their web sites, highlighting performance and success, experience, leadership, and qualifications – all stereotypical "masculine" traits. For example, Democrat Jimmie Lou Fisher, a woman running for governor of Arkansas in 2002, noted on her web site: "Jimmie Lou Fisher is the only person in the race for governor with this kind of experience."

Recalling that in their television advertising, female and male candidates emphasize both "feminine" and "masculine" traits, the focus on masculine traits on web sites seems significant. This difference in emphasis suggests that candidates recognize that the intimacy of television requires evidence of a more "feminine" style, with traits such as sensitivity, honesty, and cooperation accentuated in their messages. Because web sites, as opposed to attack and rebuttal/response ads, do not generate responses, candidates may perceive less need to balance their toughness and aggressiveness, which may be highlighted in an attack ad, with sensitivity and honesty.

Although it may be premature to suggest that web sites are a more "masculine" medium, it does seem that web sites are still a neutral institution that call for the emphasis of traits commonly associated with political office – qualifications, experience in politics, leadership, and knowledge on the issues. Surveys show that those looking for information online – and particularly from candidate web sites – may only be seeking clarification, reinforcement, or simply convenience, so it is not surprising that both female and male candidates would choose to focus on the traits commonly associated with political office.

Candidates, especially men, were also more likely to launch attacks on their web sites than in their television ads. In 2002, 56 percent of women's and 86 percent of men's web sites contained attacks. Again, the greater use of attacks on candidate web sites, as compared to television ads, underscores the difference between these mediums. As web sites are most often accessed by people already supporting the candidate, it is "safer" to include attacks. Television ads, on the other hand, have the potential of reaching all voters, who may be turned off by attacks.

Similar to their political ads, women candidates were most likely to appear in business attire on their web sites; in fact, they were in such dress in 92 percent of the photographs used. Differing from their televised advertising, however, male candidates were more likely to be seen in business attire (71 percent), as opposed to casual attire (29 percent), on their web sites. Women's dominant use of business attire is characteristic of female candidate self-presentation; that is, women choose such attire in order to establish a professional appearance that emphasizes their competence and the seriousness of their candidacy in order to convince voters of their legitimacy. However, on a web site – as opposed to television – male candidates also clearly feel the need to appeal to more traditional political expectations by establishing an image of a serious, viable political candidate.

Most of the photographs on candidate web sites included a combination of the candidate and other people, whether they were located on the candidates' home pages or in their biography sections. Male candidates were slightly more likely (68 percent) than female candidates (54 percent) to include pictures of just themselves in their candidate biography section, while female candidates were slightly more likely (73 percent) than male candidates (64 percent) to include pictures of themselves with other people, perhaps seeking to illustrate that many are supportive of their campaigns. When others were shown in the photos, female candidates were significantly more likely (92 percent) than male candidates (64 percent) to have men in their photos and, in many instances, these were men in positions of power and prestige, a strategy undoubtedly designed to lend legitimacy to the female candidate's campaign.

For example, Jennifer Granholm, Democrat candidate for governor of Michigan in 2002, featured photos of herself with former Vice President Al Gore at a rally; with Muhammad Ali, who was noted as "helping [her] get out the vote"; and with Senator Carl Levin from Michigan. Dianne Feinstein, Democratic candidate for U.S. Senate in California in 2000, included photos of herself and former President Bill Clinton. U.S. Representative Anne Northup, a Republican from Kentucky, pictured herself with U.S. House Speaker Dennis Hastert and Majority Leader Tom DeLay on her web site in her 2004 re-election campaign.

Female candidates also were more likely to feature women in their photos (85 percent) than male candidates (68 percent), and children and senior citizens played popular roles as well. Although 59 percent of male candidate sites included photos of their families, only 46 percent of female candidate sites included such images. It seems that some female candidates choose not to associate themselves with their families in hopes of not being linked with motherhood and domestic responsibilities, which can diminish their political credibility. For male candidates, however, the presence of "family" can evoke notions of stability and tradition, suggesting that because he has a family to protect, he will govern in ways that will protect the viewer's family as well.

One advantage that web sites have over television ads is the potential for interaction with Internet users, allowing the candidates to appear more personal as well as to raise money and recruit volunteers. Female and male candidates seem to be trying to take advantage of the opportunity for interactivity, although in rather limited forms. Female and male candidates in 2002 attempted to include more links from their home pages, as compared to previous election cycles, although male candidates were more likely to offer more links overall than female candidates. Almost all candidates provided a link from their home page to a candidate biography section, issues section, contribution section, and "get involved" section. Male candidates were more likely to link to a calendar of events section, which requires more frequent updates and attention than a well-established biography section, contribution section, or even issues section. So male candidates either are more aware of the need to have their web sites current and up-to-date, or they may simply have the financial ability to pay someone to do so.

Overall, the web sites of candidates running in U.S. Senate and gubernatorial mixed-gender races in 2000 and 2002 were largely similar. Notably, few gender differences emerged. Thus, it appears that the strategies used in political candidate web site design are in response to expectations for the medium rather than candidate sex. The ability to present an unmediated message to potential voters makes the campaign web site an appealing venue for female candidates in particular.

## CONCLUSION

An examination of how female and male candidates are presented in their campaign news coverage, political advertising, and web sites perhaps suggests more questions than answers. Nonetheless, there are several recurring trends that help to guide our expectations for the future role of gendered campaign communication.

Candidates do not have complete control of how the news media decide to cover their campaigns. In the past, female candidates have suffered in this particular genre of campaign information. However, it appears that the stereotypical news coverage trends of the last century are no longer dominant. In more recent campaign cycles, female candidates have achieved sufficient status as candidates to be given equal and sometimes greater coverage in newspapers than their male opponents. In fact, in 2000, female U.S. Senate candidates received more total coverage than males. Since 1998, women candidates have also been getting their share of positive coverage, and there are no longer great differences in the viability or electability quotient accorded to female candidates.

There are some areas where news coverage remains troublesome for female candidates. The tendency to emphasize candidate sex, appearance, marital status, and masculine issues in news coverage still haunts female candidates. Candidate sex is still mentioned more frequently for women, reporters still comment more often on a female candidate's dress or appearance, and journalists still refer to a female candidate's marital status more frequently.

Although neither male nor female candidates can directly control news coverage, they can have considerable influence on it. For example, by focusing on a mixture of "masculine" and "feminine" issues, a female candidate can achieve a balance that helps to ensure the media will not leave her out of a discussion of "masculine" issues. Female candidates also can use their controlled communication media – television ads and web sites – to influence their news coverage. For the past three decades, particularly since the 1988 presidential campaign, the news media have increased their coverage of candidate television advertising. So women candidates can influence their news coverage by producing high quality ads that will attract media attention. It is also likely that, as web campaigning becomes more popular and more developed, news media will expand their coverage of candidate web sites as part of the campaign dialogue.

Television commercials and web sites also provide female candidates with tremendous opportunities to present themselves directly to voters, without interpretation by the news media. Political television advertising is still the dominant form of candidate communication for most major level races in which female candidates must compete with male opponents. However, female candidates are successfully establishing their own competitive styles of political advertising. For example, women candidates have overcome the stereotypical admonition that they must avoid attacks. Even as challengers, they have been able to adopt strategies typical of incumbents to give themselves "authority." Female candidates who win also seem to have been successful at achieving a television "videostyle" that is overall positive, emphasizes personal traits of toughness and strength, and capitalizes on the importance of "feminine" issues such as education and health care while also discussing "masculine" issues such as the economy and defense/security. Winning female candidates also top their male opponents by keeping their attire businesslike and their smiles bright.

When it comes to self-presentation in the newest campaign medium, the Internet, research shows fewer differences between male and female candidates. Both men and women candidates' web sites are characterized by significant amounts of issue information. And, unlike the balance between "feminine" and "masculine" issues observed in their television commercials, web sites for both sexes seem to focus on "masculine" issues. Both female and male candidates also focus on past accomplishments on their sites.

Perhaps the "newness" of this medium has not provided sufficient development of different styles for female and male candidates. Neither sex has taken full advantage of the web's ability to provide message segmentation for different types of groups. Although the 2002 campaign web sites provided some additional use of links to solicit contributions and volunteers, both sexes are still lagging behind commercial development trends in providing interactivity and personalization on their web sites.

The web may be the best venue for female candidates wanting an equal competition with male candidates, especially in situations where resources are limited. A female candidate can do much more for much less on the web than through television advertising. Female candidates should develop sophisticated web sites that provide more specialized messages to specific groups, use innovative types of interactivity, and generate a more personalized presence with voters (e.g., through audio/visual presentations by the candidate and by providing opportunities for citizens to "tune in" for personal chats and question-and-answer sessions with the candidate or campaign representatives).

Despite continuing stereotypes held by voters and the media, women candidates can manage campaign communication tools in ways that improve their chances of success. Women candidates who present themselves successfully in their television ads and web sites may be able to capitalize on these controlled messages to influence their media coverage for a synergistic communication effort.

## NOTES

1. Alex Freyer. October 25, 2004. No-Frills Style Belies Murray's Tenacity, Competitive Streak. The Seattle Times.
2. Joni Balter. November 11, 2005. Two Women, Two Campaigns, Two Very Different Outcomes. The Seattle Times.
3. Linda Witt, Karen M. Paget, and Glenna Matthews. 1995. *Running as a Woman: Gender and Power in American Politics*. New York: The Free Press.
4. Witt, Paget, and Matthews 1995.
5. Michael Dorning. October 22, 1998. Carol Moseley Braun for Senator, Image is Asset and Curse: Though She Stresses Her Record, the Democrat Finds Her Personality and a Series of Missteps in the Spotlight. The Chicago Tribune.
6. James Devitt. 1999. Framing Gender on the Campaign Trail: Women's Executive Leadership and the Press. Washington, D.C.: The Women's Leadership Fund.
7. Devitt 1999.
8. Jennifer L. Pozner. March 13, 2001. Cosmetic Coverage. <http://www.alterntet.org./story/10592> 2005, March 11.
9. Pozner 2001.

10. Adam C. King. 2002. Harris Could Have Last Laugh. St. Petersburg Times. <http://www.sptimes.com/2002/06/02/State/Harris_could_have_the.shtml> 2004, December 6.

11. Dianne G. Bystrom, Mary C. Banwart, Lynda Lee Kaid, and Terry Robertson. 2004. *Gender and Candidate Communication: VideoStyles, WebStyles, NewsStyles.* New York: Routledge. Throughout this chapter, references to specific findings and statistics, unless otherwise referenced, are from the research in this book.

12. Bystrom, Banwart, Kaid, and Robertson 2004.

13. David Postman. January 9, 2005. Governor-Elect Says the Voters Never Got to Know Her. The Seattle Times.

14. Balter 2004.

15. Postman 2004.

16. Bystrom, Banwart, Kaid, and Robertson 2004.

17. Bystrom, Banwart, Kaid, and Robertson 2004.

# 8 State Elections

## Where Do Women Run? Where Do Women Win?

Voters in Washington state are used to seeing women's names on the ballot. Not only is Washington represented in the U.S. Senate by two women, but one-third of the state legislature is female.[1]

Elsewhere, voters face a different political environment. South Carolina is a good example. Not only do several thousand miles separate Washington from South Carolina, but the two states are worlds apart in terms of gender and politics. In South Carolina, fewer than 10 percent of state legislators are women, and voters there are much less familiar with women candidates.

The presence of women in statewide office varies across the country as well. For example, Arizona has set a number of records for women in state politics, including being the only state in the nation where a woman governor has succeeded another woman. Arizona is not typical, however. In a recent study, women held more than one-third of all statewide executive offices in some states but no statewide offices in other states.[2]

This state diversity in women and politics makes for interesting trivia. But does it matter that the presence of women officeholders varies so widely? Investigating the progress of women in the states is worthwhile for several reasons. If more women are to win seats in Congress, more women need to seek office in the states. State legislative and executive offices are rungs on the career ladder typically climbed by ambitious politicians – stepping stones to higher office including the Oval Office. Thus, the pattern of women's representation in the states is a map to the future of women's opportunities for the highest echelons of American politics.

Moreover, state policies are shaped by the presence – or absence – of women in public office. Women state legislators are much more likely than men to feel an obligation to represent women as a group and to work on legislation aimed at helping women, children, and families. Men and women officeholders bring different issues to the table and frequently take different policy positions as well.

Although Washington, D.C., typically comes to mind when one thinks about American politics, the states are major players in public policy. Most state legislators and statewide officeholders – men and women – labor outside the limelight shone on national politics. But federalism makes their role quite consequential. Not only do states have the power to ratify amendments to the U.S. Constitution, but also they wield tremendous influence over many policy areas.

Much about daily life depends on the state in which you live, including marriage, divorce, child custody, and the right to vote. One of the most controversial issues in American politics – same-sex marriage – illustrates the significance of the states. In 2004, voters in eleven states approved ballot initiatives to ban same-sex marriage. State policy choices in education, health care, and child care also vary widely. Some states have adopted more generous benefits and developed more innovative programs, while spending lags in other states. Many state policies have a distinctive impact on women. For example, some states have more restrictions than others on women's access to abortion and contraceptives. Moreover, some states have adopted constitutional amendments guaranteeing women and men equality under the law, while others have no such provision. In short: states matter a great deal.

How did women fare in the 2004 elections in the states? Why are women more likely to run for and hold office in some states than others? In the first half of the chapter, I examine the presence of women in the state legislatures and compare 2004 with previous elections. I then turn to an analysis of women in statewide office and compare women's status at the state level with their status in the legislatures. I argue that there has been significant progress compared to earlier decades when women legislators and statewide officeholders were scarce. At the same time, however, women are far from reaching parity with men in elective office. The lack of progress for women in the 2004 elections suggests that women's advancement in state politics is not a foregone conclusion. Moreover, some states continue to provide much more favorable environments for women candidates than others.

## HOW FAR WOMEN HAVE COME: WOMEN
## IN THE STATE LEGISLATURES

How does 2004 compare to past state elections? A little background is in order. It is well known that women won the right to vote in the United States in 1920. Less well known are women's milestones on the road to public office. In the 1890s, even before the national suffrage fight was won, Clara Cressingham, Carrie C. Holly, and Frances Klock were elected to the Colorado House of Representatives. The first woman to serve in a state senate – Martha Hughes Cannon – lived in Utah. Firsts for women were not limited to the West. In 1924, the first woman of color was elected to the legislature in Michigan: Cora Belle Reynolds Anderson, a Native American. The first African American woman, Minnie Buckingham Harper, was appointed to the West Virginia House in 1929. One can only imagine what these women's experiences must have been like, given how rare it was for women to hold office.

Women's presence in the state legislatures has become less of a novelty over time. Women candidates have been spurred on by women's groups dedicated to electing more women to office. And as more women have run for office, voters, parties, donors, and women themselves have become more used to the idea of women as politicians. Instead of a mere handful, a total of 1,663 women hold state legislative office today. Whereas women were less than 5 percent of all state legislators in 1971, today women are 22.5 percent of legislators (see Figure 8.1).

The number of races in which both contestants are women has also increased. These races attest to the progress women have made in increasing their presence as candidates. Moreover, these contests highlight the diversity of women candidates. In 2004, for example, two women vied for the 37th assembly district in California. The Republican candidate was Audra Strickland, the wife of the outgoing incumbent legislator, Tony Strickland, who could not seek re-election because of term limits; the Democratic candidate was Ferial Masry, who won her party's nomination through a last minute write-in campaign. Masry, a naturalized U.S. citizen born in Saudi Arabia, would have been the first Saudi-American to win elective office in the United States. In the end, Strickland won the close general election race, becoming one of only six Republican women in the California legislature.

Women state legislators are increasingly likely to be women of color. One newly elected Latina legislator from Arizona is Representative

Figure 8.1: The Proportion of Women Elected to State Legislatures Increased through the Late 1990s but Has Stagnated Since.

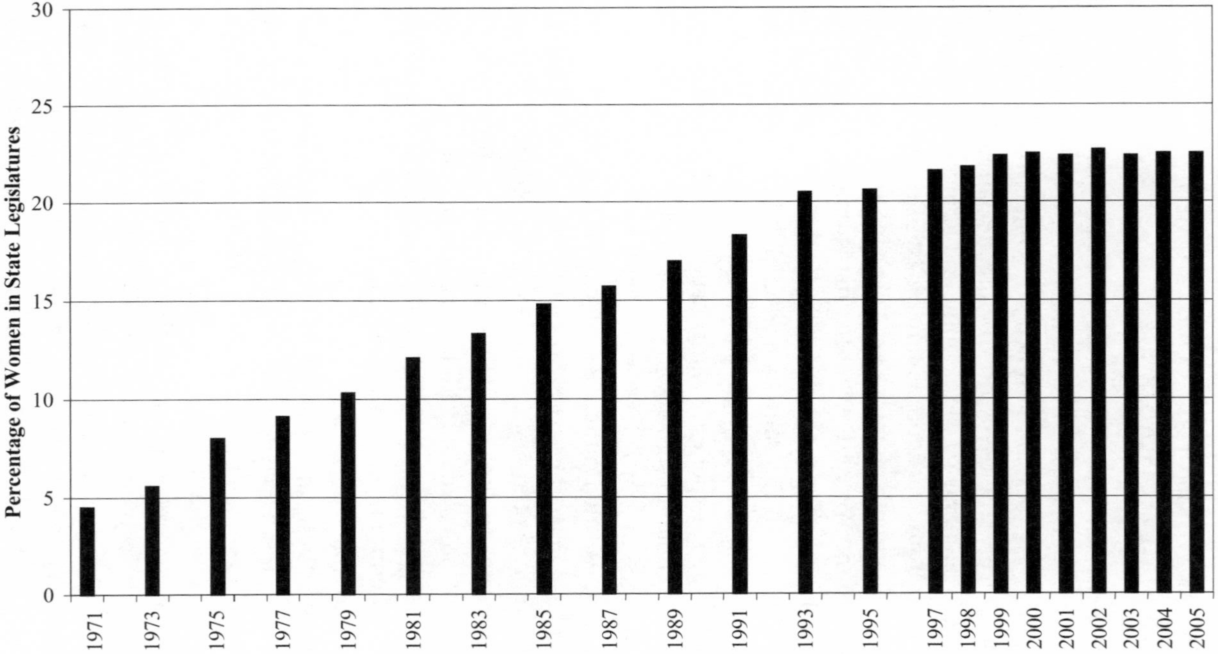

Source: Compiled by author from Center for American Women and Politics, 2005 Fact Sheets.

Martha Garcia. When surveyed on what prompted her to run for the legislature, her response was simple: "Understanding the need for women to be represented at the state level."[3] While 11.6 percent of all women state legislators were women of color in 1988, that statistic is 18.9 percent in 2005. These numbers include 215 African American women, sixty-seven Latinas, twenty-three women who are Asian American or Pacific Islanders, and nine Native American women. Almost all of these legislators of color – 296 – are Democrats; only eighteen are Republicans.

Like women of color, women state legislators in general are more likely to be Democrats than Republicans (see Figure 8.2). For most of the twentieth century, the Democratic party was the majority party and dominated the state legislatures. However, the Republican party has become much more competitive in recent years, resulting in a sea change in control of state legislative seats. Currently, Democrats have unified control of nineteen state legislatures while Republicans control twenty. In ten states, control is divided between the two parties.[4]

Legislative life depends a great deal on majority party status. By definition, the majority party has more votes and therefore more power than the minority party to enact the legislation it prefers. The majority party also controls the agenda – presiding over the legislative chamber, choosing committee chairs, and making decisions about what bills should be brought to a vote. In some states, the parties are so bitterly divided that the minority party has almost no influence at all.

Republican women have historically constituted a larger share of all Republican legislators than Democratic women (see Figure 8.3). But this has changed in recent years as women have come to be better represented among Democratic legislators. Meanwhile, Republican women have become less well represented among Republicans overall. Thus, women have become a smaller share of all Republican legislators as the Republican party has gained more power nationally, and the reverse is true for Democratic women.

Women are not just members of their political parties; in some cases, they are leading their parties. For example, women are key players in Colorado, a state where control of the legislature changed hands as a result of the 2004 state legislative elections. Democrats won majorities in both legislative chambers there for the first time since 1960. Senator Joan Fitz-Gerald helped engineer the Democrats' victory in the senate and was elected senate president after the election – the first woman ever to hold that position in the state. Meanwhile, Representative Alice Madden

Figure 8.2: Democratic Women Legislators Outnumber Republican Women Legislators.

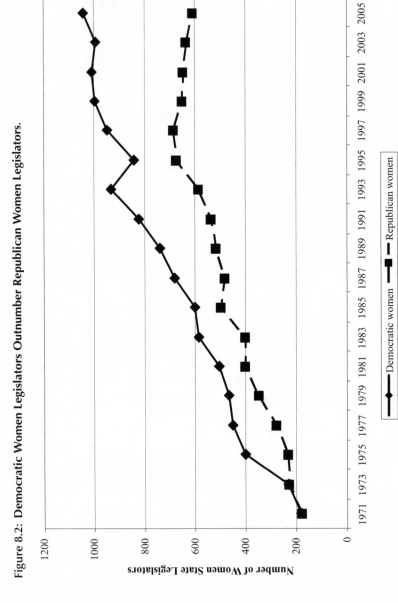

*Source:* Compiled by author from Center for American Women and Politics, 2005 Fact Sheets.

194

Figure 8.4: A Larger Share of Democratic Legislators Than Republican Legislators Are Women.

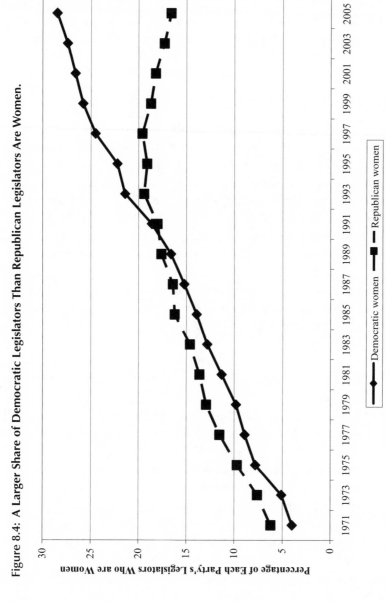

*Source:* Compiled by author from Center for American Women and Politics, 2005 Fact Sheets.

helped the Democratic party take the majority in the house. After the election, Madden "received two standing ovations from her caucus and was credited for masterminding the comeback."[5] She was unanimously elected house majority leader.

## STATE LEGISLATIVE ELECTIONS

What happens when women run for the legislature? Women typically win their races for the legislature at the same rates as men on average.[6] Women state legislative candidates, like women congressional candidates, do not appear to be at a disadvantage compared to men when other factors are taken into account. Instead, a candidate's chances of winning office depend much more on the type of race than on candidate gender. An incumbent officeholder who is seeking re-election is quite likely to win his or her race, while a challenger trying to unseat that incumbent faces long odds. Thus the most competitive races are for open seats where there is no incumbent seeking re-election. However, the likelihood of winning open seats often depends on the candidate's party affiliation since most legislative districts are likely to favor one party over the other. When a seat is thought to be safely in one party's column, the other party may not bother to run a candidate. In the 2004 state legislative races, for example, 35 percent of all state legislative seats up for election were not contested by one of the major parties.[7]

A total of 5,809 state legislative seats across the country were up for election in 2004; 2,220 women ran in the general election for these seats, slightly lower than the number of women running in the most recent comparable election.[8] Women were about 23 percent of all major party state legislative candidates, including 24 percent of state representative candidates and 20 percent of senate candidates

In 2002, a total of 2,344 women had run in the general election for state legislative office with 62 percent of these women winning their races.[9] Similarly, women won 62 percent of their general election races in 2004. Not surprisingly, women were much more successful when they ran as incumbents than when they ran as challengers or open seat candidates. Of the 1,123 female major party incumbents running for office in 2004, 95 percent won re-election. Meanwhile, over 90 percent of women who ran as incumbents in 2002 were successful, compared to only 15 percent of women who ran as challengers. Candidates who ran as challengers in 2004 won only 11 percent of their races – not atypical statistics given the difficulties of unseating a sitting legislator.

**TABLE 8.1:** More Democratic women than Republican women sought election to the state legislatures in 2004

|  | House | | Senate | |
|---|---|---|---|---|
|  | Democrat | Republican | Democrat | Republican |
| CANDIDATES |  |  |  |  |
| Open seat | 225 | 129 | 50 | 26 |
| Challenger | 327 | 226 | 64 | 37 |
| Incumbent | 557 | 379 | 121 | 66 |
| Total | 1,109 | 734 | 235 | 129 |
| WINNERS |  |  |  |  |
| Open seat | 103 | 71 | 25 | 17 |
| Challenger | 47 | 15 | 9 | 3 |
| Incumbent | 542 | 354 | 113 | 61 |
| Total | 692 | 440 | 147 | 81 |

*Note:* Cell entries are numbers of general election candidates and winners by type of race.

*Source:* Center for American Women and Politics (CAWP), 2005 Fact Sheets.

One such successful challenger was Gwyn Green in Colorado. Green, a city councilwoman and former medical social worker, was declared the winner only after a ballot recount. The close race pitted Green against a Republican woman incumbent, Ramey Johnson, who is a registered nurse. Green's narrow victory contributed to the Democratic majority in the Colorado House.

About half of all open seat candidates were successful in both 2002 and 2004. In these open seat races, where women are most likely to increase their numbers, 275 Democratic and 155 Republican women ran, and 47 percent of Democratic women and 57 percent of Republican women won in 2004 (see Table 8.1).

Democratic and Republican women state legislative candidates have usually performed similarly. For example, 60 percent of Democratic women won their races for house seats in 2002 compared to 66 percent of Republican women. Meanwhile, Democratic women were more success-ful in their bids for state senate, with 63 percent winning; only 54 percent of Republican women won their senate races. In 2004, women's success rates were even more similar across the two parties; 62 percent of Demo-cratic women and 60 percent of Republican women won their house races, and about 63 percent of both Democratic and Republican women won their senate races.

Importantly, however, in both 2002 and 2004, Democratic women candidates outnumbered Republican women, particularly in house races. In 2004, for example, 1,344 Democratic women ran in the general election, whereas only 863 Republican women did so. While women were about 28 percent of all Democratic candidates, they were only about 18 percent of all Republican candidates. Thus, because Democratic women legislators already outnumbered Republican women, and more Democratic women than Republican women sought office, the gap between the two groups of women continued to grow as a result of the 2004 election.

## CROSS-STATE VARIATION IN WHERE WOMEN HOLD STATE LEGISLATIVE OFFICE

These national statistics mask differences across the states in where women run for and hold office. Compared to 2004, seventeen states saw an increase in women legislators in 2005, but nineteen states saw a decrease. The largest percentage decreases occurred in Rhode Island, Washington, Georgia, Wyoming, Michigan, Maine, and West Virginia, while the largest increases were in Nebraska, Arizona, Delaware, Kansas, and Nevada.[10] Indeed, as a result of the 2004 elections, women set a new record in Delaware, where women are now about 34 percent of the legislature.

Women are 22.5 percent of all state legislators nationwide. But in Alabama, Kentucky, and Mississippi, women are only 10 to 13 percent of the legislature (see Table 8.2). Low numbers are not limited to the South, however, since Pennsylvania, Wyoming and New Jersey help round out the bottom of the nation's list. Meanwhile, women are most likely to serve in the legislature in Maryland, Delaware, and Arizona. These statistics reflect where women run for office.[11] For example, in 2004, women were 13 percent of all Pennsylvania candidates but 26 percent of Delaware candidates.

Why are women more likely to run for the legislature in some states than others? One of the state factors associated with where women hold state legislative office is ideology; where the public holds more liberal views, women are much more likely to seek and hold state legislative office.[12] Ideology probably matters at more than one point in the electoral process. In areas where the population is more liberal and less conservative, voters are more accepting of women in nontraditional roles, women are more likely to think of themselves as candidates, and political parties are more likely to see women as viable candidates as well.

**TABLE 8.2:** The presence of women legislators varies considerably by state

| More than 30% | 24–30% | 18–24% | 15–18% | Less than 15% |
|---|---|---|---|---|
| Maryland | Minnesota | Florida | Tennessee | Oklahoma |
| Delaware | Connecticut | Maine | Rhode Island | Wyoming |
| Arizona | Oregon | New York | Indiana | Virginia |
| Nevada | Illinois | North Carolina | Arkansas | Mississippi |
| Vermont | Hawaii | Missouri | North Dakota | Pennsylvania |
| Washington | Idaho | Michigan | South Dakota | Kentucky |
| Colorado | Wisconsin | Utah | Louisiana | Alabama |
| Kansas | Montana | Iowa | New Jersey | South Carolina |
| New Mexico | Massachusetts | Texas | West Virginia | |
| California | Nebraska | Ohio | | |
| New Hampshire | | Alaska | | |
| | | Georgia | | |

*Source:* Center for American Women and Politics (CAWP), 2005 Fact Sheets. States are listed from high to low in each column.

Many men and women who run for the legislature are ordinary citizens without elective experience. Indeed, a majority of state legislators come to the office without any prior officeholding experience.[13] But in addition to whatever formal requirements are set by the state for holding office, such as residency or age requirements, it is common for voters to have expectations about the qualifications and backgrounds of state legislators, or what are known as "informal requirements" for the office. For example, legislators often have law degrees or political experience. Not surprisingly, more women serve in state legislatures where there is a larger pool of women with the informal qualifications expected of state legislative candidates – for example, where more women are in the labor force and more women are lawyers.

Another state contextual factor that is related to the presence of women legislators is the type of legislature. Legislatures are not all alike. In some states, being a state legislator is similar to a full-time job resembling service in Congress – as in Pennsylvania, where legislators earn about $66,000 annually and meet year round, or California, which has state legislative districts that are even larger than congressional ones and where the pay is $99,000 per year. These types of legislatures are considered to be "professional." A far cry from Pennsylvania and California is New Hampshire, where legislators earn just $100 per year. In some states, like New Hampshire, legislators pride themselves on being citizen legislators who serve on a part-time basis.[14]

Women tend to be less well represented in the more professional legislatures. Why this is the case is not clear. It may be that it is more difficult for women to seek these positions because potential candidates are keenly interested in running, putting women, who are relative newcomers to electoral politics, at a disadvantage. Alternatively, there may be more recruitment by parties where the office is less desirable, and parties may turn to new groups of candidates such as women for these roles. Regardless, women tend to be more likely to hold office where service in the legislature is less than full-time. For example, of the top states for women legislators – Maryland, Delaware, Arizona, Nevada, Vermont, Washington, and Colorado – none has a full-time, professionalized legislature.[15]

The number of legislators elected from each district often matters as well. In most states, legislators are elected from single-member districts, in which only one legislator is elected per legislative district. Seats in the U.S. House of Representatives are likewise single-member. But some states, such as Arizona, Maryland, and Washington, have multi-member districts which elect more than one legislator per district. Where districts are multi-member rather than single-member, women are more likely to serve. Perhaps a woman is more likely to put herself forward to run for office when she is one candidate among many. Or, where voters are able to elect more than one representative from the district, perhaps voters seek a gender balance in who represents them.

Thus, the pattern of women's representation across states is not random, but is a function of how interested women – and men – are in serving in the legislature, whether women have the requisite informal requirements for the office, and how voters and party leaders respond to women candidates.

## CANDIDATES AND RECRUITMENT FOR THE LEGISLATURE

All of this discussion begs a larger question: why don't more women run for the state legislatures? Because men and women tend to win their races at similar rates, the crux of the problem of women's underrepresentation lies in the dearth of women candidates. Despite significant advances in the number of women holding state legislative office, women remain much less likely than men to become candidates. In recent years, women have been only about one-quarter of state legislative candidates.

Part of the explanation for the scarcity of women candidates is that women are relatively new to electoral politics, and incumbency acts as a barrier to increasing the number of women in office. Incumbency gives state legislators an advantage similar to that of incumbent members of Congress. Because most state legislators who are incumbents win re-election, and most incumbent legislators are men, women are more likely to increase their presence in office by running for open seats rather than as challengers. But because there are few opportunities to seek open seats, incumbency is an institutional constraint on the pace at which any new group of officeholders, including women, can increase their presence.

Certainly, the lack of openings and the gender gap in the pool of individuals with the informal requirements for office partially explain why more women do not run. But even in races for open seats, women remain much less likely than men to seek office. For example, for many years, those in favor of term limits have trumpeted the boon to women's candidacies that these reforms were expected to create. Fifteen states have adopted limits on the number of years individuals can serve in the state legislature. By creating more open seats, doors were expected to open for women and yield dramatically more women officeholders. Yet term limits have not led to an increase in the presence of women in office. In recent years, and despite the implementation of term limits in many states, the percentage of women state legislators has been stagnant. In 40 percent of the house seats made available by term limits, no woman has even entered either party's primary.[16] Although term limits create new openings, all incumbents – men and women – are prevented from seeking re-election after serving the designated number of terms. Women who have worked hard to achieve leadership positions can lose their positions as a result. For example, Lola Spradley, Colorado's first woman speaker of the house, could not seek re-election in 2004 because of term limits.

Moreover, among the pool of potential candidates with the informal qualifications for office, studies have shown that women are less likely to think about becoming candidates.[17] In a recent survey of potential candidates with backgrounds in law, business, and education, women were much less likely to have considered running for political office than men.

Thus, the underrepresentation of women in state legislatures remains a puzzle. To investigate why more women do not run, I conducted interviews with party leaders, state legislators, and political activists across several states. Several promising explanations related to the parties' informal recruitment practices emerged from these interviews.[18]

First, despite dramatic changes in the role of women in society, social networks remain quite segregated by gender. Among officeholders and political activists alike, talk of an "old boys network" was not uncommon in some states. The upshot of these differences in social networks is that men tend to know other men. As many party leaders and legislators argued, the leaders who recruit candidates tend to look to whom they know – people they do business with, people they play golf with, and so on. As one North Carolina legislator explained:

> I don't think it's conscious. I think that they would pick whoever they thought could win.... If the woman looked like she was the better winner, and could win more easily, I think they'd support the woman.... I don't think they really care whether they're men or women. I think it's just that they have more contacts with men, and that there are more men in leadership positions back in the community – in those important, visible, power positions back in the community.

Many other interview subjects echoed the view that gender differences in networks mean that women are not typically thought of as candidates. Others argued that men in the old boys network tend to look to people they know and with whom they are comfortable; because women are less likely to be part of that network, they are less likely to be recruited to run for office.

A second, and related, explanation for why more women do not seek office is that some party leaders have doubts about the abilities of women and their electability, which can make it quite unlikely that women will be tapped to run for office. For many years, scholars as well as women's groups have repeated the slogan that "when women run, women win" – indicating that women are as likely as men to win their races when the type of race is taken into account. Yet not all party leaders are in agreement about women and winning. Naturally, party leaders want to win elections. And women are not likely to be drafted for important races if party leaders think women are going to lose. These attitudes are important predictors of where women hold office and pose an obstacle to increasing women's representation.[19]

The combination of networks segregated by gender and doubts about women's capacity for politics means that women are typically worse off where parties are more influential in choosing the party nominee. Indeed, statistical analyses indicate that states with stronger party organizations typically have fewer women in their legislatures.[20] In contrast, where the process is more open, women are better represented. Thus, how candidates are recruited for office and whether parties are more actively involved as gatekeepers to the nomination help explain why women are more likely to seek office in some states than others.

Of course, women candidates may have strong party support in some cases. Most parties recruit candidates and help them win election in order to maintain or increase their party's share of seats in the legislature. Parties are often selective about the candidates they recruit and support.[21] Though strong parties tend to be negatively related to women's representation, parties do sometimes select women candidates for important races. In 2004, for example, Joy Padgett, a former Republican state legislator, was selected to fill a vacant Ohio senate seat. In the general election, Padgett's was one of the seats targeted by her party for victory. Indeed, the campaign set a new record for spending in a senate contest, with Republicans spending $1.4 million to ensure her success.[22]

Although being a woman can be a disadvantage in some states, depending on how women candidates are viewed, being a woman is sometimes seen as an electoral advantage, increasing the likelihood that women will be recruited to run for office. Voters perceive women as more honest and compassionate and better on education and women's issues, for example. However, other stereotypes put women at a disadvantage; men are perceived as better leaders and better able to handle issues such as foreign policy and crime. Although some voters would like to see an increase in women's representation, other voters have doubts about women's ability and would prefer to vote for male candidates.[23] For example, in Massachusetts, where the public is fairly liberal, the viability of women state legislative candidates is not an issue. In Alabama, however, voters are much less familiar with women in leadership roles.

In addition, research shows that women may talk themselves out of running, fearing they do not have the right qualifications. Thus, it is not enough for women to possess the right qualifications for office; women must also perceive themselves as qualified. As one legislative leader in Colorado observed:

> Men are much more willing to jump into it than women. You need to push women a lot harder to do it, and for whatever reason, they feel like they're not as qualified or they're not as ready. I don't know who's sending them that message necessarily, but it certainly seems to be one that's fairly universal from the folks I've talked to. And you know, it's changing a little bit.

Politics is still a career much more likely to be pursued by men than women. Indeed, studies have shown that women are much more likely to run for the legislature after having been recruited to run; meanwhile, men are more likely to run because they are "self-starters" – arriving at the decision to become a candidate without external encouragement.[24] Women are much less likely than men to report that the main reason they ran for office was that it was something they always wanted to do. As one North Carolina legislator observed, women may feel they need to have high qualifications to run and be accepted as a candidate: "They just have to be a little better qualified than men. Men can just decide, I think I'd like to go to Washington, and they run for the Congress. And they've never been [in] state, local government."

For these reasons, the recruitment efforts of parties and women's organizations are extremely valuable. Women's groups and networks have been critical to the success of women state legislative candidates. Both inside and outside the legislature, women have formed networks and political action committees (PACs) to elect more women. State versions of EMILY's List, an influential national PAC, help elect pro-choice Democratic women to the legislature in Ohio, North Carolina, Colorado, and other states. In North Carolina, Republican women state legislators have formed a PAC to bring more Republican women into the body. Other groups are bipartisan, such as Iowa's Women in Public Policy, which recruits and trains women for the legislature. Given the recent plateau in the number of women legislators, these efforts are increasingly important. The reasons that women fare better in some states than others have much to do with recruitment, the presence of women in leadership roles, and the types of networks that women have at their disposal.

## WOMEN IN STATEWIDE OFFICE

Women in statewide elective executive office, such as governor or secretary of state, are more visible than women legislators. Because their constituency is the entire state rather than one legislative district, running for statewide office typically means more competitive races and higher campaign expenditures than running for state legislature. As the federal government has devolved more responsibilities to the states, state executive officeholders have become increasingly important. Governors, in particular, are positioned to play major roles in policymaking.

Holding a statewide office can often be a stepping stone to higher office. Opportunities for statewide positions vary across states. For example, all fifty states elect governors and most states – forty-three states – also elect a lieutenant governor and an attorney general. The offices of secretary of state and treasurer are elected positions in thirty-five states. Other elective positions in some states include auditor, comptroller, chief agriculture official, and chief education official.

The women who paved the way in statewide office often did so in the footsteps of their husbands. For example, Nellie Tayloe Ross of Wyoming, the first woman governor, was selected to succeed her deceased husband in 1925.[25] It would be fifty years before Ella Grasso of Connecticut became the first woman elected governor in her own right. Madeleine Kunin, Democrat of Vermont, also made history; she was the first woman to serve three terms as governor. In 2002, with Janet Napolitano's election to governor of Arizona, a woman succeeded another woman as governor for the first time in history.[26]

Only a total of twenty-eight women have ever held the office of governor, and twenty-one states – fewer than half of all states – have ever had women governors. In 2005, eight women serve as governors, including six Democrats and two Republicans.

Women have increased their presence in other statewide offices in recent years as well. In 1971, only twenty-four women held statewide offices (including governor), 7 percent of the total. In contrast, a total of seventy-nine women currently serve, holding 25.1 percent of all statewide offices. Figure 8.4 demonstrates that the presence of women in statewide office more than doubled between 1983 and 1995; however, women's presence has leveled off since then.[27] Republican women slightly outnumber Democratic women in statewide office. Thus, although Republican women trail Democratic women as legislators, the two groups of women have more similar records in statewide officeholding.

Women have achieved even more success as lieutenant governors than as governors: six Democratic women and nine Republican women currently serve as lieutenant governors. Balancing the gubernatorial ticket by gender has become an attractive electoral strategy – particularly for the Republican party, which tends to fare better with men voters than women voters.[28]

Women of color have also increased their presence in statewide office, but they remain very few in number. A total of five women of color currently hold statewide office. These women include Denise Nappier, the Democratic state treasurer of Connecticut, who is African American, and the attorney general and secretary of state of New Mexico – Patricia Madrid and Rebecca Vigil-Giron – both of whom are Democrats and Latinas. Another Latina, Susan Castillo, serves as the superintendent of public instruction in Oregon, a nonpartisan position. Republican Jennette

Figure 8.4: The Proportion of Women Elected to Statewide Office Increased through the Mid-1990s but Has Stagnated Since.

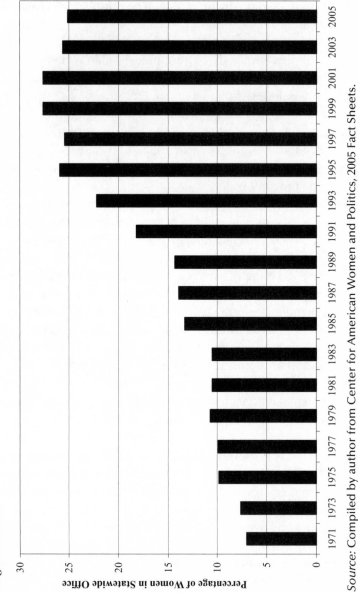

*Source:* Compiled by author from Center for American Women and Politics, 2005 Fact Sheets.

Bradley, state treasurer of Ohio, previously served as lieutenant governor – the first African American woman to hold that office in the entire country.

It is not uncommon for governors and other statewide officeholders to have previous experience in state legislatures. M. Jodi Rell, the governor of Connecticut, is a good example. Rell served in the Connecticut House of Representatives from 1984 to 1994. She was also elected lieutenant governor three times before becoming governor in 2004 after the sitting governor was impeached and resigned from office.

Women have been more likely to serve in some types of statewide offices than others. Studies show that women have been more likely to seek statewide offices that are consistent with voters' gender stereotypes; women have been less likely to run for what could be considered "masculine offices" and more likely to run for "feminine offices." One such "feminine" office is chief education official, with titles varying from state to state. This is one policy domain where voters have traditionally believed that women are more competent than men.[29] Women may be more likely to come forward to run for such positions, which are consistent with voter stereotypes. Alternatively, party leaders may be particularly interested in recruiting women for these offices.

## CANDIDACY FOR STATEWIDE OFFICE

Running for these high level executive positions presents additional challenges compared to state legislative races. It is much more common for women to run for school board or for the legislature than for governor. Studies show that voters may be more comfortable with women in legislative positions than executive positions.[30] Because executive office vests power within one individual, candidates for these offices must persuade voters that they have the requisite leadership skills and can command authority.

On the one hand, that women statewide candidates and officeholders frequently make national news attests to the hurdles that women continue to surmount. For example, Jane Swift of Massachusetts, a Republican and former state senator, campaigned for lieutenant governor while pregnant with her first child. She was expecting twins when she ascended to the governor's office several years later to fill a vacancy. When Democratic male politicians criticized her for attempting to govern while hospitalized after her delivery, women from both parties were quick to come to her defense. Meanwhile, whether men can juggle governing and fatherhood is not usually a public concern. A good example is Jim McGreevey's

campaign for governor of New Jersey in 2001. Though McGreevey and
his wife were expecting, whether McGreevey could be governor with a
new baby at home was not an issue in the campaign.

On the other hand, women in the states often generate positive headlines and excitement when they set new records. In 1998, for example,
Arizona made history by electing five women to hold the top executive
offices in the state: governor, attorney general, secretary of state, treasurer, and superintendent of public instruction. In 2004, the spotlight was
on Missouri. Some heralded the "Year of the Woman" in Missouri because
half the major party nominees for statewide office were women. Women
ran for five of the six statewide offices up for election. Thus statewide
office poses significant obstacles for women but also promises significant
rewards.


## THE 2004 STATEWIDE ELECTIONS

Election years for many statewide offices do not typically coincide with
presidential election years. In non-presidential election year 2002, for
example, there were thirty-six gubernatorial races; in presidential election year 2004, there were only eleven. In 2002, similar numbers of
Democratic and Republican women sought the most prestigious offices
in the states: governor, lieutenant governor, attorney general, treasurer,
and secretary of state. More of the incumbent candidates seeking re-
election to these positions were Republicans than Democrats, while more
of the open seat candidates were Democrats than Republicans. Overall,
Democratic women had a lower success rate than Republican women
because Democratic women were less likely to run as incumbents: seventeen of thirty-four Democratic women candidates (50.0 percent) won
their races, compared to nineteen of thirty Republican women (63.3 percent). Republican women were also more likely to win their open seat
contests.

All of the women incumbent candidates for the top statewide offices
in 2004 were Democrats (see Table 8.3). Of these candidates, six of fifteen
Democratic women candidates (40.0 percent) won their races, compared
to four of seven Republican women (57.1 percent). Democratic women
were more likely than Republican women to run as challengers. Women
performed fairly well overall; they were 22 percent of general election
candidates for these top offices and 18 percent of the winners. In the end,
the percentage of women holding statewide office remained about the
same as before the election.

**TABLE 8.3:** Twenty-two women sought election to major statewide executive offices in 2004

| Seat status | State | Office, candidate name, party, outcome |
|---|---|---|
| Incumbent | Delaware | Governor, Ruth Ann Minner (D) (won) |
| | Indiana | Lt. Governor, Kathy Davis (D) (lost) |
| | North Carolina | Lt. Governor, Beverly Perdue (D) (won) |
| | North Carolina | Secretary of State, Elaine Marshall (D) (won) |
| | Vermont | Secretary of State, Deb Markowitz (D) (won) |
| Open seat | Washington | Governor, Christine Gregoire (D) (won) |
| | Missouri | Governor, Claire McCaskill (D) (lost) |
| | Missouri | Lt. Governor, Bekki Cook (D) (lost) |
| | Utah | Lt. Governor, Karen Hale (D) (lost) |
| | Washington | Attorney General, Deborah Senn (D) (lost) |
| | Missouri | Secretary of State, Robin Carnahan (D) (won) |
| | Missouri | Secretary of State, Catherine Hanaway (R) (lost) |
| | West Virginia | Secretary of State, Betty Ireland (R) (won) |
| | Missouri | State Treasurer, Sarah Steelman (R) (won) |
| | North Dakota | State Treasurer, Kelly Schmidt (R) (won) |
| | Pennsylvania | State Treasurer, J. Craige Pepper (R) (lost) |
| Challenger | Indiana | Lt. Governor, Becky Skillman (R) (won) |
| | North Dakota | Lt. Governor, Deb Mathern (D) (lost) |
| | Vermont | Lt. Governor, Cheryl Rivers (D) (lost) |
| | Oregon | Secretary of State, Betsy Close (R) (lost) |
| | Washington | Secretary of State, Laura Ruderman (D) (lost) |
| | Utah | State Treasurer, Debbie Hansen (D) (lost) |

*Note:* The table includes candidates for governor, lieutenant governor, attorney general, secretary of state, and treasurer only.
*Source:* Center for American Women and Politics (CAWP), 2005 Fact Sheets.

The total number of women governors in 2005 is lower than in 2004 because one woman governor did not seek re-election and one was defeated in the primary.[31] Two women won their races for governor in 2004, including Ruth Ann Minner, Delaware's incumbent governor. Minner, a Democrat, had become the state's first woman governor in 2000. The other 2004 winner is Christine Gregoire, a Democrat, who ultimately won her bid to be governor of Washington in one of the most dramatic election stories of the year. Her Republican opponent, Dino Rossi, had been named the winner by an initial tally of 261 votes out of more than 2.8 million cast. An automatic machine recount narrowed his lead to just forty-two votes. However, in a stunning reversal, a statewide hand

recount put Gregoire ahead by 129 votes.[32] Minner and Gregoire join
the women governors continuing in office: Democrats Kathleen Blanco of
Louisiana, Jennifer Granholm of Michigan, Janet Napolitano of Arizona,
and Kathleen Sebelius of Kansas; and Republicans Linda Lingle of Hawaii
and M. Jodi Rell of Connecticut.

Meanwhile, state auditor Claire McCaskill lost her general election
bid for governor of Missouri. In what was considered a "hopeless race,"
McCaskill had challenged sitting governor Bob Holden in her own party's
primary. McCaskill, the daughter of a city councilwoman, had worked
her way up the political ladder, having served as county legislator and
prosecutor, state senator, and state auditor. As one Democratic official
noted, McCaskill is a "great lady . . . But she's going to lose."[33] In the history
of Missouri, a sitting governor had never been defeated. Even nationally,
the defeat of a governor is unusual and had not occurred in ten years. Yet
McCaskill triumphed in the hotly contested primary, narrowly losing in
November. In the end, only two women won their bids for five statewide
offices in Missouri, including Democrat Robin Carnahan who was elected
secretary of state, and Republican Sarah Steelman, who was elected state
treasurer.

But women in the states continue to break records and make history.
For example, 2004 saw the first woman elected to statewide office in West
Virginia: Betty Ireland as secretary of state. She attributed her success to
women voters, arguing "We've broken that glass ceiling." Her campus
visits were greeted with enthusiasm: "Young women on college campuses
have come to me and told me 'We're so glad you're doing this.' Now we
know there's something for us in West Virginia."[34] Ireland explained that
it was time for the state to elect a woman: "What kind of signal do we send
when it's all men? Do not apply if you don't fit the good old boy mold?"
Indeed, many had cheered on her candidacy: "For all these years we've
been sending seven men to the highest echelon of state government. I
don't want to risk invoking the ire of men, but even men came up to
me all during the campaign and said, 'It's time.'"[35] Ireland, a Republican
businesswoman, had run unopposed in the primary. While West Virginia
has been a Democratic stronghold, Republican candidates are becoming
more competitive. Yet Ireland was the only Republican to win one of the
five statewide offices up for election.

The 2004 statewide elections demonstrate the importance of the
pipeline of women in lower offices. Women today are more likely to
hold the highest statewide offices where women are a greater share of
state legislators. They are also more likely to hold these positions where

women have been successful in winning statewide office in the past.[36] Given the relationship between the presence of women in the pool and the presence of women in higher office, it is perhaps not surprising that the 2004 elections continue a trend of stasis in women's representation in statewide office. Similar to the current situation of women state legislators, the number of women in statewide office has leveled off as well.[37]

## GENDER AND CANDIDACY IN THE FUTURE

The states are increasingly important arenas of policymaking. And they continue to be training grounds for higher office. Compared to past decades, women have made tremendous progress in both state legislative and statewide executive office. Yet, at both levels, women's representation has reached a plateau in recent years. This leveling off suggests that the recruitment of women candidates continues to be a critical mechanism for women's representation.

In general, the 2004 elections largely saw a continuation of the pre-election patterns for women in office. In some states, women gained state legislative seats. Women now hold a record number of seats in Delaware, for example. Elsewhere, however, women lost seats. And although women from the two major parties have similar records in statewide office, Democratic women legislators outpace their Republican counterparts – a trend that continued with the recent election.

Not all electoral environments are created equal with regard to women candidates; some states provide more favorable environments for women candidates than others. For example, women are more likely to hold office in liberal states, states with less professionalized legislatures, and states with a higher share of women in the pool of eligible candidates. Meanwhile, the presence of women in the pipeline of lower offices has implications for where women have been able to achieve statewide office: women fare better statewide where more women serve in the legislature. While women have made impressive gains across the country, there are many firsts that women have yet to achieve. In most states, women leaders are missing from the highest levels of public office. Women of color, in particular, have yet to win more than a handful of statewide races.

Women candidates and women's groups have already been planning for the upcoming elections. In California, women's groups fear a decline in women's representation in 2006 because term limits will force many of the current women legislators from office. Meanwhile, women in several states are likely to seek election to the governor's mansion, including

212                                                          Kira Sanbonmatsu

Alabama lieutenant governor Lucy Baxley and Ohio auditor Betty Montgomery. Montgomery, formerly the state attorney general, a county prosecutor, and state senator, has been the top Republican vote-getter in the past
two statewide elections in Ohio. Her media consultant believes that she
may benefit from her expected status as the only woman in the gubernatorial primary: "Whenever there's one woman and several men, the
woman tends to do better. It doesn't mean she's going to win, but it gives
the woman an edge, because she stands out not just because she's different
but as a potential agent of change."[38]

As more women run for state legislative and statewide office, voters
become more accustomed to women candidates. Yet, progress for women
is occurring at an uneven pace across the country. The dearth of women
candidates continues to be a vexing problem for those who would like
the number of women officeholders to rise. Whether future elections will
see an increase or decrease in women's representation in the states will
depend on whether women put themselves forward as candidates for public office.

## NOTES

1. All data on women officeholders and candidates are from the Center for
   American Women and Politics (CAWP), Eagleton Institute of Politics, Rutgers
   University. Data on women as a percentage of all candidates and by party
   caucus were calculated by the author. The author thanks the CAWP staff and
   research assistant Heidi Bruns.
2. Zoe M. Oxley and Richard L. Fox. 2004. Women in Executive Office: Variation
   Across American States. *Political Research Quarterly* 57: 113–20.
3. Legislative Candidate Responses. 2004. Arizona Republic. <http://www.
   azcentral.com/news/election/q_legis.html> 2005, January 21.
4. National Conference of State Legislatures. 2004. 2005 Partisan Composition
   of State Legislatures. <http://www.ncsl.org/ncsldb/elect98/partcomp.cfm?
   yearsel=2005> 2004, December 15. Note that Nebraska is unicameral and
   nonpartisan.
5. Peggy Lowe. November 5, 2004. Romanoff Elected House Speaker; New Majority Promises Big Things. Rocky Mountain News.
6. R. Darcy, Susan Welch, and Janet Clark. 1994. *Women, Elections, and Representation,* 2nd edition. Lincoln: University of Nebraska Press; Richard A. Seltzer,
   Jody Newman, and Melissa Vorhees Leighton. 1997. *Sex as a Political Variable:
   Women as Candidates and Voters in U.S. Elections.* Boulder, CO: Lynne Rienner.
7. National Conference of State Legislatures. 2004. Uncontested State Legislative Seats, 2004. <http://www.ncsl.org/programs/press/2004/unopposed_
   2004.htm> 2004, December 15.

8. National Conference of State Legislatures. 2004. Legislative Seats Up in 2004. <http://www.ncsl.org/programs/legman/elect/seats2004.htm> 2004, December 15; Center for American Women and Politics. December 10, 2004. Record Number of Women Seek Seats in U.S. House; Candidate Numbers at Other Levels Don't Match Record Highs. Press release. New Brunswick, NJ: Center for American Women and Politics, Eagleton Institute of Politics, Rutgers University.

9. Note that the total number of seats up for election in 2002 differed from the number of seats in 2004 because some states have four-year terms.

10. Note that state legislative elections were not held in Alabama, Louisiana, Maryland, Mississippi, New Jersey, and Virginia.

11. Where women served prior to the election is highly correlated with where women ran in 2004 (r = .77, p < .001).

12. These results are from multivariate regression analyses of women's representation in the states conducted by the author. For other recent analyses, see Barbara Norrander, and Clyde Wilcox. 1998. The Geography of Gender Power: Women in State Legislatures. In *Women and Elective Office: Past, Present, and Future*, eds. Sue Thomas and Clyde Wilcox. New York: Oxford University Press; Kevin Arceneaux. 2001. The 'Gender Gap' in State Legislative Representation: New Data to Tackle an Old Question. *Political Research Quarterly* 54: 143–60.

13. Pew Center on the States. 2003. The Pew Center on the States State Legislators Survey: A Report on the Findings. Princeton Survey Research Associates.

14. National Conference of State Legislatures. 2004. Legislator Compensation 2004. <http://www.ncsl.org/programs/legman/about/04salary.htm>. 2004, December 17.

15. National Conference of State Legislatures. 2004. Full-time and Part-time Legislatures. <http://www.ncsl.org/programs/legman/about/partfulllegis.htm>. 2004, December 17.

16. Susan J. Carroll and Krista Jenkins. 2001. Unrealized Opportunity? Term Limits and the Representation of Women in State Legislatures. *Women & Politics* 23: 1–30.

17. Richard L. Fox and Jennifer L. Lawless. 2004. Entering the Arena? Gender and the Decision to Run for Office. *American Journal of Political Science* 48: 264–80.

18. The interviews were conducted in 2001 and 2002. Kira Sanbonmatsu. 2006. *Where Women Run: Gender and Party in the American States*. Ann Arbor: University of Michigan Press.

19. Sanbonmatsu 2006.

20. Albert Nelson. 1991. *The Emerging Influentials in State Legislatures: Women, Blacks, and Hispanics*. Westport, CT: Praeger; Kira Sanbonmatsu. 2002. Political Parties and the Recruitment of Women to State Legislatures. *Journal of Politics* 64: 791–809; Sanbonmatsu 2006.

21. Sanbonmatsu 2006.

22. Lee Leonard. December 11, 2004. Record Cash Influx Helped Padgett Win; GOP Coffers Gushed More than $1 Million for Race vs. Anderson. Columbus Dispatch.

23. Leonie Huddy and Nayda Terkildsen. 1993. Gender Stereotypes and the Perception of Male and Female Candidates. *American Journal of Political Science* 37: 119–47; Barbara C. Burrell. 1994. *A Woman's Place is in the House: Campaigning for Congress in the Feminist Era.* Ann Arbor: University of Michigan Press; Kira Sanbonmatsu. 2002. Gender Stereotypes and Vote Choice. *American Journal of Political Science* 46: 20–34.

24. Gary F. Moncrief, Peverill Squire, and Malcolm E. Jewell. 2001. *Who Runs for the Legislature?* Upper Saddle River, NJ: Prentice Hall.

25. Susan J. Carroll. 2004. Women in State Government: Historical Overview and Current Trends. *Book of the States 2004.* Lexington, KY: The Council of State Governments.

26. Center for American Women and Politics. 2004. Statewide Elective Executive Women 2004. New Brunswick, NJ: Center for American Women and Politics, Eagleton Institute of Politics, Rutgers University.

27. Carroll 2004.

28. Richard L. Fox and Zoe M. Oxley. 2004. Does Running with a Woman Help? Evidence from U.S. Gubernatorial Elections. Paper presented at the American Political Science Association Annual Meeting.

29. Richard L. Fox and Zoe M. Oxley. 2003. Gender Stereotyping in State Executive Elections: Candidate Selection and Success. *Journal of Politics* 65: 833–50.

30. Leonie Huddy and Nayda Terkildsen. 1993. The Consequences of Gender Stereotypes for Women Candidates at Different Levels and Types of Office. *Political Research Quarterly* 46: 503–25.

31. Susan J. Carroll. Women and the 2004 Elections: An Analysis of Statewide and State Legislative Election Results. *Spectrum: The Journal of State Government* 78: 23–5.

32. Sarah Kershaw. December 31, 2004. Governor-Elect Declared in Washington Recounts. New York Times.

33. Betty Cuniberti. August 8, 2004. One Thing Is Claire: Just Tell McCaskill She Hasn't a Chance. St. Louis Post-Dispatch.

34. Tom Searls. November 3, 2004. Secretary of State; Ireland Beats Hechler. Charleston Gazette.

35. Cheryl Caswell. November 5, 2004. Betty Ireland's Breakthrough. Charleston Daily Mail.

36. These results are from least squares and logistic regression analyses conducted by the author. The least squares analysis examined the pattern of where women constitute a greater share of high-level, statewide executive elective officeholders; the logistic regression analysis examined whether women hold any of these offices. Data on where women have had success in winning statewide office in the past are from Oxley and Fox 2004.

37. Carroll 2004.

38. Joe Hallett and Alan Johnson. November 7, 2002. 2006 Governor's Race; Never Too Early to Start Next Campaign. Columbus Dispatch.

# Index

| DATE | | | |
|---|---|---|---|
| | | | |
| | | | |
| | | | |
| | | | |
| | | | |
| | | | |
| | | | |
| | | | |
| | | | |
| | | | |
| | | | |
| | | | |
| | | | |

NOV  2007

BAKER & TAYLOR